Sarah P. Fox

Kingsbridge and its Surroundings

Sarah P. Fox

Kingsbridge and its Surroundings

ISBN/EAN: 9783337192716

Printed in Europe, USA, Canada, Australia, Japan

Cover: Foto ©Andreas Hilbeck / pixelio.de

More available books at **www.hansebooks.com**

KINGSBRIDGE

AND

Its Surroundings.

BY S. P. FOX.

PRINTED FOR THE COMPILER
BY G. P. FRIEND, 60 & 61, UNION STREET, PLYMOUTH,
AND MAY BE ORDERED THROUGH KINGSBRIDGE BOOKSELLERS.

1874.

THIS VOLUME

WAS TO HAVE BEEN DEDICATED

(BY PERMISSION)

TO THE RIGHT HON. MICHAEL CONRADE DE COURCY

THIRTIETH BARON KINGSALE,

WHO DIED, AFTER A VERY BRIEF ILLNESS,

APRIL 15TH, 1874.

AS A SMALL TRIBUTE OF REGARD FOR HIS MEMORY,

THE WRITER NOW VENTURES TO OFFER IT, VERY RESPECTFULLY,

TO HIS MOTHER.

PREFACE TO FIRST EDITION.

This little book makes no pretension to originality. It is not much beyond a selection of materials culled from various sources, and strung together in a connected form. The works of Polwhele, Risdon, Prince, and many others, have been consulted, while Hawkins' "History of Kingsbridge" has been borrowed from extensively. Valuable aid has also been received from several of the inhabitants, and others, to all of whom the writer tenders her very sincere thanks. She is indebted to Mr. H. Nicholls, taxidermist, for most of the information on the Natural History of the district, it having been kindly furnished by him for the purpose. The Photographs, with which some of the copies are illustrated, are the work of her brother.

Kingsbridge, 1864.

PREFACE TO THE SECOND EDITION.

"KINGSBRIDGE ESTUARY, with Rambles in the Neighbour-bourhood," was published about ten years since.

The writer has now prepared a second edition; and having endeavoured to render it more complete as a local history, she trusts it will be found better worth perusal than its predecessor, from which it differs in so many respects that it has been deemed best to alter the title to "KINGS-BRIDGE AND ITS SURROUNDINGS."

She desires to offer her best thanks to those kind friends who have so readily responded to her inquiries for infor-mation, either by the loan of books, or by written or verbal communication.

Some additional information, in connection with pages 61, 88, and 112 to 114, which was received too late for insertion in the body of the work, will be found in the appendix.

Fore Street Hill, Kingsbridge, 1874.

Kingsbridge and its Surroundings.

CHAPTER I.

"I am very sure that the plan of reading *general* history by the light of *local* is one that may be applied far more widely than has hitherto been attempted. * * * Every parish has its church, seldom without some relic, some carved tomb, some mouldering achievement, or heraldic shield, which may be made to tell its own story of the past. In most there is the old manor house, the revolutions of which, as Southey has somewhere told us, would be as interesting and as full of instruction as those of England herself, could they be as fully chronicled; and even where these are wanting, the open country, the woods, the moors, and above all, the ancient roads, may be called on for assistance."— *R. J. King's Dartmoor.*

ABOUT ten years ago—that is, in the spring of 1864—a Bill was presented to Parliament, praying for the authorization of a branch railway, to connect the town of Kingsbridge with the South Devon line. This Bill was passed, but not acted on. A *second* Bill was presented and passed in 1866. The line was commenced; a bridge was built (the first stone of which was laid amidst rejoicings); then—difficulties arose, and the work was abandoned. Again, in 1873, a *third* Bill was presented; but this was ultimately, and very reluctantly, withdrawn, from causes which it is not needful to enter upon here. Notwithstanding this discouraging state of things, another scheme has been discussed. We extract from an article in the *Kingsbridge Gazette*, dated October 24th, 1873.—"The promoters of the new Coast Line of Railway express great confidence in the success of their scheme, and hope they may be able to carry it out without an Act of Parliament. We believe that if they get the consent of all the landowners through whose property the line passes, they can proceed to make it without parliamentary sanction; and seeing that when the Brent line was before the public, the major part of the landowners along the line of the proposed coast railway hung back from the Brent scheme, and advocated such a one as now proposed, it is only fair to argue that at least they will not object to this being carried out, even if they do not actively support it. Kingsbridge people now will not care much which line is made: they want railway accommodation, and how it comes they will not greatly care." Whether any of the present generation will live long enough to see locomotive engines bustling in and out of a railway station at this place, remains to be proved. In the meantime, let us enquire a little about "Kingsbridge and its Surroundings."

Kingsbridge is a small market town and parish, but the *metropolis* (one may say) of the Union to which it gives its name.* It is in the Deanery of Woodleigh, Archdeaconry of Totnes, Diocese of Exeter, and Hundred of Stanborough, South Devonshire; distant five miles north from Salcombe Harbour, nine miles and a half south from Kingsbridge Road Station (on the South Devon Railway), twenty miles from Plymouth, and about 231 miles from London.

---

* The Union House is in the parish of Churchstow.

"Stanborough Hundred is a long, narrow district, extending more than twenty-two miles southward from the
river Dart, in Dartmoor Forest, to the English Channel,
between Bolt Head and Bolt Tail, and the mouths of
Salcombe Creek and the Avon, but averaging only about five
miles in breadth. It stretches into the hilly region of
Dartmoor on the north-west, and is bounded by the river
Dart as low as Totnes, where it is crossed by the South
Devon Railway. It is traversed southward by the Avon,
which receives several smaller streams; and the haven and
creeks from Kingsbridge to the sea form its south-western
boundary."*

A fine navigable estuary runs inland about five miles,
from Salcombe to Kingsbridge. Fifty years ago few
vessels were seen here but sloops; now, however, the
sloops are few in comparison with vessels of larger class
and tonnage. This estuary has also several navigable
creeks, branching from either side, and affording the
adjacent parishes the means of importing lime, sand,
and other manures; and of exporting their produce.

Frazer, in his Survey, in 1794, spoke of the district about
Kingsbridge, Dartmouth, and Modbury, as remarkable for
the produce of barley; and observed that it was exported
from Salcombe in quantities scarcely to be credited: and
Kingsbridge is mentioned by White as one of the chief
corn markets in the county—the others being Exeter,
Tavistock, Totnes, Plymouth, and Barnstaple. The cider
of the South Hams is considered superior to any other,
and it is largely exported from hence.

"The most uniformly fertile soils are in the red sand-

* White's History of Devonshire, published in 1850.

stone district; but the richest are those occurring in
contiguity with limestone or greenstone rocks, in many
parts of the slate district; especially in that beautiful
southern district, commonly called the 'South Hams,' and
sometimes the 'Garden of Devon,' and having for its
natural boundaries Dartmoor and the heights of Chudleigh
on the north; the river Plym on the west; Torbay and
Start Bay on the east; and Bigbury Bay and the other
parts of the coast of the English Channel, on the south.
The red colour which characterizes the best soils, both in
the South Hams and the eastern division of the county,
and which seems to be so closely connected with the
principle of fertility, proceeds from an abundant mixture
of iron, in a highly oxidated state. The soil of that part
of the South Hams which is bounded by the Erme and
Dart rivers is generally a rich friable loam, of a hazel-nut
brown colour, mostly on a substratum of slate; but that
on the east of the Dart, as far as Torbay, is richer and
redder, and generally on a substratum of marble rock."*

Polwhele says, "In regard to the South of Devon, its
climate has often been compared to the South of France.
The hills that, overspread with verdure, more frequently
rise with a gentle swell than with that rocky abruptness
which is a feature of the north, are favoured by tepid
breezes; and the green vallies, sometimes covered with
wood, though open to the sea, indicate the softness of
the atmosphere." He also remarks that in Devonshire
the summers are cooler, and the winters warmer, than in
any other part of England, except Cornwall.

With respect to the Rainfall in this immediate neigh-

* White's Devonshire.

bourhood, it is slightly in excess of some other parts of South Devon. The register from which our data are taken is from a gauge under the care of the writer's brother (G. Fox), and is fixed at an elevation of 60 feet above the sea level. The rainfall for the last seven years gives a mean of 35 inches. We believe the nearest station to this is on the Bolt Tail, where the readings are somewhat less than the above. The *Kingsbridge Gazette* has, from the commencement of the observations, published the monthly returns.

The climate and soil about Kingsbridge are particularly favourable for the culture of vines : probably there is no other town of its size in England where there are so many green-houses expressly devoted to this branch of horticulture ; and grapes in abundance find their way to less favoured parts of the adjacent counties.* A Cottage Garden Society, established some years since, has been the means of demonstrating the great capabilities of our fertile soil, and the mildness of our climate. Besides the orange and lemon, the myrtle and magnolia flourish in great perfection. The myrtle sometimes attains the height of twenty or thirty feet; and the magnificent cream-white flowers, and bright green laurel-like leaves of the magnolia may be seen reaching even to the roofs of some of the houses.

The neighbourhood of Kingsbridge is also favourable for bees, if we may judge by the large number of hives in the gardens of cottagers and others. But that there is a great diminution of *good* years is evident ; for we

---

* As many as 99 green-houses were counted very recently in Kingsbridge and Dodbrooke ; but these are not *all* specially devoted to vines, although a great number of them are so.

seldom now hear of very large "supers" of honey. This
may be owing to the increased cultivation of the land, and
consequently the lessening of wild flowers, which form the
best pasturage for bees. In 1863, G. Fox (who practises
the *humane* system of bee-keeping) took the following
large quantity of honeycomb from two of his hives, viz.,
112 lbs., and 109 lbs. 8 oz. (nett weight of honey). These
boxes, or rather glass cases, were placed on the top of
the stock hives; which, after these astonishing "supers,"
as they are called, were removed, remained untouched and
well filled with stores, for the winter use of the industrious
inhabitants. It must be understood, however, that this
was quite an exceptional year, such surprising quantities
never having been obtained here before or since; so that
the wonderful display created quite a sensation when it
formed a part of the *first* exhibition of the Cottage
Garden Society.

Robert Dymond, Esq., F.S.A., says—"Kingsbridge is
the smallest parish in Devonshire. Some of the Exeter
parishes are smaller, but they are not, strictly speaking,
in Devonshire, as Exeter is a county of itself." Hawkins'
statement, that "its whole contents are no more than
thirty-two acres," was in accordance with the general impression, but we have been informed by Mr. William Jarvis
that this is considerably below the mark, and that fifty-two
acres would be more nearly correct.

Leland, the librarian of Henry VII., observes of Kingsbridge, in his Itinerary, that it was "sumtyme a praty
town." Blome, in 1673, less courteously, mentions it as
"a meane Towne, but hath a great market for provisions
on Saturdays."

Nothing is known with certainty regarding the origin

of the name *Kingsbridge*. The various theories respecting it are too vague to be in any way relied on, and it is not likely we shall ever have much light thrown on the subject.

In Directories and Gazetteers you generally find Kingsbridge and Dodbrooke mentioned as *one* town : they are, in fact, only separated by a rivulet, which, however, is also the dividing line between the Hundreds of Stanborough and Coleridge, in which the parishes of Kingsbridge and Dodbrooke are respectively situated.

Hawkins stated that in 1791 the population of Kingsbridge (without Dodbrooke) amounted to 972. At the census of 1841 the numbers reported were...1,561

1851 1,679

1861 1,585

1871 1,557

Emigration may, perhaps, partly account for a diminution, but probably the *chief* cause is the absence of railway communication.

Risdon, who died in 1640, says that "Kingsbridge was long since the lands of the Earl of Devon, until by the attainder of the Marquis of Exeter (the 3rd of December, 1531), it came to the Crown, and was purchased by Sir William Petre, Knight, now the Lord Petre's inheritance." Sir William Pole, who died in 1635 or 6, also says, " Kingesbridge belonged unto therles of Devon, and after thattainder of Henry Marques of Exceter, purchased by Sir William Petre, and is nowe the Lord Petre's"; but it is stated elsewhere that "this manor, and that of the adjoining parish of Churchstow, belonged to the Abbey of Buckfast as early as the year 1333. After the dissolution of monasteries, they continued in the Crown till after the 4th and 5th Philip and Mary, A.D. 1558, a period of twenty-five years; when they were sold to John Drake and Bernard Drake, Esquires, who, in the same month, conveyed them to Sir William Petre, the ancestor of the Right Honourable Lord Petre, of Writtle. From that time till the year 1793, when the late Robert Edward, ninth Lord Petre, sold the said manor to a relative of the present proprietor, it continued in that family."

The Manor of Kingsbridge belonged for many years to Colonel Scobell, of Nancealvern, near Penzance, Cornwall. He died June 16th, 1866, in his 88th year. He was the son of the Rev. Mr. Scobell, Vicar of Sancreed, Cornwall. At an early age he entered the Marine service, and was in action at the battle of the Nile. According to the statement of the late Mr. Robert Cox,* (who was steward to the Lord of the Manor), Colonel Scobell was born at Nutcombe, in the parish of East Allington, originally the property and residence of the Scobell family. When a child, he was a favourite of an uncle, a barrister, and Lord of the Manor of

---

* On the 31st of March, 1870, the Portreeve wrote to George Scobell, Esq., to inform him of the death of his steward, Mr. Robert Cox, and received the following reply :—

"Montvale House, Hallatrow, Bristol,
4th April, 1870.

Dear Sir,

I am obliged by your note of the 31st ult., addressed to my brother, Mr. George Scobell, upon the death of the late manor bailiff and town crier. The settlement of a new appointment has been referred to me, as trustee of the manor property at Kingsbridge. These offices having been held by the Cox family for the last three generations, as I am informed, we should naturally favor any other member of the same family, if entirely fitted for the business. It has been proposed that the widow should retain the offices, with Mr. John Veale as her deputy. Still, I am open to any recommendation or information on the subject, my only object being to appoint some one suitable for the interests of the manor and the requirements of the town.

I am, dear sir,
Yours faithfully,
J. USTICKE SCOBELL."

[The appointment was made as above suggested.]

Kingsbridge, who resided at the Manor House (now called Knowle House), which was then a part of the Manor, but was sold to Sir Edwin Bayntun Sandys. He (Col. Scobell) lived with his uncle, and went to our Grammar School until he was seventeen years old.

Colonel Scobell's eldest son, John Usticke Scobell, Esq., who now owns Nancealvern, although he generally resides near Bristol, is Trustee for the Manor of Kingsbridge, but George Scobell, Esq., the Colonel's younger son, receives the rents of this property. His residence is at Lower Poltair, near Penzance.

The Steward holds a Court Leet and Court Baron on alternate years, and appoints a Portreeve, Constables, and *Ale Tasters*. At the Manorial Court held in 1865 (which was the last preceding the death of Colonel Scobell) Mr. William Parkhouse was re-elected Portreeve, an office he had already held for a number of years, and which he held up to the time of his decease, having been again elected in October, 1873.* On the occasion above referred to, he informed the newly-appointed *Ale Tasters* that it was "their duty to taste the ale of every brewing at the various breweries and inns in the town (each Ale Taster having the power to demand half a pint), and if they did not consider it good, they might set the tap running, that the bad ale might be

---

* From the *Kingsbridge Gazette* of November 29th, 1873 :—"The late Portreeve.—During the past week one, erewhile, of our most prominent public men has been removed by the hand of death,. Mr. W. Parkhouse, senr., represented the parish of Kingsbridge at the Board of Guardians for some years ; and so diligently and heartily did he transact all such business as modern institutions have left to be performed by the Court of the Lord of the Manor, that he was unanimously re-elected, for a considerable number of years to the office of Portreeve. The remains of the deceased were followed to their last resting-place, in Dodbrooke Churchyard, on Wednesday last, by a large number of townsmen." [In December, 1873, Mr. John Port was elected to fill the vacant office.]

got rid of."* On the Manorial Court days, the Portreeve and officials, and other gentlemen invited, make a perambulation of the manorial property, and afterwards dine together. A few years ago, a robe and cocked hat, as appropriate for a Portreeve on state occasions, were purchased, and presented to Mr. Parkhouse.

Hawkins thus describes the town of Kingsbridge. "The principal street, Fore Street, which is full 60 feet broad, runs nearly the length of the parish from south to north, and, rising from the estuary like the crest of a helmet, commands a delightful view of the water and its verdant shores, almost to the harbour of Salcombe, being obstructed only by the creek's suddenly turning from south to south-west, and leaving the prospect to be terminated by the parish church and green hills of Portlemouth. Behind the several houses are gardens and orchards; and as this street is on the brow of a hill, these grounds decline to the east and west, at the extremities of which, on each side of the town, run two brooks, which form a junction of the best portion of their waters near the bottom of the hill on the west side, and there become of sufficient force to turn the Town Mills. * * * Nearly at the lower end, Fore Street is crossed at right angles by Mill Street and Duck [now called Duke] Street, the former on the west side, leading to West Alvington and Salcombe; the latter on the east, in the direction of Totnes and Dartmouth, and uniting the towns of Kingsbridge and Dodbrooke by a very small bridge.† These, with a

---

* Ale Tasters were also appointed formerly at Dartmouth. In White's "Devonshire" we find the following:—"The Ale Taster is an officer appointed by the Corporation; and formerly he tasted every brewing of the publicans, and proclaimed at their doors, with a loud voice and 'uplifted leg and arm,' whether the ale was good or not!"

† Alvington Road (now Mill Street) was once the aristocratic end of the town: here lived the Crockers and the Holdyches.

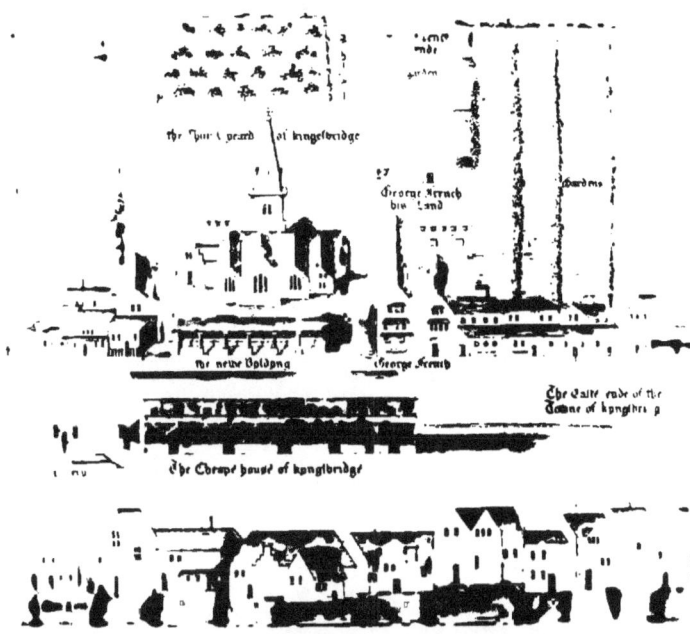

The Thurl prand of kingesbridge

George Ferrich bis Land

Gardens

the newe Buldyng

George Ferrich

The Baile ende of the Towne of kingsbri g

The Churche house of kingsbridge

double line of houses branching off from the east side of Fore Street towards the north end, formerly called Sigdure Lane, since that, by corruption, Sugar Lane, and more recently, Duncombe Street (in compliment to the founder of the Lectureship), together with the gardens, orchards, a few small closes, and a genteel villa and pleasure grounds, called Knowle House, at the north end, compose the whole parish." The foregoing, although written by Hawkins many years ago, is a pretty accurate description of Kingsbridge at the present time.

Robert Dymond, Esq., F.S.A., says, "From the few ancient buildings that remain, and from an old engraving, dated 1586, it may be inferred that Kingsbridge formerly wore something of that quaint, foreign aspect, still in some degree characterizing the neighbouring port of Dartmouth. The 'Cheape House,' in the middle of the main street, was the southernmost market place in the county."

The *old engraving* referred to has been considered of sufficient interest to be reproduced by photography. Hawkins speaks of it thus : " The birds-eye view of Kingsbridge, taken in 1586, and now preserved among the archives of the Feoffees of the town lands, has been engraved to satisfy local curiosity ; it may be proper to mention, however, that what has been there marked 'The Wester parte' is the south, and the 'Easter end' is the north. This error is in the original."

Kingsbridge was formerly a part of the parish of Churchstow, and at what period the separation took place is uncertain. They, however, still form one vicarage. The ecclesiastical history of Kingsbridge is rather complicated. There is an old document, bearing date 1309, which is a memorandum of the deposition of witnesses taken at Exeter, concerning the rights and services of the chapel of St.

Edmund, king and martyr, at Kingsbridge; and the first witness states that it has had a parish and parishioners separate and distinct from a time *beyond all memory,* and that the said chapel possesses Canteria, or Chantry, and all other Divine service complete, the rite of burial alone excepted. It is recorded that the parishioners represented the inconvenience of attending the Mother Church, which they stated " is founded on the summit of a high mountain, and the direct way between them for carrying dead bodies to be there buried proceeds through a troublesome and tedious ascent of the said mountain." Probably it was in consequence of this representation that M. Litlecumb, rector of the church of Churchstow, "granted unto the Abbot and Monks of Buckfast permission to build a church in their demense, in the vill of Kingsbridge, upon condition of their granting all the profits of the said vill, belonging to the church, for the maintenance of a chaplain to celebrate Divine service there; and that all the inhabitants might enjoy every ecclesiastical right therein, so that they visited the Mother Church, with offerings, at least once in every year, to wit, on the Assumption of the Blessed Virgin Mary, or within eight days after." The present parish church was thereupon erected, and on the 26th of August, 1414, it was dedicated to St. Edmund, king and martyr, and the cemetery was consecrated on the following day.*

A few words respecting the patron saint of the church. " St. Edmund, King of the East Angles, having been attacked by the Danes, and being unable to resist them, heroically offered to surrender himself a prisoner, provided

---

* A copy of the original grant for building the church (with the translation) may be found in the " Notes and References," at the end of Hawkins' History of Kingsbridge."

they would spare his subjects. The Danes, however, having seized him, used their utmost endeavours to induce him to renounce his religion. Upon his refusing to comply, they first beat him with clubs, then scourged him with whips, afterwards bound him to a tree and shot at him till he was completely covered with their arrows, and then finally struck off his head.—A.D. 870." Many years afterwards his body was removed to London, and subsequently was brought back to Suffolk, to be there enshrined and honoured; and in process of time a vast abbey and a large and wealthy town, now known as "Bury St. Edmund's," gathered around his venerable dust. In confirmation of the story that he was shot in the manner, related, it has been *said* that when an old tree in Hoxne Wood, Suffolk, which had been known as St. Edmund's Oak, fell in 1848, an arrow was found imbedded in the heart of the tree.

The following is an extract from Dr. Oliver's account of Buckfastleigh Abbey, in his Monasticon Diœcesis Exoniensis:— "26 Aug. 1414, Bishop Stafford dedicated the chapel of St. Edmund, King and Martyr, a daughter chapel of Churchstow, and on the next day blest its cemetery. Roger Bachelor, then rector of Churchstow, made his will Aug. 30, 1427, and desired to be buried 'in cancello de Kingston' [Kingsbridge?], and left to its store 10 marks. To the store of St. Mary de Churchstow he gives 12 sheep and 1 cow, and also 2 marks 'to paint the image of the blessed Mary of Churchstow, namely in the chancel.' On the dissolution of the abbey, in the time of Henry 8th, Gabriel Donne, the last Abbot, granted a lease to John Southcot, of Bovey Tracey, of the rectory of Churchstow, and its dependant chapel of

Kingsbridge." Edmund Stafford, Bishop of Exeter, and Lord Chancellor of England, died in 1419. In the north wall of Exeter Cathedral there is a stately monument of alabaster, with a latin inscription to his memory. The name of the Abbot of Buckfast, at this time, was William Slade.

Kingsbridge Church stands in a cemetery, on the west side of Fore Street. The edifice is of stone, and built in the form of a cross. The bells (six in number) were made in London, in the year 1761, at which period the old set having been taken down and shipped for the capital, to be re-cast, were captured by a French privateer, and carried off as a lawful prize. It certainly cannot be said that the present bells were chosen for sweetness of tone; and the question of a new set has been mooted, and may, perhaps, at no very distant time be carried out.

On Sunday, the 22nd of June, 1828, there was an awful thunderstorm, which came on about one o'clock p.m.: the lightning struck the spire of the church, descending by the iron bar which supports the top and carries the vane; it exploded with a tremendous crash, knocked out a large hole about fifteen feet from the summit, and shifted a considerable portion of the spire from its centre. The stones, which were *blown to shatters*, flew over the houses, and into the gardens adjacent. Providentially, no person was injured; but if it had occurred one hour sooner, the consequences might have been very serious, as many people were then in the church. The lightning came down, and after partially fusing a small bell used for calling the attention of the ringers, and knocking out the staples with which the communion table was secured, then escaped through a window, the glass of which was smashed. The damaged portion of the spire was taken down the same year, and re-built.*

In reference to the clock in the church tower, Hawkins says, "The present clock was set up in the year 1786, to replace one of ancient date and *mendacitous* notoriety." We might remark that this present clock has not established for itself a much better character for correct time-keeping than its predecessor; consequently it will be a great boon to the inhabitants when it is superseded by one which will render inapplicable the old saying, "As great a liar as Kingsbridge clock." Some time ago, Mr. Thomas Peek offered £100 towards a new town clock for Kingsbridge. Soon after his handsome offer was made, he died, but it appears that his gift is still available. Plans have, accordingly, been drawn, and estimates made, in preparation for its erection.

There is within the church a monument, executed by Flaxman, in Carrara marble, to the memory of the wife of a Major Hawkins, of the East India Company's Service. A marble tablet, with a Latin inscription, may also be seen, to the memory of the Reverend George Hughes, B.D., vicar of St. Andrew (commonly called the Old Church) in Plymouth. He was one of the 2000 ministers who, two years after the restoration of King Charles II. (which took place in 1660) were deprived of their benefices for refusing to subscribe to the Act of Uniformity passed in 1662. It seems that he was not only silenced, but committed a prisoner to St. Nicholas Island. After a considerable time, his health having suffered by long confinement, he was permitted to pass the remainder of his days in Kingsbridge. He died the 9th July, 1667. Thomas Crispin, the founder of the Free Grammar School, erected this monument to his

* Information from the late W. Millar.

C

memory. The Latin inscription is said by Hawkins to
have been written by Duncombe; others attribute it to
the Rev. John Howe, the Chaplain of Cromwell, and son-
in-law of Hughes.

Hughes was the author of several works; and a sermon
of his, preached before the House of Commons, is still
preserved.

The remains of George Geffery, A.M., Incumbent of
Churchstow and Kingsbridge, were deposited in the same
place twenty-seven years before. He died 12th May, 1641.
A translation of the inscription, as given by Hawkins, is
here copied, as a specimen of the pompous style of
epitaph adopted formerly :—

"To the redolent, immortal, and ever-to-be-respected
memory of that most excellent man, George Hughes,
B.D., late of Plymouth: highly vigilant to unfold the
hidden truths of the Holy Scriptures: to incline man-
kind by his preaching, the Almighty by his prayers,
being particularly learned; who (like the luminary of
day) auspiciously commencing his career in the east
(having received his birth in London), thence beamed
a star in the west for a long time, diffusing light on
every side by his life, and wailing by his death. His
earthly course (truly useful) having been extended to 64
years, contributing good and enduring ill, he at length
found pure rest—for his soul in the skies, his body in
the grave beneath, on the 9th day of July, in the year of
grace 1667, with his fellow pastor, long most dear,
George Geffery, A.M., whose remains, thrice nine years
before, were deposited in the same place, and being first
turned to dust, are now to mingle with fresh ashes."

(We omit the six poetical lines which accompany this).

To the memory of Duncombe, Master of the Grammar School, and founder of the Lectureship, the following is inscribed on a tablet:—

"Here lieth the body of Mr. William Duncombe, the son of John Duncombe, of Buckinghamshire, Esq., who was some time fellow of King's College, in Cambridge, and the first schoolmaster of the Free-school in Kingsbridge, and taught there twenty-eight years, and brought up many young gentlemen, who, by his industry, became useful members both in Church and State, and died the last day of December, 1698, and left all that he had to pious uses."

The attention of strangers is sometimes directed to a tablet just outside one of the doors of the church, which has the following inscription:—

"Underneath
Lieth the body of Robert,
Commonly called Bone Phillip,
who died July 27th, 1793,
Aged 65 years.
At whose request the following
lines are here inserted:—
Here lie I at the chancel door;
Here lie I because I'm poor;
The further in the more you'll pay;
Here lie I as warm as they."

These lines were *supposed* to be written by the person whose name they commemorate, but Murray, in his "Guide to Devon," intimates that they are, or were, also to be found at Hartland, North Devon, consequently their authorship may be considered somewhat doubtful.

In a book entitled "From the Thames to the Tamar,"

is the paragraph which follows:—"Robert Phillip, who
died in 1793, was commonly called Bone (Bon?) Phillip,
and was by trade a cooper, but preferred to obtain his
livelihood by collecting herbs, which were then used as
specifics, and by receiving beatings at thirty strokes for
a penny."

The Church was enlarged and improved about the beginning of this century: again it was partially restored in
1845, and subsequently in 1860.

Over the communion table is a handsome window of
stained glass. The upper centre compartment represents
the Ascent of the Saviour, and the lower one has a figure
of St. Edmund (the patron saint). The side compartments
are filled with various saints and apostles. Underneath
is an inscription to this effect:—"Presented by John
Millar and Tryphena Toby. Prebendary Luney, Vicar."

A beautiful memorial window has just been inserted, and
on a brass plate underneath, the following inscription is
engraved. "This window is presented by the youngest
daughter of Thomas and Harriot Harris, in affectionate
remembrance of much-loved parents, three brothers, and a
sister. A. N. Hingston, Vicar, 1873." In the centre is a
figure of the Saviour bearing a lamb in His arms, and below
is the injunction "Feed my sheep." The screen was
removed from the church long ago. On a fragment of it
might be seen these words, cut in relief—

O SANCTE EDMUDE ORA PRO NOBIS.
(O, Saint Edmund! pray for us.)

The following is a list of the Vicars of Kingsbridge, as far
as we have been able to ascertain the names:—

Rev. Robert Spark 1636

„ George Geffery, A.M. ... ... *died* 1641

„ Nathaniel Seaman 1695

[In an old baptismal register, belonging to the parish of Kingsbridge, commencing, we believe, at the date 19th June, 1636, there is an entry to this effect: "The first entry upon y° old rigester, by Nath. Seman, minister." This is under date 1695. There are also entries of the baptisms of twelve of his children.]

Rev. — Freke... ... ...

„ — Baron ... ...

„ Richard Jones 1754

„ — Andrews ... ...

„ Edward Michell ... ... 1763 or 4

„ John Wilcocks, A.B. 1779

„ George Furlong Wise, .B. 1809

„ — Pott ... ... *died* 1842

„ Richard Luney, M.A., 1842 ... *died* 1865

„ Alfred Nottage Hingston, M.A. (the present Vicar)

The vicarage house stands very near the turnpike gate, at the head of the town, as you enter the Plymouth road. It is a good, modern, stone dwelling, and was erected by the late Rev. Richard Luney, M.A., Vicar of Kingsbridge *cum* Churchstow, and Prebendary of Exeter Cathedral. Mr. Luney was a native of Launceston, in Cornwall, and received his early education at Dr. Cope's school, in that place. He manifested great aptitude for learning, and displayed talents of no ordinary character. Ultimately, he went to the University of Oxford, took orders in the Church, and shortly became the preacher at St. Andrew's Chapel, Plymouth. In Kingsbridge he soon became very popular, not only as a preacher, but as

a lecturer and public man in general.   In 1842, the Rev. Mr.
Pott, the Vicar of Kingsbridge, died, and this living, which
is in the gift of the Lord Chancellor, was handed over to the
Bishop, who presented it to Mr. Luney.   For several years
he was incapacitated by ill-health from attending to the
duties of his office, and he died December 19th, 1865.   His
remains were deposited in a vault in Churchstow churchyard,
and on a white stone cross is inscribed the following :—

> RICHARD LUNEY, M.A.,
> Vicar of Kingsbridge
> and Churchstow,
> Prebendary of Exeter;
> Born March 5th, 1800;
> Died December 19th, 1865.
> Jesu Mercy.

After the death of Mr. Luney, the Rev. Alfred Nottage
Hingston, M.A., received the appointment of Vicar of
Kingsbridge and Churchstow.

CHAPTER II.

"Can we so describe,
That you shall fairly streets and buildings trace,
And all that gives distinction to a place?"
                                    Crabbe.

ABOUT the centre of Fore Street, and obstructing a view of the church, stand the Shambles, which were built in 1796. Hawkins says, "Five of the six granite pillars which support the present butchery are the very same that upheld the late corn market, and are represented as sustaining "𝕿𝖍𝖊 𝖓𝖊𝖜𝖊 𝖇𝖞𝖑𝖉𝖞𝖓𝖌," between the two church styles."

In the same year (1796) footways were added on each side of the street; but these were mostly paved with round pebbles, and in process of time they became very uneven and much out of repair. They were consequently replaced by good Yorkshire stone some years ago, at a cost of about £600. Not long since, a considerable quantity of the "tar pavement" was laid down, both in Kingsbridge and Dodbrooke. Perhaps the less said respecting this the better.

The Town Hall, which immediately adjoins the church steps, on the lower side, was erected in 1850, by a company of shareholders. The spacious area, paved with stone, is used for the weekly butter and poultry market; it also serves as a covered drill-room for the 26th Devon Volunteer Rifle Corps, and various other purposes. A long passage at the farther end leads to the lock-ups, to apartments for the

sergeant of police resident in the district, and also to club
rooms. A flight of stone stairs at the west end leads to the
Public Rooms, which are used for magistrates' meetings,
sittings of the County Court, lectures, concerts, bazaars,
&c. &c. Another staircase takes us to the reading room,
which is well supplied with books, newspapers, maps, and
other requisites. One of the rooms is devoted to a museum
of stuffed birds and other objects in natural history, presented
to the town by the late Charles Prideaux, Esq., and intended
as the nucleus of a larger collection as other donors come
forward.

The Petty Sessions, which were formerly held at Morley,
were discontinued there in or about the year 1858, and are
now held in the Town Hall, Kingsbridge, and the adjourned
meetings take place at Totnes instead of Kingsbridge. There
are meetings of magistrates held alternately at Kingsbridge
and Totnes, monthly; at the Public Rooms, Kingsbridge, and
the Guildhall, Totnes.

The names of the present magistrates (1874) are—

Sir H. P. SEALE, Bart., Mount Boon, Dartmouth;
J. ALLEN, Esq., Coleridge House, Stokenham;
A. B. E. HOLDSWORTH, Esq., Widdicombe, Stokenham;
R. DURANT, Esq., Sharpham, Totnes;
M. FORTESCUE, Esq., Weston House, Totnes;
H. L. TOLL, Esq., Street Gate, Blackauton;
Capt. A. RIDGWAY, Shipley, Blackauton;
A. CHAMPERNOWNE, Esq., Dartington House, Totnes;
R. H. WATSON, Esq., Dorsley, Totnes;
C. S. HAWKINS, Esq., Triton Lodge, Plympton;
A. F. HOLDSWORTH, Esq., Widdicombe, Stokenham;
S. E. CARY, Esq., Follaton, Totnes;
Com. T. S. TWYSDEN, R.N., Charleton;
T. KING, Esq., Manor House, North Huish;
Major-General BIRDWOOD, Woodcot, Salcombe;
W. CUBITT, Esq., Fallapit, East Allington.

Magistrates' Clerk—THOMAS WYSE WEYMOUTH.

The County Court of Devonshire, holden at Kingsbridge, was opened in the year 1847, William Mackworth Praed, Esq., Judge, who died in or about the year 1857; when Matthew Fortescue, Esq., the present Judge, was appointed.

Thomas Harris was Registrar to the time of his decease; when the present Registrar, John Henry Square, was appointed.

The Court is held once in two months, on Saturdays. Until the present year it was held once a month, on Fridays.

Formerly, that old instrument of punishment, the pillory, stood about the centre of Fore Street; but it was removed in the eighteenth century.

From Hawkins' account of the inns in Kingsbridge, we extract the following:—"The chief inn, prior to the year 1775, was the 'Prince George,' in Fore Street, close to the north style, or gate, of the church, and north end of the butchery, * * * conspicuous in the ancient view engraved to accompany these pages, where the site is marked 'George French's land,' and clearly shows the foundation to have been before the year 1586. In consequence, however, of legal disputes, 'The Old Tavern,' as it was familiarly termed, remained some years untenanted; another inn was opened in opposition, in Fore Street, a little below Duncombe Street, and the 'George Inn' was put up for a sign. This continued open for many years, but at length was disposed of, and became a private residence. After this, a dwelling-house and shop were fitted up and opened as the 'King's Arms' Inn, by Mr. Richard Stear, in 1775, on the opposite side of the way to the Old Tavern, or Prince George, and this has from that period been the principal house of entertainment. Mr. Stear resigned in 1787, and Mr. Andrew Winsor succeeded him." It is now kept by Mr. Robert Foale. The present Ball or Assembly Room was built by Mr. Winsor in 1809.

Not very long since, the "George Inn" being for sale, it was purchased, and a portion of it was converted into the "Parochial Rooms." The Rev. E. A. Lester (Duncombe's Lecturer) says, "We had no place of our own where we could have a Bible class, or anything of the kind, except the church. * * * I took the rooms, and converted them into tolerably respectable ones, to supply the above much-felt want, where our Sunday School can be held, our Young Men's Society can meet, and where we can have our missionary meetings, &c."

There are several other inns in Kingsbridge, but none which require particular notice.

In former times, four water conduits stood, nearly at equal distances, in the middle of the main street. They were constructed of stone, and were six feet square, and ten or twelve feet high. The upper conduit stood nearly opposite the Free Grammar School; another faced the door of the "King's Arms" inn; a third, a little below the Shambles; and a fourth, towards the lower end of the same street. These supplied the town with water, brought thither in pipes from Combe Royal Estate, which now belongs to John Luscombe, Esq. The oldest of these conduits had on it the date 1611. All of them were demolished by the Feoffees, with the consent of the Lord of the Manor, in 1793; others were placed on the side of the street, not far from their former position, and a reservoir was built at the upper end of the town. The removal of *these* "water taps," however, was resolved upon in 1853, and effected as soon as pipes were conveyed into the different courts and houses.

Over the smaller of the reservoirs (for there are two) is

the shed appropriated to the fire engines of the West of England Company. Happily, the services of the fire brigade are, however, seldom required, except for the purpose of exercising the engines by washing windows, when troops of noisy boys are splashed to their hearts' content.

The water supply for this town being a subject of great importance, and one which has been occupying the attention of the inhabitants for a considerable time, we enter upon it at greater length than would otherwise have been the case.

Hawkins says, "The first lease of the water now extant bears date 14th October, 1677, and was made by John Gilbert, of Combe Royal, Esq., to Joseph Bastard and others, feoffees and inhabitants of Kingsbridge, for ninety-nine years absolute; but the writer (Hawkins) feels confident that in the year 1791 he saw a more early lease of the water, granted by one of this family, and bearing date in 1607. * * * The existing lease of this water is dated 2nd May, 1775, and was granted for a like term of years (to commence on the expiration of the former) by the late John Luscombe, Esq., to Mr. John Adams and others, feoffees and inhabitants of Kingsbridge, under the yearly rent of five shillings."

There seems to have been a trying deficiency of water in 1861, for in August of that year "it was resolved that application be made to John Luscombe, Esq., of Combe Royal, to enquire if he will allow the water which now runs to waste to be conveyed into the town reservoir," &c.

And again, in 1867, it was resolved that Mr. Appleton, of Torquay, should be written to, and requested to survey the Combe Royal valley, for the purpose of getting a larger supply of water for the town. He did so, and pronounced as his opinion that the valley was not large enough to get the desired supply from, on the theory that its area was too small for a sufficient rainfall. He recommended that the supply should be taken from the neighbouring valley of Mary Mills. There was, however, a strong opposition to this scheme, on the part of many of the inhabitants, on the ground of expense.

In the meantime, "a plan and estimate of a proposed alteration in the Combe Royal valley, with a view to increase the supply of water to the town, was produced by Mr. Thomas Moore, and it was resolved that the same should be submitted to Mr. Luscombe for his approval." This was done; and his consent having been expressed, "Mr. Moore was requested to get the work proceeded with at once."

In 1872, a new lease was granted by John Luscombe, Esq., for the term of 99 years, from the termination of the existing lease of the water in Combe Royal Valley, to Trustees, twenty-five in number.

Notwithstanding the improvement in the supply of water since Mr. Moore completed the work he undertook, there is still a deficiency, which *might* be attended with very serious results. It was, therefore, resolved in October, 1873, " that application be made to John Luscombe, Esq., to allow the pond in the lawn at Combe Royal, to be drawn, and the water therefrom conducted into the town reservoir, according to a plan suggested by Mr. Pulliblank, in the case *only* of a fire occurring in the town of Kingsbridge; the committee undertaking to use all necessary precaution to prevent the said pond-water from flowing into the reservoir on any other occasion, or for any other purpose than to be used in case of fire."

This application was granted, " subject to the condition

that some provision must be made to prevent the pond from being entirely emptied, so as to preserve the fish.*

We may now turn our attention to some other topic. There is an erection in Fore Street, known by the name of the "Timber House," of which some remarkable things are said. Listen to this—"I am told that Mr. Lavers reversed the usual order of things, by commencing at the *top*, and building downwards." "Yes—so he did." "How did he manage this architectural feat?" "Can't tell'ee, but *so he did*." We should think this problem as difficult of solution as Euclid's "Pons Asinorum." Once upon a time, a man really kept his donkey on the roof of this house. Although not remarkably *up* in the world himself, yet he took care that his "Mulley,"† at least, should occupy an elevated position in life, and so he had his stable on the flat roof; and the animal used to walk up and down the long flights of stairs which connected his home with the street below, (as our informant said,) "like a Christian." The eccentric owner of the donkey also had a sort of garden laid out upon the house-top.

Hawkins mentions *six bridges* within the limits of the town: it would puzzle a stranger to find them, for they are *now* little more than covered water-courses. They were as follows:—the first called pre-eminently "The Bridge," was near the bottom of the town, the second is Gallant's bridge, at the further end of Mill Street; the third, Duck's bridge; the fourth, Quay bridge; the fifth, Duncombe's bridge; and the sixth is that which crosses the stream dividing the two parishes. Previous to the

* This information is mostly gathered from minute books belonging to the Water Trust.

† Provincial name for a Donkey.

construction of some of these *bridges,* foot passengers were dependent on stepping-stones, while horses and carriages waded the brooks. Some years ago, when an alteration was made in the course of one of these streams, an engagement was entered into, that the owners of the land through which the new channel was made, should be allowed, by way of compensation, to have their corn ground at the mill, *gratis,* "for ever."

There are records of transactions relating to houses in Mill Street, in the first half of the fourteenth century; one such is dated 1337. The mill was there at that time, for the north boundary of the said property is "the mill-stream of the Abbot of Buckfast." In a feoffee deed of 1601, it is called Mill Street, but the name is doubtless older than that.

In 1798, Messrs. Walter Prideaux and John Roope erected extensive machinery here, and converted the mills into a woollen manufactory, where for a number of years the serge or long-ell trade was carried on, to supply the East India Company with goods for India. This branch of the trade gradually lessened, and when Messrs. Walter W. and George Prideaux took the business, they commenced making blankets and other woollen goods for Newfoundland, and for some years this was carried on to a considerable extent. This has, however, been long discontinued, and the mills were, in 1845, turned again to their *original* use, that of grinding corn. There was, at the beginning of this century, another manufactory erected by Mr. John Lavers, for making serges and other woollen goods, but that has also been long given up. It was situated in Duncombe Street.

Tokens, principally in connection with the woollen trade, were at one time struck in this district.

A paper by H. S. Gill, Esq., on "Devonshire Tokens issued in the 17th century," was read at the meeting of the Devonshire Association for the Advancement of Science, Literature, and Art, in July, 1872. He says, "The local tokens so universally circulated in this kingdom about two hundred years ago present to the student a very singular episode in the history of our national currency. They were introduced by private enterprise, without the consent of the Government, to meet a pressing want of 'small change,' which had existed for a long period. These tokens, chiefly copper, but sometimes brass, began to appear in London at the close of the reign of our ill-fated King Charles 1., gradually spreading from place to place during the Interregnum, and for twelve years after the Restoration, until at length they were issued in nearly every city, town, and important village, in England, Wales, and Ireland. * * * More than ten thousand varieties of our local tokens are known to have been coined; the earliest date to be found on them is 1648, the latest 1672, in this country; and although never legally sanctioned, yet for just that quarter of a century they were allowed to circulate in their respective localities, each coin passing for a farthing, half-penny, or penny, according to the value set upon them by the persons for whom they were struck; and scarcely any other small money being then obtainable, they supplied to the poorer classes, while they lasted, almost the only means of obtaining the cheaper necessaries of life; but in 1672, Charles II. sent out a very stringent proclamation, forbidding the further use of them throughout the kingdom, and declaring that all offenders in that respect should be 'chastised with exemplary severity.' "

In the list of local tokens appended to Mr. Gill's

paper, nine different ones are described as belonging to
Dartmouth, two only to Kingsbridge, two to Modbury,
two to Salcombe, and one to Aveton Gifford.

Mr. William Parkhouse, the late Portreeve, had in his
possession some time since, a book containing fac-similes
of some of the tokens in the collection of the late Mr.
John Gibbs, who was an assistant to Colonel Montagu.
We noticed *three* belonging to Kingsbridge, *three* to Modbury, two to Salcombe, and one to Aveton Gifford.

Doubtless the old monks of Buckfast knew perfectly
well what they were about when they settled themselves
so comfortably amongst the rich pastures of South Devon.
We find traces of them in various parts of the town
and neighbourhood even now. Towards the top of Fore
Street Hill, on the west side, there was, some years ago,
a house which had been a banqueting house, where the
Abbot of Buckfast used to keep Lent. In the front room,
on the first floor, there was a large cupboard, behind
which was a considerable hollow, intended as a hiding
place. That part of the house was taken down many
years ago, and we believe that there is no portion of
it now remaining. When the late Mr. Walter Light,
druggist, purchased these premises, he discovered in the
cellar, a large open space, something in the shape of an
inverted limekiln, about which remained some appliances
which led to the belief that it had been a chimney, used
for roasting oxen, and other animals, whole. The materials
of this building were used for repairs, and none of it is
in existence now.

There is also a house at the lower end of Fore Street,
which is said to have been an occasional residence of these
monks, and where there is still retained some finely-carved

wainscoting (of the kind termed *linen-carving*) of a monastic character. Some years ago, a portion of it was taken down from the wall, when repairs were needed; and after having a thorough cleansing from the coats of paint with which it was encrusted, it was tastefully transformed into a magnificent sideboard or bookcase; and it now ornaments the dining-room instead of remaining almost hidden away behind the legal documents of T. W. Weymouth, Esq., solicitor.

There are not many houses now remaining of what may be termed ancient Kingsbridge; the hand of improvement has gradually swept them away. Perhaps No. 40, Fore Street Hill, may be considered a pretty fair sample of the style of abode once prevalent in the town. We remember when there used to be many houses with these broad, low windows, and projecting attic lights; but the old buildings have in many instances been superseded by good modern ones. "Old Inhabitants" speak of penthouses projecting from the house fronts into the street, forming a sort of open shop, where goods were exhibited for sale. "Joe" Pritchett's cloth stall seems to be the one more especially remembered. There is a deed still extant, relating to a house, or rather the *site* of a house, the property of the late J. Elliot, Esq., surgeon, of Tresillian;*

---

* In the *Kingsbridge Gazette* of February 1st, 1873, appeared the following notice :—" We regret to announce the death of John Elliot, Esq., which took place on Wednesday evening, after a very brief illness. Deceased had not been well for some days, but nothing serious was apprehended until Tuesday, when his symptoms became alarming, and he gradually got worse until the closing scene. Mr. Elliot had for many years taken a prominent part in public affairs in Kingsbridge, although of late an increasing deafness had caused his partial withdrawal ; but at the time of his death he held the offices of Guardian of the Poor, Churchwarden, Feoffee, Duncombe's Trustee, and he was the sole survivor of the Water Trust.* His uniform courtesy

* We believe this is a mistake, and that Mr. Peter Randall, since deceased, was the last survivor of the Water Trust.

which dates back to the thirty-fifth year of Edward I., 1306.
The *earliest* date on any of the public documents belonging
to the town is 1309; consequently the former is very
valuable from its antiquity. Tresillian House was called
after an Estate of that name in Cornwall, which belonged
to the late Major Bennett, of the Cornwall Militia, and
who was at one time stationed here.

Previous to the year 1461, the weekly market at Kingsbridge was held on Fridays. It was at that period changed
to Saturdays. A fair is held annually, and begins on
St. Margaret's Day (20th of July), or following Thursday.

The late Portreeve kindly lent a *copy* (both in Latin
and English) of the original charter for holding Kingsbridge
Fair and Market. We here give the translation.* Whether
the various modes of spelling *Kingsbridge* exist in the
original document, we have no means of knowing.

THE CHARTER GRANTED IN THE REIGN OF HENRY VI., TO HOLD A MARKET AND FAIRS AT KINGSBRIDGE AND BUCKFASTLEIGH, DEVON.

"The King to the Archbishops, Bishops, &c., greeting.
Know ye, that of special grace we have granted and given
license, and by these presents do grant and give license,
for us and our heirs, as much as in us is, to our beloved
in Christ, the Abbot and convent of the house and church
of the blessed Mary, of Buckfast, in the county of Devon,
and to their successors, that they and their successors,

---

had made him much respected, and his kindness to the poor will make his
loss much felt by them, as well as by a large circle of friends." Mr. Elliot
was buried on the Tuesday following his death, at South Milton. Nearly
all the shops in Kingsbridge were wholly closed for several hours on that
day, as a mark of respect for this much-esteemed gentleman.

* Being a curious specimen of abbreviated Latin, we give that also in the
appendix.

hereafter, for ever, shall have one market every week, to
be holden on Saturday, at their manor or lordship of
Kingesbrygge, in the county aforesaid, and also two fairs,
for ever, each to continue for three days in every year,
namely, one to be holden at Kyngesbrigge aforesaid, on
the day of Saint Margaret the Virgin, and the two days
next following, and the other to be holden in like manner
at their manor or lordship of Buckfastleigh, in the county
aforesaid, on the day of Saint Bartholomew the Apostle,
and the two days next following, with all liberties, rights,
and free customs, to such market and fairs belonging or
appertaining, unless the same market or fairs be to the
injury of neighbouring markets and fairs. Wherefore we
will and firmly command, for us and our heirs, as much
as in us is, that the aforesaid abbot and convent, and
their successors, for ever, shall have one market at their
manor or lordship of Kyngsbrigge, in the county aforesaid,
to be holden on Saturday, in every week, and also two
fairs, every year, for ever, to last each for three days,
that is to say, one to be holden at Kyngesbrigge aforesaid,
on the day of Saint Margaret the Virgin, and the two
days immediately following, and the other to be holden
at Buckfastleigh aforesaid, in the feast of Saint Bartholomew
the Apostle, and the two days immediately following, every
year, for ever, with all liberties, rights, and free customs,
to such market and fairs belonging or appertaining, unless
the same market and fairs be to the injury of neighbouring
markets and fairs, as is aforesaid, these being witnesses:
the venerable fathers, Thomas of Canterbury and W. of
York, archbishops; Thomas of London and W. of Exeter,
(our chancellor) bishops; and our most dear cousins,
Richard of York and John of Norfolk, dukes, Richard of

Warwick and Richard of Salisbury, earls; Henry Bourgh-chier, treasurer of England; also our dear and faithful John Nevill, our chamberlain, and Walter Scull, treasurer of our household, knights; and others.

"Given by our hand, at Oxford, the 16th day of September.

"By the King himself, and of the date aforesaid, &c."

A meeting of the parishioners of Kingsbridge was held in the vestry on Friday, the 20th of July, 1855, pursuant to a public notice, to take into consideration the propriety of altering the day and days on which the Fair shall in future be held. 1st, it was proposed by Mr. Robert Cox, and seconded by Mr. Reuben Toms, that the Fair, in future, shall be held on the first Thursday after the nineteenth day of July, and continue on the two days (only) following, in each and every year, commencing in the year 1856, and carried unanimously.

The following letter from the Lord of the Manor having been read, 2nd, it was proposed by [name illegible, from paper being torn], and seconded by the Rev. Prebendary Luney, that the Portreeve be requested to give proper publicity to the above resolutions. The letter from the Lord of the Manor is as follows:—

"Nauccalvern, July 17, 1855.

DEAR SIR,

I have great pleasure in complying with your and other inhabitants of Kingsbridge's request, with respect to the Fair, and have written to Mr. Cox, my agent, to that effect.

Yours truly,

W. SCOBELL.

W. Parkhouse, Esq., Kingsbridge."

During the time of the Fair, a stuffed glove is extended on a pole, at the Market House, and continued there until its conclusion, to designate the right.*

Formerly, there was an extensive business transacted in woollen goods at the time of the annual fair, but this is no longer the case. Cattle and horses are brought for sale on the first day only; and on the other days, when wild beasts, acrobats, bands of music, Punch and Judy, sweetmeats, and various other attractions, *used* to be present, there is now very little to draw the people from the country, save the pleasure of exchanging an annual greeting. The fair, at least that part of it known as the "pleasure fair," is gradually dwindling away. Witness the report of it in the *Kingsbridge Gazette* of last year (1873). "The fair this season has been, with the exception of the first day, one of the smallest we have seen for years. There was but one show, and a rifle shooting tube, besides the usual fairing stalls; and the

---

* In explanation of this old custom, we copy the following from a newspaper of last year (1873):—"Judges used to be prohibited from wearing gloves on the bench, and gloves were not tolerated in the presence of royalty. The covered hands were considered discourteous in the latter case because, the first gloves being *gauntlets*, it was equivalent to presenting the mailed and, consequently, threatening hand to the king. If we carry the matter a little further, we here find the reason why it is at present considered discourteous to shake hands with gloves on. In many parts of England it was common to hang out a large gilt glove from the Town Hall in fair time, as a token of freedom from arrest while the fair lasted. Here, again, we have the hand and the glove representing power and protection. This typical use of the glove probably originated at Chester, a city which was noted for its glove manufacture for several centuries. The annals of the city shew that Hugh Lupus, the first Norman Earl of Chester, granted to the Abbot and Convent of St. Werburgh 'the extraordinary privilege that no criminals resorting to their fairs at Chester should be arrested for any crime whatever, except such as they might have committed during their stay in the city.' Hence this sign. A glove was hung out from the Town Hall, at the High Cross, while the fair lasted ; and under its safeguard non-freemen and strangers carried on a roaring trade, which at other times was restricted to the citizens. The custom ceased about thirty years ago."

consequence was that very few people were in on the
Saturday. Everything passed off quietly, and there was
not even a case for the interference of the police."

Mr. J. F. Earle, of Upton, has kindly given the following
account of an institution of considerable importance to the
neighbourhood:—

"The Kingsbridge Chamber of Agriculture was established
about six years ago, for the purpose of discussing all
questions affecting agriculture, with the view of influencing
legislation, by petitioning Parliament, so as to prevent
the agricultural interest from having an undue share of
burthens placed on it. The following are a few of the
subjects dealt with by the Chamber. The unfairness of
charging local real property only with rates which are
spent for Imperial purposes, and should be supplemented
by funds from the Imperial Exchequer. The desirability
of abolishing turnpikes. The formation of County Financial
Boards, so as to give the ratepayers a voice in the expendi-
ture of the county rates. The improvement of farm leases
and agreements which are become obsolete. The necessity
of allowing the occupiers of land to destroy rabbits. The
propriety of adopting the 'Metric' system of weights and
measures, in lieu of the present numberless systems and
customs of buying and selling, by which it is impossible
to ascertain the real value of an article in any particular
market of the kingdom, the same terms being frequently
used to express different weights and quantities."

A Branch Bank of the "Plymouth and Devonport Banking
Company" was opened in Kingsbridge in 1832, under the
joint management of Messrs. George Fox and John Nicholson. The name of this establishment was afterwards changed
to that of the "Devon and Cornwall Banking Company."

On the retirement of Mr. Nicholson, in consequence of ill-health, Mr. Fox became sole manager. He continued to hold that appointment until 1870, when he also retired from it, on account of the infirm state of his health. His relinquishment of this office was thus noticed in the *Western Weekly News* of October 8th, 1870:—" Mr. George Fox has- resigned the managership of the Kingsbridge Branch of the Devon & Cornwall Banking Co., and is succeeded by Mr. Benjamin Balkwill. At a meeting of the Kingsbridge Board of Guardians, on Saturday, a vote of thanks to Mr. Fox was unanimously carried, for his attention to the duties as Treasurer of the Kingsbridge Union, which office he has held for thirty-four years. His reason for resigning this is that he is going to remove to Plymouth. Mr. Fox has always taken a great interest in the well-being and prosperity of Kingsbridge, and will be greatly missed in that town."

A Branch of the "West of England & South Wales District Bank" was established here several years since. It is under the managership of Mr. William Boucher Davie.

The agent for the "Devon & Exeter Savings' Bank" is Mr. W. H. Balkwill; and the "Post Office Savings' Bank" has been available for a considerable time in Kingsbridge.

"About the middle of 1865, 'The United Kingdom Telegraph Co.' extended their line from Totnes to Kingsbridge, the wires being carried along the turnpike road between the two towns; the receiving office being at Mr. G. P. Friend's. Towards the end of 1868, Sir William Mitchell, the proprietor of the *Shipping Gazette*, also carried a wire from that office to his signal station at Prawle, thus being enabled to supply his paper with early shipping intelligence. This line was worked with a single wire;

the return current being obtained by 'going to earth,' as
it is termed. Sir William Mitchell's station at Prawle,
and that of the Messrs. Fox, of Falmouth, at the Lizard,
Cornwall, are, perhaps, two of the most important on our
coasts.*

"The United Kingdom Co.'s line fell into the hands
of Government, February 5th, 1870, but the Prawle line
still continues private property; it is, however, kept in
working order by Government.

"A wire was also carried to Torcross, the Prawle insulation
being available as far as Frogmore, where the line branches
off. An important line has also been extended to Salcombe,
along the main road; the Brest line being suspended to
the same poles. These also carry a wire which was to
have joined the Channel Islands cable; but as that cable
was landed at Dartmouth, instead of on the Salcombe
coast, as at first intended, this wire is not used. The
Post Offices at Kingsbridge, Salcombe, and Torcross, are,
as is now usual, the receiving offices for messages."

The mention of Telegraphs and Post Offices seems to
take us back to the time when Kingsbridge letters were
delivered by a *woman*, and that woman extremely deaf,
and unable to read writing. How she managed to take
the letters to their right destination is a kind of mystery;
but she did so much better than could have been expected.
When "Jenny" became superannuated, a post*man* was
appointed to succeed her, and he (as well as the letter
carrier for Dodbrooke) is now attired in the orthodox
livery of blue and red, which certainly does look more
business-like than the black bonnet and little woollen
"turnover" of his predecessor.

---

* "The Lizard telegraph station, worked by Messrs. Fox & Co., of
Falmouth, passed into the hands of Government, October 1st, 1873."

A local newspaper, the *Kingsbridge Gazette,* printed and published by George Pearson Friend, has been in existence for nearly twenty years, the first number having been issued in 1854; but in November, 1873, on his removal to Plymouth, Mr. Friend disposed of his interest in this paper to Mr. Charles Fox, of London.*

The *Kingsbridge Journal,* printed and published by Alfred Davis, first appeared in 1867.

The "Foresters," "Odd Fellows," and sundry other clubs, have *lodges* in Kingsbridge. The "Independent Order of Good Templars" (the "Star of Kingsbridge") has only recently been established here.

The shops in this place can vie with those of most other small country towns; many of them have plate-glass windows, and all are lighted with gas, which was introduced here in 1834. The gas works are in the Union Road.

There is still a great want unsupplied; viz., a *Public Library.* True, there are reading societies and libraries on a small scale; but it would be a great benefit to the town if a library of a more general character was established.

* Not related to the writer of "Kingsbridge and its Surroundings."

CHAPTER III.

CHARITIES AND ENDOWMENTS.

"Ye have the poor with you always, and whensoever ye will ye may do them good."—Mark xiv. 7.

THE late Sir John Bowring, in a paper read at the meeting of the Devonshire Association for the Advancement of Science, Literature, and Art, July, 1872, when speaking of the Cathedral Yard, at Exeter, says:—"In the same Cathedral Yard lived Thomas Crispin, one of those public benefactors, founders of schools and alms-houses, who did for Exeter what Gresham accomplished in London, and Colston in Bristol. * * * Crispin was born in Kingsbridge, where he endowed a school, still prosperous, and ornamented with his portrait. Of the charities left for the encouragement of the woollen trade, several will, ere long, have to be devoted to other purposes. They represent the conditions and requirements of bygone times, and their appropriation must be accommodated to new-born wants."

In the portrait alluded to by Sir J. Bowring, Crispin is represented "with a large hat, grey hair, and a crutch stick."

Crispin's Free Grammar School is situated in the higher part of Fore Street. Over an arched entrance in the front of the building, is the following inscription, cut in stone—

This Grammar School was
Built and Endowed 1670
By
Thomas Crispin of the City of
Exon, Fuller, who was born in
This Town, the 6 of Jan: 1607-8
" Lord what I have, 'twas thou that gavest me,
And of thine own I this return to thee."

There is a good dwelling-house attached to the school, for the residence of the master, and accommodation of pupils. In 1688-9, Thomas Crispin (who died the following year) " by his will bequeathed this grammar school and house, with the appurtenances thereunto belonging, to trustees; and he charged an estate of his in fee, called Washbearhays, in the parish of Bradninch, in the county of Devon, with the payment of an annuity of thirty pounds to the said trustees, for them to give five pounds thereof yearly for teaching twenty-five poor children of the town of Kingsbridge English; five pounds more for instructing twelve poor children of the said town to write and cipher; five pounds a year for repairing the grammar school, and to defray the expense of collecting the money; and fifteen pounds per annum, for ever, to be paid to the master of the said school (such an one as shall be chosen and appointed by the trustees), who is to teach at least fifteen boys of the said town (grammar); and in case so many are not to be found in that place, then the number may be filled up at the discretion of the trust. He also bequeathed twenty pounds, the interest of which was to be expended in buying books and paper for the children of the school; but this sum is said never to have been received."*

* A copy of Thomas Crispin's Will may be found in the Appendix to Hawkins' History of Kingsbridge.

In consequence of dissensions among the trustees, the house was for many years uninhabited, and the school deserted. At length, in 1779, the trustees appointed the vicar of Churchstow and Kingsbridge, the Rev. John Wilcocks, A.B., formerly of Merton College, Oxford, to the mastership. This gentleman dying in August, 1809, the school was again suffered to remain vacant for nearly two years ("no ostensible holding of the establishment, at least," says Hawkins, "was apparent"). In June, 1811, the Rev. Robert Lane, A.B., formerly of Baliol College, Oxford, and perpetual curate of Salcombe chapel, received the appointment; and since that time several other masters have had it in succession.

We will here introduce a letter, which was addressed to the master of the Grammar School in the year 1700, by Henry Hingeston, a man who boldly and conscientiously lifted up his voice, and wielded the pen, against many of the evil practices which prevailed in this town in his day.

"Respected Friend,

      * * * The occasion of this, at present, was from my hearing, two days since, of a cock-match shortly to be fought by the scholars, and I am apt to think, not without thy approbation, either directly or indirectly, which hath occasion'd me to think it my duty to request thee to silence it, and that for many reasons, not only from the duty incumbent on thee as a *master*, but more especially as a professed minister of a self-denying Jesus.

I was last year grieved on the same account, when I heard of the same action then going on in the school * * * inasmuch that I made bold to acquaint my neighbour,

N. S.* of my dissatisfaction, who candidly told me he thought the action inconsistent with Christianity; however,· it lay not with him to suppress it, as being subjective to thy government. I am certain thy predecessor, and my master, W. D.,† did detest this action, and directly forbid it, so as not to suffer it to be done. I have also been informed that thy predecessor, E. E., a man to be honoured for his faith and piety, thought it his duty, for some years past, publickly to reprehend the abettors of cockfighting. * * *

HENRY HINGESTON.

17th 12th mo., 1700."

The writer of this letter was the son of William Hingeston, an upright, faithful man, and one of the first in Devonshire who embraced the principles of "Friends." He suffered much for conscience sake during the long period of their persecution. His son Henry was the author of a book entitled "A Dreadful Alarm, &c., an Address to England, containing sundry warnings and admonitions to the inhabitants thereof, of all degrees and persuasions, but more particularly to those of the town of Kingsbridge, in Devon (the place of my nativity and abode), and parts adjacent." In this part of his work the writer severely condemns the vices and follies of his neighbours in such matters as throwing at cocks, bull-baiting, and wrecking; and includes in his condemnation the pastimes of football, shooting, keeling (i. e., skittle playing), carding, dicing, dancing, and the prevalent feasting and drunkenness of his day.‡

* Rev. Nathaniel Seaman.

† William Duncombe.

‡ Probably H. H.'s objection to *some* of these pastimes was on the ground of the betting and drinking which usually accompanied them.

A great change has taken place in the habits of people generally since the period when this book was written, and we cannot be too thankful for the altered times in which we live.

In the absence of a *biography*, we can gather but little respecting Henry Hingeston's history, but believe he was a merchant of good standing and considerable importance.

William Duncombe, who was the *first* master of the Free Grammar School, and appointed by the founder himself, bequeathed by will, in 1691, certain lands to trustees, "in order to pay fifty pounds a year to a lecturer, *to be chosen by the major part of the said Trustees, with the consent of the inhabitants of the said town;* who shall every Sunday supply the place of the vicar on that part of the day when his duty requires his attention at Churchstow, and also to preach once a month on one of the week-days which he shall judge most convenient; that the lecturer so chosen shall be neither the master of the free school, the usher, nor the incumbent or pastor of the place, but some other clergyman of good moral character. Besides the annual stipend of fifty pounds, he ordered that the lecturer should be paid an additional three pounds yearly, to give away, or buy books to present to the poor parishioners, as an encouragement to learn catechisms, &c. He also directed that ten pounds a year (if the estate would permit) should be allowed for four years, to one, two, or three scholars, being poor, and educated at the free school before mentioned, who should go from thence to Oxford or Cambridge, with the approbation of the major part of the trustees, and the master, as a help towards their maintenance at the university. If any surplus remained, he ordered that it should be applied in binding out poor scholars, of not less than two years' standing at the said free school, to good trades; but that no larger sum than eight pounds should be given with each, and a like sum at the expiration of their apprenticeship (provided they behaved well) to set them up in business."*

There have been changes in the administration of both these charities since the first foundation, and doubtless there will be more as time advances, and new plans are found desirable, in place of the old.

The *Kingsbridge Gazette* of March 29th, 1873, says:— "It has been felt by Kingsbridge people, for some time past, that the salary of Duncombe's lecturer should be increased, either by money, or by the provision of a residence. Duncombe's Trustees appear to have taken the same view, and have applied to the Charity Commissioners to be allowed to give the lecturer possession of Duncombe House at a nominal rent; and we are glad to say the request has been granted."

The National and British Schools for the two parishes of Kingsbridge and Dodbrooke are both situated in the latter place, and will be referred to bye-and-bye.

About the year 1814, the Rev. John Tucker opened a school, under the name of the "Kingsbridge Classical, Mathematical, and Commercial School." This, when it fell into other hands, became known as "St. Edmund's School." It is a very old building, if we may judge by the low stone archway at the entrance.

We believe that it was on these premises that John Morris, a native of Ringwood, in Hampshire, followed the profession of a schoolmaster for many years, with great

* For copy of W. Duncombe's will, see appendix to Hawkins' History of Kingsbridge.

success, and died in 1788, at the age of seventy-one. He was a member of the Society of Friends. Hawkins describes him as "a good classical scholar, beloved and respected through life by all his pupils and neighbours, for sound learning, virtuous worth, and unassuming manners."

It was probably in John Morris's time that a certain Dr. Phillips, by will, left some property in trust to the Society of Friends, for charitable purposes, more especially for the endowment of a free school in Kingsbridge. It appears, however, that the will was disputed by the *heir*, and a proposal was made to him that he should "give the sum of £1,500, in case William Cookworthy would re-convey the Barton of Malston and the mills, in lieu of the charity intended to be charged thereon. That a thousand pounds capital stock should be purchased therewith, as an endowment of a free school," &c. The arrangement was agreed to; and the sum received just covered the law expenses! so that the Friends lost the Barton of Malston, the mills, *and* the free school.

Lands in several parishes have been given, and vested in feoffees in trust, for keeping the church in repair, and for the relief of the poor. The oldest deed concerning the feoffee property dates 1309.

There is an old Seal belonging to the feoffees of these parish lands, as they are termed, on which is engraved the town arms, viz., a bridge of three arches, with a crown over it, and in a legend around are these words,

Sigillvm Regis Pontis.*

---

* The representation of the Seal, which appears on the cover of this book, was copied from Lewis's "Topographical Dictionary"; but it differs somewhat from the carving over the church porch, although both are intended to portray the same subject.

One of these bequests of land deserves notice as a curious relic of ancient superstition. By the original *deed of grant* now extant, dated the 1st of April, in the 20th year of the reign of King Henry VIII. (A. D. 1528), "one John Gye grants to Robert Toly and others, a close of land near Wallingford, in the parish of Dodbrooke, in trust, to pay part of the profits to the churchwardens of Kingsbridge, to buy cakes, wine, and ale, to be spread on a table in the chancel of the church of St. Edmund in the said town, for the priests and others attending, who are to proceed from thence to the west end of the church, near the font, and there pray for the souls of the donor, his wife, father, mother, &c., who there lie buried. Further, on every Good Friday, to pay ten poor people one penny each in honour of the Passion, when it is sung or said in the church, who are to say five Paternosters, five Ave-Marias, and one Credo: and a half-penny each to twenty other poor persons for nearly similar purposes, &c., &c."

There appear to have been *two* grants, or at any rate, two deeds of grant concerning John Gye's charity—one dated 1522, and the other 1529, and although not clearly expressed, yet we rather fancy there was something to be given to the poor besides the cakes and ale, the pence and the half-pence. In the deed of 1522 he intrusts to feoffees two several half acres of land in Kingsbridge, "for the use of the wardyns of the store of St. Edmund." The first half acre lies between his own house and "that of the Abbot of Buckfast, and runs down so far as the Lord Abbot's meadows, called Norton Meadows." The other half acre is on "the other side of the street, higher up, and runs down to the bed of the current which divides Kingsbridge and Dodbrook."

E

The family of the Gyes were people of consequence in the fifteenth and sixteenth centuries.

In connection with the bequest of John Gye, Hawkins says:—"As the inhabitants of Kingsbridge have, from time immemorial, made use of a liquor called *white ale*, known only in their own neighbourhood, and give the name of *beer* to what is elsewhere denominated *ale*, it is natural to conclude that old Gye meant the beverage peculiar to his native place, and which is of such ancient date as to have established, by long usage, a tithe thereon in the adjoining parish of Dodbrooke, payable to the rector. This malt liquor has much the albugineous appearance of egg-wine, and is always lutulent. A principal ingredient made use of in the brewing, called *grout*, is a secret composition, ·known only to a few people, who make and sell it to the ale-house holders."

Among the benefactors of the town and neighbourhood, we find the name of Sir John Acland, who was knighted 15th March, 1603, by King James I. Prince says, in his "Worthies of Devon":—"He settled on the Mayor and Chamber of the City of Exeter, in trust, for ever, the rectory and sheaf of Churchstow and Kingsbridge, * * * for them to dispose of the profits thereof, as he had appointed. The greatest part whereof is to be distributed in bread, weekly, to the poor of divers parishes in Exeter and Devon (which are enumerated). * * * If, after all this, any overplus should remain, it is ordered to be divided (except what is settled upon the minister that serves the cures)" amongst towns and parishes also mentioned by name, Kingsbridge and Dodbrooke being included in the list. Prince goes on to say:—"Next, let us consider his piety towards the church; and herein he was also considerable.

For whereas, before was reserved to the minister that is to officiate in the parishes of Churchstow (the mother) and Kingsbridge (the daughter) but twenty nobles a year, he was pleased to settle upon him twenty pounds. Which being duly and entirely paid by the Chamber of the City of Exeter, is much better than a greater sum, to be received only out of the small tythes, as they come due."

In May, the 21st year of Henry VII., 1505, Nicholas Osant gave a tenement in trust to feoffees to pay an annual rent of four shillings to the wardens of the store of St. Edmund.

Hawkins also mentions among the charitable donors the names of Robert Mydwynter and Johan his wife, who, in 1568, left houses in trust, to provide dwellings for four poor people; Joseph Leigh, who left land for the church and poor; and John Peters, rent charge for the benefit of the poor.

The following is gathered from an Inspector's report. "In or prior to the year 1626, certain lands were held in trust in the parish of Kingsbridge, part being the gift of one Joseph Leigh, and part being given to superstitious uses. They were subsequently conveyed to Pascoe, Lapp, and others, inhabitants of Kingsbridge, for the good of the town and its inhabitants, and for the payment of all contributory charges and impositions wherewith the said town might be charged, as might be agreed upon by the chief inhabitants. When the feoffees died, others were to be elected by the inhabitants of Kingsbridge; but those feoffees were not to convert the charity to any other purposes without the consent of the inhabitants. The fact of the charity having been applied to the repairs and sustentation of the parish church was first mentioned in 1679; but the Inspector believed this came within the intention of the donors. The last conveyance to new trustees was made about twenty years ago. * * * The Inspector remarked that this was only technically a charity. It was not like an eleemosynary charity; but was rather for the benefit of those who paid the rates than those who received it. * * * The Commissioner observed that as this charity was held for parish purposes, it would have been allowable to apply the money to the relief of persons receiving parochial relief. * * * During the enquiry into this charity, the Commissioner expressed incidental opinions that one of the most valuable and admirable objects to which a charity could be applied was to give the poor medical relief by means of a dispensary, to which, however, they should contribute some small sum, so that they might feel they had a right to the relief; that this money might have been applied to the poor rate or church rate; that the Churchwardens were not bound to apply this money in exactly the same way as they must church rates, out of which they could not pay an organist or any officers, as he thought this trust allowed such a disposition, if a majority of the parishioners consented; * * * that it would be legal to apply some of the money to erect a clock, or bring water into the town. * * *"

Various institutions—scientific, literary, charitable, &c.—have long been in existence in Kingsbridge and Dodbrooke. The "Benevolent" Society was established in 1810; the "Dorcas" Society in 1819; and the "Blanket" Society in 1832. A biennial Repository-sale of fancy work has been held for about forty years. It was originally held for the purpose of increasing the funds of the "Bene-

volent" *only;* but of late years the proceeds have been
divided between the *three* charities named.

In the *Kingsbridge Gazette* of June 21st, 1862, a letter
appeared, the principal part of which is here copied.

" Sir,

Of all the 'wants' of Kingsbridge set forth of
late by yourself and your zealous correspondents, you have,
I conceive, overlooked the greatest want of *all,* namely, a
sanatorium, or hospital (none being nearer than Plymouth)
for bodily injuries, difficult operations, and for such
diseases as require *special* treatment, dietary, baths, &c.

Places of worship, schools, reading rooms, a Town Hall,
a popular *Gazette,* and improved walks round the Quay,
you have already; and the time may not be far distant
when you have a line of healthy, convenient dwellings for
the labouring classes, a railway station, and even a park.
But the town, with its populous district of six miles round,
without a *sanatorium,* scarcely deserves the name of a
town. A *sanatorium* must surely be regarded as the next
want to places of worship (of which you have already
seven), for it is certain Our Lord, in His Divine mission
to this our fallen and suffering world, next to the salvation
of souls, devoted much of His time in ministering to
the bodily afflictions of our race; and, with his first
commission to his disciples to preach the gospel, com-
manded them to heal the sick, and as freely as they had
received, freely to give. * * * Any Christian, therefore, having the means, and daily receiving God's blessings
of life, health, and comfort, who would 'pass by on the
other side,' and evade the claims of suffering humanity
(we are assured by our Lord Himself), is not worthy the
name of neighbour, much less of a *Christian brother.* But

here it may be asked, where is the money to come from?
I reply, from the *wealth* and *benevolence* of the locality.
* * * Should any one shrink from their pecuniary
duty to the cause, let me remind such that a hospital
has been compared to a universal bank, which has all
the wealth of the universe for its security, and which
pays the highest interest; *vide* Proverbs, chap. xix., v. 17.
* * * And now, Mr. Editor, I must leave the undertaking, with all its arrangements and details, to yourself
and your zealous friends, so laudably engaged in supplying
the wants of Kingsbridge; only adding, as a suggestion,
that although I have a large family, and have not a penny
but what I have earned, under the blessing of Providence,
by my hand and brain labour, I will (D. V.) contribute
£100, if met by four others, each in a similar amount,
and subscribe myself

A NON-RESIDENT INVALID."

After the publication of this letter, the "Kingsbridge
Invalid Trust" fund was founded by the late William
Peek, Esq. (the "Non-resident Invalid"), by the gift of
£600 in New South Wales five per cent. bonds, for the
purpose of "aiding poor persons residing in Kingsbridge,
or at any place within six miles from the parish church
thereof by the main road, and not receiving any relief
from the parish to which they belong, and who may be
deemed proper objects of the bounty hereby contemplated,
to go to and return from one of the hospitals at Plymouth,
or Devonport, or Exeter, or the Free Hospital at Bath;
and moreover for the purpose of enabling or assisting
poor invalids residing within the limits aforesaid, and not
receiving relief from the parish to which they belong, to
go to the sea side for any space of time not exceeding

six weeks, and to return therefrom, and for supplying them while at the sea side with a weekly allowance of not less than four shillings, or more than six."

Eight hundred pounds in the same kind of bonds was placed in trust by the late Mr. Thomas Peek, to be added to the above fund, and to be applied to the same purposes, on the death of his only surviving child.*

In case a sanatorium should be hereafter established, we believe it was the desire of the "Non-resident Invalid" that the monies now vested for the "Invalid Trust" should be transferred to the object at first contemplated; but as the Charity *at present* exists it is a most useful and highly appreciated one.†

The "Hazelwood Chapel Trust," founded by James Peek, Esq., by which several inhabitants of Kingsbridge and others are greatly benefited, is spoken of in connection with Richard Peek, Esq., and his residence, Hazelwood.

---

* She died January 30th, 1874.

† A pamphlet, entitled "Kingsbridge Invalid Trust Fund," was printed by Mr. G. P. Friend, to which our readers are referred for particulars.

CHAPTER IV.

DISTINGUISHED MEN.

"What is the city but the people?"
Shakespeare.

THE first in chronological order who may be mentioned, is

DAVID TOLLEY,

or as he is variously called, Tolbey, Towle, Trevelgus, and Tavelegus, who was a native of Kingsbridge. Tradition says he was born in Mill Street. "He commenced student at St. Mary's Hall, Oxford, about the 9th of Henry VIII., and became a considerable proficient in the Latin and Greek languages. The Progymnasamaŧa Grammaticæ Græcæ was written by him for the use of Prince Edward. He was also the author of Themaŧa Homeri; and other works." "In 1547, or thereabouts," says Anthony Wood, "I find this David Tolley to be made one of the senior students of Christ Church, by the name of David Towle, being then forty-one years of age, at which time, or before, he taught grammar to young students of this University." When he died is not known, nor is anything further recorded of him, except that his name occurs among the senior students who were theologians of Christ Church in 1551, and the following year.

WILLIAM COOKWORTHY.

One of the names most intimately connected with the early history of the porcelain manufactures of this kingdom is that of William Cookworthy, to whom that art was indebted for the discovery of the two most important of its ingredients (the native Kaolin, and the Petunse), and to whose successful experiments and labours its excellence was, and is, in a great measure, to be attributed. At the time when he first made his experiments—although Dwight had patented his invention for making transparent porcelain, although Van Hamme, and others, had also secured their rights for similar purposes, although Chelsea and other places made their china (it is said of Chinese materials), and although many experiments had been made on the nature and properties of the earths supposed to be employed for its manufacture—the art of china-making from *native* materials was unknown, and Cookworthy pursued his course of study, unaided by the experience of others; and though beset with difficulties at every turn, brought it to a perfectly successful and satisfactory issue.

William Cookworthy was born at Kingsbridge, on the 12th of April, 1705, his parents being William and Edith Cookworthy, who were members of the " Society of Friends." His father died, leaving his family but ill provided for, in 1718. Thus young Cookworthy, at the age of thirteen, and with six younger brothers and sisters, was left fatherless. His mother entered upon her heavy task of providing for, and maintaining her large family with true courage, and appears to have succeeded in working out a good position for them all. She betook herself to dressmaking, and thus maintained them in comparative comfort.

In the following spring, young Cookworthy was apprenticed to a chemist in London, named Bevans, and he walked there on foot. This task, no light one in those days, or even now, for a boy of fourteen, he successfully accomplished. His apprenticeship he appears to have passed with extreme credit, and on its termination, he returned into Devonshire, not only with the good opinion, but with the co-operation of his late master, and commenced business in Notte Street, Plymouth, as a wholesale chemist and druggist. Here he gradually worked his way forward, and became one of the little knot of intelligent men who in those days met regularly together at each other's houses, of whom Cookworthy, Dr. Huxham, Dr. Mudge, and the elder Northcote, were among the most celebrated.

Here he brought his mother to live under his roof, and she became, by her excellent and charitable character, a general favourite among the leading people of the place, and was looked up to with great respect by the lower classes whom she benefited.

In 1745, an American brought William Cookworthy some specimens of China Clay (Kaolin) and China Stone (Petunse) found in Virginia; and of Porcelain made therefrom. This seems to have stimulated his enquiries respecting the art of china-making; but the death of his wife, which appears to have taken place the same year, entirely took away his attention from business, and his researches into china-clays were thrown aside. He retired into seclusion at Looe, in Cornwall, where he remained for several months, and on his return to business, took his brother Philip into partnership. This arrangement enabled Cookworthy to prosecute his researches while his brother took the commercial management of the business. Left thus more to the bent of his scientific inclination, he pursued his enquiries relative to the manufacture of porcelain, and lost no opportunity of searching into, and experimenting upon the properties of the different natural productions of Cornwall; and it is related of him that, in his journeys into that county, he has passed many nights sitting up with the managers of mines, obtaining information on matters connected with mines and their products. The information given him by the American had never been lost sight of, and he prosecuted enquiries wherever he went. After many searchings and experiments he at length discovered the two materials, first, Polwhele says, "in the burrows of a mine near Helston"; another account says "in Tregonning Hill, in the parish of Germs.;* next, in the parish of St. Stephens; and again at Boconnoc."

Having made this important discovery, Cookworthy appears to have determined at once to carry out his intention of making porcelain, and to secure the material to himself. To this end he went to London, to see the proprietors of the land, and to arrange for the royalty of the materials, and in this he succeeded.

Cookworthy determined to make his porcelain equal to that of Sevres or Dresden, both in body, which he himself mixed, and in ornamentation, for which he procured the services of such artists as were available. To this end he engaged a Mons. Saqui, from Sevres, who was a man of rare talent as a painter and enameller, and to whose hands, and those of Henry Bone, a native of Plymouth, who was apprenticed to Cookworthy, and afterwards became very celebrated, the best painted specimens may be ascribed.

* St. Germans?

During the time he was engaged on the manufacture of china-ware, his ever active mind seems to have been busied with other things as well, and he appears to have been sought, and much esteemed by the *savans* of the day.

Smeaton, the builder of the Eddystone Lighthouse, was an inmate of his house while the lighthouse was in progress; Dr. Wolcot (Peter Pindar) was a frequent guest for days together; Sir Joseph Banks, Captain Cook, and Dr. Solander, were his guests just before the famous "Voyage Round the World," and also on their return; Earl St. Vincent was his attached friend; and he was looked up to by all as a man of such large understanding, such varied and extensive knowledge, and such powers of intellectual conversation, that, as Lord St. Vincent is said often to have remarked, "whoever was in Mr. Cookworthy's company was always wiser and better for having been in it."

He carried on considerable experiments to discover a method by which sea-water might be distilled for use on board ship; he was also an accomplished astronomer, and an ardent disciple of Izaac Walton.

In 1780, Cookworthy, then seventy-five years of age, died in the same house, in Notte Street, Plymouth, which he had occupied from the time of his first starting in business; and a touching testimony to his character was given by the "Monthly Meeting" of Friends. He was interred, with every mark of respect, at Plymouth; and his memory is still warmly cherished in the locality.

As is well known, his china, which has become scarce, is eagerly sought after, and produces the most extravagant fancy prices. A few pieces, at an auction, will bring people from great distances, eager to purchase. The mark upon the coloured specimens is the astronomical symbol for Jupiter, or the chemical for tin. The white specimens have no mark. Cookworthy's China-works were situated at Coxside, Plymouth. After a time, he sold the patent right to Mr. R. Champion, of Bristol, who established a manufactory at Castle Green, in that city.*

JOHN WOLCOT, M.D.,

usually known by the name of "Peter Pindar," was a native of Dodbrooke. Hawkins speaks of "a smart little mansion, with a white front, on a gentle verdant declivity, extending to the water's edge at the flow of the tide;" and he says that Dr. Wolcot "first drew his breath within the precincts of these premises." The house now called Pindar Lodge stands on the *site* of this "little mansion," and is not, as many suppose it to be, the *actual* birth-place of the satirical bard. In the road which passes behind Pindar Lodge is a barn, which Wolcot rendered conspicuous by addressing to it various sonnets, one of which concludes thus—

"Daughter of thatch, and stone, and mud," &c.

Dr. Wolcot received a classical education at the Grammar School, which was under the able direction of John Morris; and after pursuing his studies here, and finishing his education at Liskeard and Bodmin, he was apprenticed to his uncle, a respectable surgeon, at Fowey. This uncle was employed as an apothecary by Sir William Trelawny, and consequently the nephew was introduced to the notice of that family, who soon formed a high opinion of his

* Account mostly extracted from "Art Journal." William Cookworthy was great-great-uncle to the present writer.

abilities. In 1769, when Sir William was appointed Governor of Jamaica, Wolcot obtained a diploma, and accompanied him in the capacity of physician. After a time, he returned to England, procured ordination as a *clergyman*, and went back to Jamaica.

On the death of Sir W. Trelawny, he returned to England, gave up a clerical life, and settled at Truro, in the medical profession. He afterwards fixed his abode in London, where he became an acknowledged satirist, and the tormentor of old King George III. We can feel but little respect for the memory of this clever, but unscrupulous man. It is only fair, however, to state that "he nobly threw up the pension with which Government silenced him, when he found that he had to write for the administration he despised." In the latter part of his life, Dr. Wolcot's literary pursuits were impeded, though not entirely suspended, by cataracts in his eyes, which occasioned sufficient blindness to prevent his reading, which had been one of his greatest sources of enjoyment; and an increasing deafness rendered much conversation fatiguing to him. He died on 14th of January, 1819, in his eighty-first year, and was buried in St. Paul's, Covent Garden; his coffin, at his special request, being placed touching that of Butler, the author of Hudibras.

There was in the possession of the late C. Prideaux, Esq., a beautifully-executed miniature of Dr. Wolcot, the work of W. S. Lethbridge, of whom we shall speak in due time.

GEORGE MONTAGU, ESQ., F.L.S., M.W.S.

Knowle House, which is at the head of the town of Kingsbridge, was, from the year 1799 to the middle of 1815, occupied by the late Colonel Montagu, who was the author of the Ornithological Dictionary, Testacea Britannica, a Treatise on Gunpowder and Fire-arms, and other works. His various discoveries in this neighbourhood, particularly of birds and nondescript marine animals, were detailed in the papers of the Linnæan Transactions, and Memoirs of the Wernerian Society. He was the younger son of a gentleman of good family and fortune, and was born at Lackham, in Wiltshire, the seat of his ancestors. He entered early into the army, and served as a captain in the 15th Regiment of Foot in the American war, till the year 1778, when the death of his elder brother recalled him to Europe to take possession of the paternal estates. He then accepted a company in the militia of his native county, under the command of the late Henry, Earl of Carnarvon, in which he obtained the rank of lieutenant-colonel. He quitted the service in 1799, and retired to this spot, wholly devoting himself to those scientific pursuits which rendered him so distinguished a member of the Linnæan Society. He died on the 20th of June, 1815, in consequence of a wound received in the foot, by accidentally stepping on a rusty nail, which brought on lockjaw, and speedily terminated his life. The valuable collection of British birds and animals which the colonel had gathered and preserved, was purchased after his death for upwards of £1,100, by William Elford Leach, M.D., F.R.S., for the British Museum.*

JOHN CRANCH.

In *Notes and Queries* for June 6th, 1868, appeared the following account, which seems to have been drawn up from information collected from different sources:—

"John Cranch was born at Kingsbridge, in Devon, on

---

* Abbreviated from Hawkins.

12th October, 1751. Having made extraordinary progress as a boy, in writing, music, and drawing, he was invited by John Knight, of Axminster, Esq., to accept the situation of a writer in his office, at a salary of £15 a year. Whilst at Axminster, the Catholic Priest, the Rev. William Sutton, took pleasure in teaching him Latin, &c. At the end of three years, Cranch engaged himself with a Mr. Bunter, an attorney of the town, who gave him his clerkship, and by his will left him £2,000, and even appointed him his executor and trustee. With this property, Cranch settled in London, where he published a book on the 'Economy of Testaments,' painted pictures, and became one of the Fellows of the American Society of Arts and Sciences. He died at Bath, 24th January, 1820 or 21, unmarried. (The foregoing is derived from information afforded by the late Dr. Oliver, of Exeter).

It further appears, from other sources, that Cranch's best picture, on the 'Death of Chatterton,' was formerly in the possession of Sir James Winter Lake, Bart.; and that a story is current in the town of Axminster, to the effect that, on one occasion, during the absence of his employer (Mr. Knight) from his office on a winter's day, Cranch amused himself in front of the fire-place by executing a design on the panels of a large oaken chimney piece, with the end of a red-hot poker, producing an effect of boldness of style and execution which was generally admired. This drawing is believed to be still in existence somewhere in the neighbourhood of Axminster."

JOHN CRANCH, NUMBER TWO.

In a paper on ancient Exeter, and its trade, read by the late Sir John Bowring, in Exeter, July, 1872, he speaks of his cousin, Mr. John Cranch, of Kingsbridge, as follows:

"Among remarkable Exonians connected with the same trade [the woollen trade] the name of John Cranch is well entitled to notice." Hawkins states that John Cranch was born at Exeter, in 1785, of Kingsbridge parents, and died 4th September, 1816, aged thirty-one.

Sir J. Bowring supplements this by saying, "He was *not* born of Kingsbridge parents. His father (Richard) was a journeyman fuller, and he married Jane, eldest daughter of John Bowring, my grandfather." He goes on to say, "A short biography of this remarkable man will be found in the introduction (written by Mr. Barrow, Secretary of the Admiralty, for whom I furnished the materials) to the narrative of the proceedings of the Congo expedition, under Captain Tuckey, also a Devonian, which Cranch accompanied as zoologist, and there perished, with most of the party. He was particularly patronised by Col. Montagu, of Kingsbridge, and by Dr. W. E. Leach (another Devonian) the Curator of the British Museum, whose over-enforced studies brought with them insanity and premature death. Richard, the father of John Cranch, was a fuller, fond of music, and one of the many who benefited by the instruction of Jackson, the organist of the Exeter Cathedral. * * *

Being left an orphan, John Cranch was bred by an uncle to the humble trade of a shoemaker, in which capacity he visited, and had a stall at the country fairs in the neighbourhood; but he deserted the employment for the study of Natural History.

He passed whole nights with the dredgers on the Devon-

F

shire coast; wrote articles in a local periodical, called *The Weekly Entertainer*, and assisted Col. Montagu in his researches, particularly in the capture of rare and curious birds."

There is a tablet to the memory of John Cranch, in the Independent Chapel, Kingsbridge.

Sir John Bowring, in the paper from which we have quoted, says :

" The daughter of John Cranch has also taken her place in the literary world, and has written some observant descriptions of the times of the persecuted Puritans, with whom her ancestors were associated.* The three Presidents Adams, of the United States—John, John Quincey, and Charles, were connected with the Cranch family through Judge Cranch, who migrated to America."

CHARLES PRIDEAUX, ESQ., F.L.S.

On the site of the four new houses, exactly opposite the Free Grammar School, there stood formerly an old, long, low, house, with a grey, unstuccoed, stone front, almost hidden by the luxuriant branches of vines. This house was for a great number of years the abode and property of some of the Prideaux family, and was the birthplace of the late Charles Prideaux, Esq., of whom a brief account was prepared at the request of the Secretary of the Linnæan Society, and with very slight alteration it is here inserted.

"Charles Prideaux, Esq., F.L.S., who died in his 88th year, at his residence, Kingsbridge, on the 19th of July, 1869, was born at 'Vine House,' January 2nd, 1782.

During a considerable portion of his early life he

* "Troublous Times," by Jane Bowring Cranch.

resided at Plymouth, but afterwards returned to his native town, Kingsbridge, where he continued until his death. He took great interest in pursuits connected with Natural History, and was for upwards of half a century a Fellow of the Linnæan Society. His collection of British shells was an excellent one, and his persevering labours in dredging for curiosities were the means of bringing to light rare and previously unknown specimens in Marine Zoology. There is a small Hermit, or Soldier Crab, to which his friend and relative, Dr. Leach, gave the name of Pagurus Prideauxii: another is named Hippolyte Prideauxiana. Many years ago Mr. Prideaux presented to the Museum of the Plymouth Institution a very good collection of these crustacea—a large proportion, if not the whole of them, having been collected by himself, chiefly in Plymouth Sound, Bigbury Bay, and Kingsbridge Estuary.

He always took a warm interest in every thing connected with the welfare of his native town, giving liberal aid both in public and private charities, and he will long be greatly missed by his poorer brethren. Some years since he presented his collection of stuffed birds and other curiosities to the town, intending it to form a nucleus for a more general museum. Late in life he was appointed a Magistrate, but he never qualified for the office, or took his seat on the Bench.

Although confined to his bed for many years, through illness and infirmity, his intellect remained bright to the last. He frequently spoke with deep humility of his own unworthiness; and after a time of great suffering, borne with much patience, he departed, in full reliance and trust in the merits of his Saviour. He was interred in the Friends' burying-ground, at Kingsbridge."

In 1773, George Prideaux, Esq., solicitor, grandfather
of the above, was accidentally killed by the upsetting of
his carriage in Aveton Gifford.

He is spoken of by Hawkins as "a gentleman of great
antiquarian research and strong mental abilities, and particularly celebrated for his skill in deciphering and reading
ancient writings." He appears to have been the first of
the Luson branch of the Prideaux family who settled in
Kingsbridge. We have no intention, however, of tracing
the pedigree back to old Paganus de Prideaux, who came
over from Normandy with William the Conqueror, and who
was Lord of the Castle of Prideaux, in Cornwall.

HUGH CUMING.

From the *Athenæum* of August 19th, 1865, we extract
the following:—

"We have this week to record the death of one of the
most distinguished of Natural History travellers, and the
possessor of the finest and most extensive conchological
collection that has ever been formed. In both these capacities the name of Hugh Cuming has long had a world-wide
celebrity; and few men, if any, have contributed so largely
to the material extension of the Natural Sciences, which,
from his infancy, formed the subject of his eager and
almost passionate pursuit. Mr. Cuming was born at
[Washbrook, in the parish of] West Alvington, near
Kingsbridge, Devon, on the 14th of February, 1791. Even
as a child his love of plants and shells displayed itself in
a remarkable manner; and under the friendly patronage
and encouragement of Col. Montagu, the celebrated author
of 'Testacea Britannica,' who resided in the neighbourhood,
it was largely fostered and developed. Apprenticed to a

sailmaker he was brought into contact with seafaring men, and in the year 1819 he made a voyage to South America, and settled in business at Valparaiso. Here his passion for collecting shells found an ample field for its development. * * In 1826 he gave up his business, in order to devote himself wholly to his favourite pursuit. He built a yacht, expressly fitted up for the collection and stowage of objects of Natural History; made a cruise of twelve months among the Islands of the South Pacific; afterwards he visited the western coast of America; spent several years amongst the Phillipine Islands, Malacca, Singapore, and St. Helena, as well as other places; and returned to England with the richest booty that had ever been collected by a single man. Mr. Cuming had long been subjected to a chronic bronchitis and an asthmatic affection, and he died on the 10th of August, 1865, at his residence in Gower Street, London."

JOHN SCOBLE.

This well-known Anti-Slavery Lecturer was a native of either Dodbrooke or Kingsbridge, probably the former. His parents were quite in a humble station. When a young boy he one day fought vigorously on Dodbrooke Quay with a boy much bigger than himself, in defence of a little fellow whom he was persecuting and ill-treating. This brought him under the notice of the child's parents, who from that time took him by the hand, and finding him very desirous of acquiring knowledge, they lent him books, and were in various ways kind and helpful to him. Step by step he rose, until he became eminent as a lecturer. Mr. Scoble long since removed to Canada, where he is, or has been, a Member of the Canadian House of Commons;

but until the death of his widowed mother he continued to pay occasional visits to his Kingsbridge friends.

WALTER STEPHENS LETHBRIDGE,

the celebrated miniature painter, was born in the village of Goveton, and parish of Charleton. He served his apprenticeship with a house painter named Drew, in Duke Street, Kingsbridge; and while quite a boy he evinced such a natural talent for drawing that it attracted the attention of a gentleman called Place, who took him to Edinburgh and elsewhere. After remaining with him for two years, he commenced portrait painting on his own account. He met with great success in the West, particularly at Falmouth; but for many years he lived in London, where he ranked high as an artist, more especially as a miniature painter.

JAMES LACKINGTON,

the London bookseller, was *not* a native of this district, or even of Devonshire, but a portion of his life was passed in Kingsbridge.

He was born at Wellington, in Somersetshire, and was bound apprentice to a shoemaker at Taunton. After his time was expired he went to different places seeking work: he was for a while at Exeter, of which place he soon tired, and, to use his own words, " being informed that Mr. John Taylor, of Kingsbridge, wanted such a hand, I went down, and was gladly received by Mr. Taylor, whose name inspires me with gratitude, as he never treated me as a journeyman, but made me his companion. Nor was any part of my time ever spent in a more agreeable, pleasing manner than that which I passed in this retired place, or I believe more profitable to a master. I was

the first man he ever had that was able to make stuff
and silk shoes; and it being known that I came from
Bristol, this had great weight with the country ladies,
and procured my master customers, who generally sent
for me to take the measure of their feet." But his great
ambition from the first seems to have been to become a
bookseller; and although his beginning in this line was
very small, yet ultimately his sale of books amounted to
more than one hundred thousand volumes annually, and
his shop, of enormous size, called "The Temple of the
Muses," was at the corner of Finsbury Square.

CHAPTER V.

What is a Church? let truth and reason speak,
They should reply, "The faithful, pure, and meek;"
From Christian folds the one selected race,
Of all professions and of every place.

Crabbe.

IN the old days of Nonconformist persecution, great sufferings were endured by many peaceable people in Kingsbridge and the neighbourhood, for their religious convictions.

The Conventicle Act, forbidding religious meetings, caused much strife and persecution; and many of the inhabitants, on account of such meetings, were heavily fined, while others had their furniture and beds sold from them, and some were immured in Exeter Gaol.

George Reynell, Esq., of Malston, in the parish of Sherford, and John Beare, Esq., of Bearscombe, in the parish of Buckland-tout-saints, were two magistrates most rigid in carrying the law against conventicles into execution; while Matthew Hele, Esq., of Halwell, and William Bastard, Esq., of Gerston, two other justices of the peace, were mild and tolerant; so much so, indeed, as to incur prosecution for not being sufficiently active to suppress these religious assemblies.

Several of the ejected ministers sought refuge in Kingsbridge, among whom was the Rev. John Hicks. He was born in 1633, at Moorhouse, Kirklywick, near Thirsk, in Yorkshire. He became minister of Stoke Damerel, Devonshire, which being in the gift of the crown, he was obliged to quit at the restoration of King Charles, when he removed to Saltash, in Cornwall, but at the passing of the Bartholomew Act of 1662, he gave up his benefice, and came, with his wife and children, to Kingsbridge.

Here he held religious meetings, and took all opportunity that offered for preaching; but for many years he met with great persecution, especially from Justice Beare, and he was harassed by the Bishop's Court; but his great spirit carried him through with cheerfulness. He seems to have been generous, frank, and daring to a fault; and for some things he suffered, he had reason to blame himself. On one occasion, when a warrant was out against him from the Kingsbridge justices, for preaching, and two messengers came to take him in charge, he answered their abusive words by lifting his cane and thrashing them soundly. After this, he determined to reach the ear of the King; and took his horse, and rode to London. By means of one whom he well knew, and who was then a favourite at court, he was introduced to the King's presence, and laid before him the state of things at Kingsbridge. The king told him he had abused his ministers and the justices of the peace. He replied, "Oppression, may it please your Majesty, makes a wise man mad. The justices, beyond all law, have very much wronged your Majesty's loyal subjects, the Nonconformists, in the west." He instanced several particulars, and spoke with such presence of mind and ingenuity, that the King heard him with

patience, and promised that they should have no such cause
of complaint for the future. Soon after this the Dissenters
had some favour shown them, and liberty was given to
build meeting-houses.   Hicks had a congregation afterwards at Portsmouth, and continued there until he was
driven away by fresh persecutions; and his last place of
residence is ascertained from an old indictment, in which
he is described as " John Hicks, clerk, of Keynsham, near
Bristol."

At length, being led on by the impulses of his ardent
nature, he joined in the Duke of Monmouth's rebellion,
for which he suffered death in 1685; but he seems to
have been firmly impressed to the last with the belief
that Monmouth had the prior claim to the throne, and
not the Catholic Duke of York. His brother, Dr. George
Hicks, became Dean of Worcester.

The atrocities perpetrated by the Royalist troops after the
suppression of this rebellion, in the reign of James II.,
were for many long years bitterly remembered in the West
of England. Few cases excited at the time more com-
miseration than that of the Lady Alice Lisle, who was
actually executed for giving shelter to this same John Hicks.
She was the widow of John Lisle, a man (says T. B.
Macaulay) "who had sat in the Long Parliament, and in
the High Court of Justice; had been a Commissioner
of the Great Seal, in the days of the Commonwealth, and
had been created a Lord by Cromwell. Lady Lisle was
generally esteemed, even by the Tory gentlemen of her
county, for it was well known to them that she had deeply
regretted some violent acts in which her husband had
borne a part, that she had shed bitter tears for Charles I.,
and that she had protected and relieved many cavaliers
in their distress."

After the engagement at Sedgemoor, John Hicks, and Richard Nelthorpe, a lawyer who had been outlawed for his share in the Rye-house plot, sought refuge at her house. [In the account of the trial, Lady Lisle is described as "of Moyle's Court, near Fordingbridge."] "The same womanly kindness," continues Macaulay, "which led her to befriend the Royalists in their time of trouble, would not allow her to refuse a meal and a hiding-place to the misguided men who now entreated her to protect them. She took them into her house, set meat before them, and shewed them where they might take rest. The next morning her dwelling was surrounded by soldiers; strict search was made; Hicks was found concealed in the malt-house, and Nelthorpe in the chimney." Lady Lisle was also herself captured by Colonel Penruddock, brought to trial for harbouring the fugitives, condemned by Jefferies, and executed — thus adding another to the long list of atrocities perpetrated by the "unjust judge."* From this historical incident Ward has painted one of the frescoes in the Houses of Parliament, in which picture may be seen represented the Lady Lisle, John Hicks, and Richard Nelthorpe.

The following ejected ministers are also associated with Kingsbridge. Of the Rev. George Hughes, the friend of Crispin and Geffery, mention has already been made. Anthony Wood, in his "Athenæ Oxoniensis," says he entered Corpus Christi College, Oxford, in 1619, and took the degree of B.D. in 1633, about which time he became vicar of St. Andrew's, Plymouth. Wood says that "he exercised a kind of patriarchal sway in Devonshire," and

---

* "In the first year of William and Mary, the attainder was removed, and Lady Lisle's two daughters were restored to all their former rights."

that, "on his obtaining permission to remove from St.
Nicholas Island to Kingsbridge, he was welcomed to the
house of one Daniel Elley, in that town, in whose house
he died."

"The Rev. John Quicke, M.A., of Exeter College, Oxford,
was born at Plymouth, anno 1636. He went to Oxford
about 1650, and left it 1657, when he returned to his
native county, and preached for some time at Ermington.
He was ordained at Plymouth, February 2nd, 1658, being
called to be minister of Kingsbridge and Churchstow.
From thence he was called to Brixton, where the Act
of Uniformity found and ejected him. After imprisonments
and persecutions, he died in the seventieth year of his
age, April 29th, 1706."

"The Rev. Christ. Jellinger, M.A., was born in the
Palatinate of the Rhine, near Worms, in the hereditary
dominions of Frederic, King of Bohemia, at whose court
he was when he was in Holland. After being in various
parts of England, he settled at South Brent, from whence
he removed to Marldon, not far from Totnes, and then
to Kingsbridge. He continued to preach when he was
very old, and died at Kingsbridge, at about eighty-three
years of age."

"The Rev. James Burdwood, of Pembroke College, Oxford,
was of an ancient family which had an estate at Preston,
in West Alvington, near Kingsbridge, which hath been in
the name of the Burdwoods for many generations. He was
born at Yarnacombe, in that parish, of religious parents, and
had his grammar learning at Kingsbridge school. When
he left the University, he was for awhile minister at
Plympton St. Mary, near Plymouth. From thence he
removed to St. Petrox, Dartmouth, where he continued

till the Act of Uniformity ejected him. He then rented an estate at Batson, in the parish of Malborough. There he stayed five years, and preached in his own house, as long as he was permitted, to great numbers who flocked to hear him, and when his house would not receive them, in his orchard; * * * but one Beer, or Bear, (who had been for some time the head of the informers, and now, for his good service in disturbing conventicles, was advanced to the degree of a justice of the peace), together with another justice, and a crew of informers, who were at their beck, occasioned him much trouble and vexation, unhung his doors, rifled his house, seized and carried away his goods, ripped off the locks of his barn doors, and put others on, and obliged his wife and children to seek shelter among the neighbours. He was also heavily fined. He removed from Batson to Hicks Down, near Bigbury, and finally back to Dartmouth, where he died, August 21st, 1693, in the sixty-seventh year of his age."

"The Rev. Edmund Tucker, of Trinity College, Cambridge, was born at Milton Abbot, near Tavistock, in 1627. His father had a good estate. He was first settled at Dittisham, and was a man of good natural abilities. He succeeded Mr. Hicks at Kingsbridge, where, for his nonconformity, he suffered much from the barbarity of Justice Beare and his informers, who seized all his household goods, his bed, and even his children's wearing apparel. He died July 5th, 1702, in the seventy-fifth year of his age, and was succeeded at Kingsbridge by the Rev. John Cox."*

There is a pamphlet still in existence, which was printed

* The foregoing accounts are extracted from the "Nonconformists' Memorial."

in 1671, bearing the following title:—"A True and Faithful Narrative of the Unjust and Illegal Sufferings and Oppressions of many Christians, Injuriously and Injudiciously called FANATICS, holding all the Fundamentals of the Christian Religion, believing all the Articles of the Christian Faith, and whose Lives and Conversations are as Consonant and Agreeable to the Laws of God, as theirs that persecute them, &c., &c." This pamphlet is in the hands of the representatives of the late Jeremiah Cranch, and a reprint was issued in 1821, by Mr. Joseph Cranch.

In those days of pains and penalties, the early Nonconformists used to meet for worship, by appointment, at Sorley Green (then called Surley Butts) and Lincombe Cross (then known as Linckam Hill Head), and perhaps in other places, in the open air, where they could meet undiscovered, or from whence they should be able to escape, if discovered by those who sought them out for punishment and disgrace.

The first *meeting-house* of which there seems to be any account stood on the west side of Fore Street, a little south of Duncombe Street. This was taken down towards the end of the last century, and a new Independent Chapel was built on the east side of Fore Street, by Millman's Lane, in the year 1780. This chapel was enlarged during the pastorate of the Rev. Edward Newton. The present handsome and commodious chapel was erected in 1858: Mr. J. Pulliblank architect.

We have been supplied with a list of the Independent ministers, as far as can be ascertained.

APPOINTED.		RESIGNED.
—	Rev. Alexander Walker	—
1775	„ William Evans ...	1794 or 5

APPOINTED.			RESIGNED.
1805	„	George Denner...	—
1816	„	John Angear	1820
1823	„	Josiah Davies	1829
1829	„	Hugh Watts	1840
1841	„	William Skinner Keale ...	—
1845	„	Edward Newton	1849
1849	„	John Averick	1850
1850	„	Michaiah Hill	1853
1853	„	George H. Hobbs ... ...,	1857
1857	„	John Jack	1861
1861	„	John Elrick, M.A.	1862
1862	„	James C. Postans	1868
—	„	John Stewart (the present Pastor)	

In the chapel are tablets to the memory of deceased Pastors, viz., Rev. Josiah Davies, Hugh Watts, Edward Newton, &c.

The Independents have recently purchased a house in Fore Street, for the use of their minister.

The celebrated George Whitefield visited Kingsbridge more than once. On one of these occasions, whether in 1749, or at an earlier date is not quite clear, he preached out of doors, near the spot now occupied by Quay House.* A youth named Philip Gibbs (great uncle to the individual of that name, who for many years conducted a school in Kingsbridge, and who afterwards removed to Canada) went to hear Whitefield preach, and he says "being little of stature, I got up, *not* into a sycamore, but into an elm tree." The words of the preacher took such a hold

---

* It was probably at this time that Mr. Nathaniel Cranch lent a table for Whitefield to stand upon, while preaching. This table Miss J. B. Cranch has caused to be restored, and a plate inserted with an inscription showing the honoured use to which it was applied.

upon him, that he appears to have entered, as it were, on a new life. He afterwards became an eminent minister, and was Pastor of the Baptist Church at Plymouth for fifty-one years. He was highly and very generally respected, and at his funeral, which took place 5th of December, 1800, the Rev. Dr. Hawker, Vicar of Charles Church, and another Clergyman, together with four Independent and two Baptist Ministers, supported his pall.

In connection with the account of Philip Gibbs, it may be mentioned that the Hon. T. N. Gibbs, who was educated in Kingsbridge, at the school of his uncle (the late Mr. Philip Gibbs), has for some years been a member of the Canadian House of Commons, and recently accepted a seat in the Canadian Cabinet as Minister of Inland Revenue.

The Baptists have existed in Kingsbridge from a remote period. In the published denominational list of Churches, the date of the Baptist Church, Kingsbridge, is given as 1640. On the accession to the pastorate of the Rev. Martyn Dunsford, in 1700, the Baptists resolved on building the chapel in Meeting Lane. This still stands, but is now turned into a chapel-keeper's dwelling, and into two large rooms, which are used for the elder Bible classes.

In 1798, a larger chapel was erected several feet lower down the lane; this was enlarged and altered in 1852, at considerable cost. On the walls are tablets, with inscriptions, which form almost a continuous history of the pastorate from the year 1689.

To commemorate the names of
Leonard Kent, Philip Weymouth,
and Arthur Langworthy,
who with others in the reign of Charles II.,
laboured and suffered for the truth's sake,
in connection with this Church.

Also, that of
Rev. Samuel Hart,
Who held the pastorate of this Church in 1689;
and of the
Rev. Martyn Dunsford,
who accepted the call of this Church about the close of the
seventeenth century. He died in 1713, and was buried in the
old Meeting House.
The Rev. Crispin Courtis
succeeded him in the pastoral office, and ministered to this
Church and congregation during a period of fifty years:
He died December 14th, 1768, aged 86,
and was buried in Venn Yard.
"They rest from their labours and their works do follow them."

Rev. H. Penn,
nineteen years a beloved and successful pastor of this Church,
Died 25th October, 1802, aged 44,
By whose exertions
(Crowned with the Divine blessing,)
This house was erected,
and his ardent desires for its exoneration were gratified.
The righteous shall be had in everlasting remembrance.
His remains are deposited at the door.

Rev. John Nicholson,
Twenty-nine years the beloved pastor of this Church,
Died August 26th, 1832,
aged 71 years.
He possessed a vigorous understanding,
Extensive knowledge, and solid piety.
The memory of the just is blessed.—Prov. x. 7.
His remains are deposited in Venn yard.

The following are the names of Pastors succeeding the
Rev. John Nicholson, to the present time.

Rev. Edmund Hull.
„ James P. Hewlett.
„ Thomas Applegate.
„ Enoch Williams, M.A.
„ Robert Clarke.
„ Elias H. Tuckett.

G

Rev. Thomas Peters.

„   J. Upton Davis, B.A.

„   John O'Dell, (the present Pastor).

In 1673, the Baptists seem to have become a numerous and permanent religious body, for in this year Arthur Langworthy, Esq., of Hatch, bequeathed to them by deed of gift, a piece of land near the village of Venn, for the quiet burial of those amongst them who were removed from those troublous times.   This yard is still occasionally used.

A convenient Minister's house is situated at the entrance of Meeting Lane; and one or two small endowments also belong to the Society.

The first Sunday School set on foot in these towns was at the Baptist Chapel, in the year 1812.   In the following years schools were opened, and are still carried on, in connection with almost each place of worship.   It is impossible to suppose that several hundreds of children have received religious instruction every Sunday, in the various churches and chapels, for so many years, without an important influence on the population.

We are indebted to Robert Dymond, Esq., F.S.A., for most of the following information respecting the "Society of Friends" in Kingsbridge.

George Fox's journal relates that he first entered this county from Dorsetshire in 1655, in the company of his trusty friend, Edward Pyot, of Bristol, ex-captain in the army.   Passing somewhat rapidly through the southern parts of the shire, these companions sowed the first seeds of Quakerism in the towns of Topsham, Totnes, Kingsbridge, and Plymouth, and then crossed the Tamar into Cornwall.

G. Fox says, (on the occasion of this, his *first* visit) "the next day we got to Kingsbridge, and at our inn enquired for the sober people of the town. They directed us to Nicholas Tripe and his wife, and we went to their house."

These "sober people" appear to have adopted the views entertained by their guests, for G. Fox says afterwards, "and since, there is a good meeting of Friends in that country."

After passing several months in the pestilential dungeon of Launceston Castle, the two pioneers of Quakerism again traversed Devonshire, on their eastward journey, propagating their views in the central towns of Okehampton, Exeter, and Collumpton, G. Fox's second visit to the county was in 1659, ·the third in 1663, when he again came to Kingsbridge. In his journal he says that he went "at Kingsbridge to Henry Pollexfen's, who had been an ancient justice of the peace." This Henry Pollexfen, of West Alvington, joined Friends at an early date, and was imprisoned at Totnes in 1657.

In 1680, an enquiry was made as to the more prominent oppressors of Friends. It appears, from an old record belonging to the Society, that, at that time, there were but two persecuting magistrates in West Devon: "the one," says this record, "is called by his surname, Champernown of Modbery, and the other is called by surname, Bare, dwelling near Kingsbridge. These are both very wicked to friends, and meetings, in these westarne parts, and, indeed, also to other professors, both priestbiterjans and baptists. The one of the two espetially, namely Champernown, he doth glory greatly in his acts of wickedness, who said to a baptist at whose house the said Champernown was, inquiring his name, I am one Champernown who

persecuteth the Saintes. This is as farr as wee can say
in this matter att the p'sent."

We find under date 1684, that "a justice called John
Bare, keeps Friends out of their house." [This was a
house they *rented* for the purpose of holding their meetings
in.] In the first month of 168⅝ the prisons of Devonshire alone held no less than 104 members of the Society
of Friends; the fines also were ruinous: for one small
"First day" meeting alone, of Kingsbridge Friends, in
1670, goods were levied by distress to the value of
£85 11s. 8d., and in consequence of this severe opposition,
it was not until 1702 that they could assemble here in
a building of their own.

The Friends of Kingsbridge had, in 1693, purchased a
plot containing twelve perches in Sugar, (or Sidger) Lane,
for a burying place, and in 1697 they obtained for the
site of their present meeting house and burial ground,
a plot called Old Walls, or Cutler's tenement, also an herb
garden behind the said Old Walls, and a meadow or quillet
of land, lying below the herb garden, and divided from
it by a "lake of water, that runneth to the town mills
of Kingsbridge."

The monthly Meetings of the Western division of the
County continued to be held at Kingsbridge in rotation,
till the end of 1871; but the migration of Friends from
the town has now so reduced their numbers that it has
been found necessary to close the Meeting House.

The information respecting the Wesleyan body, was
supplied by Mr. J. Pulliblank. He says, "Although Kingsbridge possesses interesting *souvenirs* of the preaching of
George Whitefield, there is no reason to believe that either
of the brothers Wesley, or their coadjutors, ever visited

this locality. That branch of Methodism which perpetuates the name of Wesley was introduced into the town about the beginning of the present century by a few pious Welshmen, who were stationed here in one of the militia regiments from the principality. They having met together in a cottage, in Dodbrooke, for social prayer in their native language, invited the townspeople to join them, and conducted religious worship in English. The times of meeting were announced by the town-crier, and the services thus commenced amidst much obloquy and scorn, resulted in the gathering of many converts, who formed the nucleus of a society which attracted the notice of the Methodist conference, who appointed a duly-qualified minister to labour in Kingsbridge, Dartmouth, Modbury, and all the intermediate country, under the denomination of the South Devon Mission. A school-room was hired in Kingsbridge, where regular services were held every Sabbath-day during several years, when the Methodists having lived down the opposition which met their first efforts, and considerably increased in numbers, purchased the site which they at present occupy, together with the house adjoining, and in the year 1813 erected a commodious place of worship, which for some time was known exclusively in the town as *the Chapel;* the preaching places of the Independents and Baptists being at that time designated respectively the Higher and Lower Meetings. Kingsbridge became the head of what is known in Methodism as a circuit, extending from Salcombe on the one side to Modbury and Ermington on the other, and containing at the present time seven chapels, besides several other preaching places, with each of which is connected a Sunday-school.

In the early part of the year 1870, the chapel built in

1813-14 was very considerably enlarged and improved. It was lengthened thirteen feet, had a new roof with a circular ceiling (by which increased internal height was secured), new doors and windows throughout, and the internal fittings restored on a more modern construction."

A place of worship for the Plymouth Brethren was built in 1853. It has a neat stone front, with a colonnade before the principal entrance. The chapel stands back from the street, from which it is separated by a grass lawn and handsome iron railing. The Brethren have no burying-place in the town, but they mostly use a small cemetery in the village of Galmpton, or one at Chillington.

About fifty years since, several persons holding Calvinistic doctrines opened a room for worship in Ebrington Street, Dodbrooke, which was continued until about twenty years ago, when they removed to a large room near Gallants' Bridge; but in 1872, the Friends' Meeting House being vacant, they resolved to endeavour to rent that place of worship, and after some little difficulty, permission was given for the "Calvinistic Baptists" to hold their services there.

DODBROOKE.

CHAPTER VI.

Cities and towns, the various haunts of men,
Require the pencil, they defy the pen.
Could he who sang so well the Grecian fleet,
So well have sung of alley, lane, or street?

Crabbe.

DODBROOKE, which is so closely connected with Kingsbridge that it is not easy to define the boundaries, is more ancient than the latter place. At Domesday survey, the Manor of Dodbrooke belonged to the widow of Edward the Confessor, and after her it was held by the family of De Dodbrooke, whose heiress married Alan Fitz Roald, ancestor of the family of Fitz Alan, who were possessed of it for five descents. The heiress of this family brought it to Champernowne. The manor now belongs to John Froude Bellew, Esq.

Sir William Pole says: "Dodbrooke descended from the Lady Alis de Dodbroke, by Rohant, unto Sir Richard Champernon, of Modbury."

In 1801, the number of inhabitants in Dodbrooke amounted only to 608. As far as we can ascertain, we believe the numbers reported at the census of

1841	amounted to	1,229
1851	„	1,302
1861	„	1,184
1871	„	1,245

The living of Dodbrooke is a rectory. The advowson
was appendant to the manor till 1790, when it was severed
and sold separately to the Rev. Benjamin Kennicott, at
that time rector (nephew of the celebrated Hebraist, B.
Kennicott, D.D.) The Rev. James Dewing was for many
years rector of this parish; and on his removal to another
part of the country, the Rev. John Power, M.A., the
present rector, became his successor.

The Rectory House, which is an attractive-looking
dwelling, is situated almost close to one of the entrances
to the churchyard.

The parish church, dedicated to St. Thomas a Becket,
is at the north end of the town. The tower was formerly
surmounted by a spire, which was taken down in 1785.
Many have remarked that the south side of the church
has a more finished appearance than the north side. This
is accounted for by the fact that the church is a nave and
south aisle only, which, perhaps, was thought sufficiently
large for the population at the time of its erection; and
it was, no doubt, expected that a north aisle would be
added at some time afterwards.

There are a few tablets on the walls of the interior.
One of them has an epitaph in Latin to the memory of
Elizabeth, wife of John Beare, Esq., of Bearscombe (usually
spoken of as "Justice Beare"). She died in June, 1666.
Hawkins gives the following translation :—

> " What grief is this, O marble, say?
> A public loss, see ! shrouds the day :
> Of purity the model true,
> And modesty,—devotion too,
> Is gone, (O sad !)—who does not sigh,
> Must more unfeeling be than I."

A stained glass window has been placed at the south

side of the church, the subject being the Adoration of the Magi, and at the lower part is this inscription:—"To the glory of God, and in pious memory of Prestwood Pearse, who died on the 10th May, 1862, aged 77 ; and of her sister, Mary Hele Pearse, who died on the 28th of October, 1862, aged 76 years."

On the opposite side of the church is a window of stained glass, erected by the widow of Thomas Harris, Esq., to the memory of her husband, who died in December, 1861 ; and also in remembrance of other relatives.

A small diamond-shaped tablet is to be seen, in memory of the Rev. Thomas Lampton Chilton Young, A.M., of Emmanuel College, Cambridge, who succeeded the Rev. Simon Webber, A.B., of Wadham College, Oxford, in 1817, as rector of the parish.

When the Rev. Mr. Owen was Rector of Dodbrooke, he effected some alterations in the church, and it was also re-seated in 1846.

A board hangs in the vestry, on which are painted the arms of John Peters, Esq., "who gave twenty shillings every year, for ever, to the poor of this parish of Dodbrooke. He was buried at St. Thomas, Exon."

In the present year, 1874, considerable improvement is being effected by the restoration of the chancel, and the removal of the old window of wood over the Communion Table, and replacing it with stone and stained glass, representing the Ascension. A window has also been placed in the *Well Aisle* (as it is called), by J. K. Gillard, Esq. Many members of the Gillard family lie in the vault underneath the family pew, and also under the pavement of that portion of the church.*

* Well, or Langwell House, the residence of J. K. Gillard, Esq., will be alluded to presently.

In the churchyard, which is surrounded by tall elm trees, there are several old monuments and tombstones.

The following appeared in a newspaper of the time, respecting Mrs. Prosser, who was interred in Dodbrooke churchyard; as also was Sir John Savery Drake, her brother.

"At Kingsbridge, in 1822, died Mrs. Ann Pollexfen Prosser, aged 76, widow of Capt. Prosser, of the Royal Marines, and last surviving child of John Drake, formerly collector of customs at Plymouth, the lineal descendant of Sir Francis Drake, Bart., and sister to Sir John Savery Drake, with whom the title became extinct, he dying without issue, and from whom the last Sir Francis cut off the entail of the property given to his ancestor by Queen Elizabeth for his services and discoveries, and gave it to the late Lord Heathfield, after him to Sir Thomas Trayton Fuller Elliott Drake, Bart., High Sheriff of Devon."

The late Mrs. Pearce, widow of William Lyfe Pearce, Esq., was the last survivor of Mrs. Prosser's family of eleven children.

Beyond the bottom of Duncombe Street, and facing a pleasant row of houses, called Waterloo Place, stands Langwell House, or as it is generally called, Well. It is a very old mansion, which has been partly rebuilt, but there are still remains of what appears to have been a monastery, probably belonging to the Monks of Buckfast. But there is no authentic record remaining to tell the history; all the old documents and deeds relating to it, as well as to some other church property, are supposed to have been accidentally destroyed by a fire which occurred in the house of the churchwarden about a hundred years ago. In confirmation of the idea that Langwell was originally monastic in its character, is the fact that one of the aisles in Dodbrooke Church belongs to that estate, and that the proprietor is bound to keep the same in repair. The ancient portions of this place, now mostly used as farm buildings, are situated at the entrance of Wallingford Lane. In John Gye's deed of 1529, Well appears under the name of La Wyll, hence perhaps Langwell. In a feoffee deed 1601, Well occurs as Will-yeate. Yeate is used on Dartmoor for a running stream, and thus Will-yeate would mean that stream which comes down by Will. Well is probably an ancient Saxon word for a spring of water. Again, we find the following, "It is spoken of by tradition that there was a holy spring of water at the once religious establishment, at Well, in Dodbrooke, near Kingsbridge, which the priest affirmed, with his prayers and incantations, would relieve whatsoever complaints were brought to it; and it seems that there were numbers of people from all parts of the neighbourhood who resorted thither, and no doubt considered it infallible. * * * There is no doubt but that the place received its name from this famous well; and there are many other places in the county, called Holywell, Halwell, &c., which perhaps may be derived from the like circumstances." There is an ancient road leading from this house to the religious house at Leigh, near Hatch Bridge.

In Oliver's History of Exeter, he says, "There was in ancient times, a hermitage at Dodbrooke:" and in Polwhele's account of this parish we find these words, "In a place called Court Green, near Court House, are the remains of an old chapel, and the vestiges of a burying place belonging to it. It is situated in a triangular plot, where three ways meet. The walls are still standing, but roofless." This, however, is not the case at the present time. We believe

every portion of the ruins has been removed, and that
pieces of the stone may be seen built into hedges and
walls in the immediate neighbourhood. Some of the larger
stones, probably the upright sides of arches, we rather
think have been laid down as steps in the Dodbrooke
churchyard. With regard to Court House, it has been
stated that it was the original residence of the Champernon
family, whose seat is now at Dartington; and in J. Gye's
deed of gift of that field now called Gye's Field, 1529,
it was spoken of as Champernon's property; but Prince
says that "Sir Arthur Champernon, Knight, was born at
Court House, at the western end of Modbury Town in this
county."

Leaving Wallingford Lane on the left hand, and Batt's
Lane, as it is usually called, on the right, we proceed
towards the National School, which was established in
1847, and of which James and Dorothy Weekes were the
first master and mistress. The building, which can boast
of no architectural beauty, was originally a malt-house,
but was purchased for the purpose of being converted into
a school-house. "The managers of the National School,"
says the *Kingsbridge Gazette* of September 5th, 1873, "have
determined to erect a new class-room adjoining the present
building, so as to meet the Government requirements."
This decision has accordingly been carried out.

Just outside the school-house there is a clear spring of
water, which flows through a pipe, causing a tiny waterfall.
Many of the inhabitants come to "the shoot," as it is
familiarly termed, for a supply of this necessary of life,
which, we believe, never entirely fails, even when other
springs are dry. It is truly a refreshing "brook by the
way."

Instead of mounting the hill towards the church, we will turn round the point elegantly termed "Bellow's Nose," and we soon reach the British School, which (as well as the National) appertains to the children of both Kingsbridge and Dodbrooke.

The piece of land on which the British School now stands was purchased in 1841, by the late Richard Peek, Esq., of Hazelwood, from George Prideaux, Esq., once of Plymouth, but during the latter part of his life a resident in Kingsbridge.

The indenture describes the property as "all that close or parcel of land, with the appurtenances, called or commonly known by the name of Hill Close, *alias* Hill Parks, situate or lying within the parish and manor of Dodbrooke." The indenture also "witnesseth" that Mr. Peek conveys a certain portion of this land to individuals whom he named, "upon trust, to permit the said premises and all buildings thereon erected, or to be erected, to be for ever hereafter appropriated and used as and for a school or schools, for the education of children or adults, or children only, of the labouring, manufacturing, and other poorer classes, in the parishes of Kingsbridge and Dodbrooke, and their vicinity, and as a residence for a schoolmaster and schoolmistress, if required; which said school shall always be conducted upon the principle of the British and Foreign School Society, established in London, and shall be under the general management and control of the committee for the time being of the subscribers to the said school, and shall be at all times open to the inspection of the Government Inspector or Inspectors for the time being." The school was first opened in 1842.

In December, 1850, Richard Peek, Esq., conveyed to

the Trustees the *remainder* of the before-mentioned Hill
Close, or Hill Parks, the income arising from which was
to be applied to the purpose of "reparation of the school
buildings."

A raised causeway extends the whole length of the
main street of Dodbrooke; and in some parts it mounts
up to such a height above the roadway that it has been
described as "suggestive and provocative of broken bones,
being entirely destitute of fence or hand-rail;" and yet we
scarcely ever heard of a catastrophe of the kind occurring
in this locality. At the foot of this bank is a broad
open space of sloping ground, on which the monthly cattle
market is held, and where temporary sheep pens are pitched.
There were formerly *weekly* markets, both in Kingsbridge
and Dodbrooke; the former granted about the year 1256,
and the latter about 1461. Dodbrooke *weekly* market
became obsolete about the close of the last century, after
the establishment, in 1773, of a great cattle market, which
is still held on the third Wednesday of every month.
There is also a fair on the Wednesday before Palm Sunday.

Whereabouts the Dodbrooke Pillory was situated we
know not, but it is left on record that "in the reign of
King Henry III., Henry Fitz Alan impleaded Matthew Fitz
John, with forty others," for throwing it down.

In the main street there are two tanyards; also the
station of the Dodbrooke fire engine. There are a few
good houses, but the greatest number are small, and some
of them very old.

A parchment deed has been placed in the hands of the
writer, relating to buildings in Dodbrooke which are no
longer in existence. It is an indenture made the 24th
day of December, 1797, between Sir Jonathan Phillipps,

of Newport, in the county of Cornwall, Knt., and Richard
Hawkins, of Highhouse, in the parish of Dodbrooke, Esq.,
of the one part, and Thomas Luscombe, of Kingsbridge,
cordwainer, of the other part, concerning the sale to the
latter of "all that messuage called the Cheap House, of or
situate in the Borough and Parish of Dodbrooke," together
with various other buildings; but we find that part of this
property was reserved, viz., "the little shed or room erected,
and built up against, and resting upon, and fastened to
the north wall of the said Cheap House; as the same now
is, and many years last past hath been used as a Toll
House, or place for collecting the Tolls, Dues, and Duties
of the Fair and Market of Dodbrooke aforesaid, which
belong to the said Richard Hawkins," &c.

What portions of these buildings still stand, we know not,
but the property remains in the possession and occupation
of different members of the late Mr. Thomas Luscombe's
family.

In former times, the parish stocks stood in front of
the Cheap House, which erection was a part of the Manor
of Dodbrooke.   .

Hawkins, in 1819, wrote of "the butchery, which still
stands at the market cross, between the sheep-pens, and
what, since the year 1804, has been called Barrack Street,
though enclosed on every side long since, and at present
converted into separate dwellings, had, within memory,
and perhaps still retains, many parts of the interior, to
show for what purposes it was originally used." Doubtless
these are the premises referred to in the deed just mentioned.

Not long before his death, Richard Peek, Esq., contributed
£190 towards the erection of a chapel in Dodbrooke, to
be used by the "Bible Christians." One was accordingly

built near that part where three streets branch off in different directions, viz., Duke Street, Bridge Street, and Ebrington Street.

In Duke Street is situated Lidstone's iron foundry, which it seems, is in Kingsbridge; but as the stream which divides the parishes is *underneath* Duke Street, it is not easy to discover to which some of the houses belong. Mr. Lidstone's foundry stands on the site occupied by the same business in possession of the same family for more than a century. The blacksmith's department was first founded, but has been gradually increased and added to, and at present iron-founding, smithery, and practical engineering are all carried on, with the assistance of the varied appliances of modern machinery, turning lathes, iron-planing machines, boring and punching machines, all of which are worked by steam.

All kinds of edge tools, agricultural machines, and implements, as well as steam engines, are manufactured on the premises. Salcombe being the nearest port to the Channel Islands, a large trade (principally in edge tools) is carried on with them, in connection with the fisheries of Newfoundland and Labrador, and there is also a considerable amount of business with the whole of the South Hams.

Here we find ourselves on Dodbrooke Quay. In November of the year 1825, there was so high a tide that several men went in a boat from the quay to the "King of Prussia" Inn (which is situated just at the junction of the three streets), and through Duke Street and Mill Street.

And again, in 1869, there was a very similar inundation. The quays were covered, and in a very short time, Bridge Street, and a considerable part of Duke Street, Mill Street, and a part of Union Road, were completely flooded; large pieces of timber floated in every direction, and boats were rowed through the streets.

In reference to the death of one of the inhabitants of this part of the town, the following appeared in the *Kingsbridge Gazette* of June 17th, 1865:—

"LONGEVITY.—'The oldest inhabitant' of Kingsbridge, who died last week (we allude to Mrs. Gard), was one of three old ladies, who, singularly enough, are mothers of three tradesmen living close adjoining each other in Duke Street, viz., Messrs. Gard, Lidstone, and Oxenham. The united ages of the three were 274 years; and two of them have lived most, if not all, their lives at the lower end of the town, which is frequently said to be less desirable, in a sanitary point of view, than the higher part."

The *only* name on the Registrar's books as that of a *centenarian* is Grace Tucker, who died at Kingsbridge, in December, 1815; aged 102.

Although Kingsbridge is so conveniently situated for commerce, being exactly at the head of an arm of the sea which is navigable for vessels of burden, yet neither of the quays for landing goods belong to the parish; Dodbrooke Quay being in the parish of that name, and Square's Quay in that of West Alvington. There used to be a creek at right angles with these two quays, but some years ago it was covered in, and superseded by the "Prince of Wales' Road," to the manifest improvement of the sanitary condition of that portion of the town, where the receding tide left anything but a fragrant perfume. Besides many schooners, sloops, barges, and boats, two steamers ply up and down the Estuary; one, the "Kingsbridge Packet," runs to and from Plymouth twice a week; the other which is smaller, called the "Queen," is only used as a *river*

II

steamer. During the summer months this last, in addition
to the regular trips between Kingsbridge and Salcombe,
makes frequent excursions to the North and South Sands,
near Salcombe; thus affording the inhabitants the benefit
of a day's enjoyment at the sea-side, in an easy and in-
expensive way.

Let us cross, by the "Prince of Wales' Road," to Square's
Quay. This road runs in front of the house formerly
occupied by the late Roger Ilbert Prideaux, and which
was then surrounded by a high stone wall, but has been
laid open, and it is now separated from the road by a
handsome iron railing only. We now come to Quay
House, which was erected in 1789, by Lieutenant-Colonel
William Elford Ilbert. It stands near one end of the
quay, from which it is separated by a low wall. On
this side of the Estuary is West Alvington.

WEST ALVINGTON.

CHAPTER VII.

Scenes must be beautiful which daily viewed
Please daily, and whose novelty survives
Long knowledge, and the scrutiny of years.

Cowper.

JUST appearing above the brow of the hill on your right hand, the pinnacles of West Alvington Church tower may be seen. One of these pinnacles was struck by lightning in the winter of 1833, when one of the large granite stones at its base, weighing more than a hundredweight, was blown out. It was afterwards replaced.

Risdon says, "The manor of West Alvington, which had been an ancient demesne of the crown, was given by King John to Alice de Rivers, Countess of Devon. After the death of Alice, wife of Patrick de Chaworth, and daughter and heir of William de la Ferte, it escheated to the crown, and King Henry III. granted it to Matthew de Besils." The lords of this manor had the power of inflicting capital punishment.

The vicarage of West Alvington includes also the parishes of Malborough, South Milton, and South Huish. The present Vicar is the Ven. Archdeacon Earle, M.A., Prebendary of Exeter.

The church, which is dedicated to " All Saints," has a fine embattled tower, and there are within the church some memorials of the Bastard and Holditch families, and a vault belonging to Bowringsleigh. At the time of the restoration of this edifice, a handsome painted window was placed over the communion table, in memory of the late William Ilbert, Esq.

On a headstone in the churchyard is an inscription, which Polwhele says is transcribed *verbatim et literatim.* It is a curiosity in its way:—

> " Here lyeth the Body of
> Daniel Jeffery, the son of Mich-
> ael Jeffery, and Joan his Wife he
> Was buried ye 2nd day of September
> 1746 and in ye 18th year of his age
> This youth when in his sickness lay
> did for the minister Send * that he would
> Come and With him Pray * But he would not atend
> But when this young man Buried was
> the minister did him admit * he should be
> Carried into Church * that he might money geet
> By this you see what man will dwo * to geet
> money if he can * who did refuse to come
> and pray * by the Foresaid young man."

" Upon setting up this stone, the churchwardens immediately waited on their minister, representing to him the offence which the epitaph had given to themselves, and to the parishioners in general, from the scandalous falsehoods it contained, and the stigma intended to be fixed on his character; for they knew that the deceased had died of a virulent smallpox, and that so suddenly, that there was scarce time for giving notice of his illness before his death confirmed it. They, therefore, begged the epitaph might be obliterated, and that they might be supported by his concurrence in doing it. But he, having gratified the churchwardens' indignation, and his own curiosity, by looking at the inscription, begged it might be permitted to remain, for he could not allow himself to have a share in the destruction of such poetry, of which, probably, he chose to be the *subject rather than the composer.*"* This minister was the Rev. and learned Mr. Pyle, the incumbent of the parish at that time, and a Prebendary of the Church of Winchester. We believe the hand of Old Father Time has since swept over the offending inscription, and effected the desired obliteration.†

When the Rev. A. Earle succeeded to the living in 1866, he found the Church affairs of the united parishes in a very critical condition. Three of the churches were in a dilapidated state, and the school-houses required extension and re-building. The churches of West Alvington, Malborough, and South Huish, were considered positively unsafe, and formidable as the enterprise appeared, the restoration or the re-building had to be set about. West Alvington Church has been restored, at a cost of £2,600; new schools have been built in the parish; and a public-house converted into a reading-room for the working classes. Malborough Church has been restored at a cost of £2,500, and handsome new school-rooms also erected. The Church at South Huish was in such a perilous state that it had to be abandoned, and a new one was built at Galmpton to replace it.‡

The Vicarage House is pleasantly situated near the village of West Alvington; and the vicar is assisted in

---

* Polwhele.

† It was afterwards re-cut.

‡ See chapter on Bigbury Bay.

this, his more immediate *locale*, by a curate. A resident minister has been placed by him in each of the other parishes. Formerly, when the vicar, or curates, had to travel from one parish to another, the services were few; now there are either two or three services each Sunday, besides those on week days, in all of them: nor are other means of influence neglected; such as harvest thanksgivings, penny readings, and other social gatherings.

Combe Royal, which is about one mile from Kingsbridge, is in the parish of West Alvington. The Rev. John Earle says, " There is a very old document almost consumed by rot, which, however, has a sound piece with the name Combe Royal on it. Roger Efford remits, releases, and for ever cries quits to Richard Chiceli of all his right and claim in Kingsbridge, Dodbrooke, and *Come-royel*. The date of this is 1373."

It may be mentioned that at this date the Archbishop of Canterbury was a member of this family of Chiceli.

This beautiful place, Combe Royal, is the property of John Luscombe, Esq. The mansion was enlarged and restored some years ago, and it is now the most attractive residence in the neighbourhood.

After passing the lodge, which is a pretty ivy-covered building, you enter on a winding carriage road, bordered by magnificent rhododendrons, hydrangeas, and other fine evergreen shrubs. The sloping grounds are beautifully diversified with wood and water : the orange walk presents great attractions to strangers, unaccustomed as they probably are to the sight of oranges, lemons, and citrons, flourishing in the open air, and bringing their fruit to perfection, with only the occasional protection of straw mats placed against the recesses in the walls at night.

In the *Journal of Horticulture* of August 31, 1871, there is an interesting paper describing Combe Royal. It is here inserted, with one or two corrections.

"'Who are you?' 'Visitors to Combe Royal.' 'Ha! Ha!' Such was the query, reply, and final laugh which occurred at the door of the Malster's Arms, at Harberton, where we pulled up on a 120°-in-the-sun day of this present month of August, to give our horses a few mouthfuls of water. If our interrogator had been even a better authority than a parrot we should not have been deterred from proceeding to our destination, for we were assured by good judges that we should be well recompensed for enduring a drive of thirty miles under such a sunshine: those judges were right, without any reference to the specially excellent cider made in the parish. That parish is West Alvington, in Devonshire, about a mile from Kingsbridge. The Manor was an ancient demesne of the crown in the time of the Norman monarchs, if not even previously, and was given by King John to Alice de Rivers, Countess of Devon, but reverted to the crown, and was subsequently granted by Henry III. to Matthew de Besils. Afterwards it was divided into various smaller estates, one of which was certainly 'all that barton known as Combe Royal,' for a barton was the demesne lands of a manor, and is named in an existing deed of the time of Edward III. This barton passed to various possessors until the Gilberts became its possessors, and one of the Gilberts of Holwell sold it in 1722 to an ancestor of the present proprietor, John Luscombe Luscombe, Esq.[*] Luscombe is a truly Devonian name (and is Anglo-Saxon for 'a valley of delight'), and the Luscombes of Luscombe,

---

[*] "*Great great* grandfather of the present proprietor. He was High Sheriff of Devonshire in 1740."—J. L.

in the parish of Rattery, held there a knight's fee in the time of Henry IV. and were residing there in 1630.*

The family were never ennobled, but they have always borne 'the grand old name of Gentleman,' and we can add, from experience, that the Luscombe of the present fully sustains Westcote's character of the Devon gentry, 'they are civil, affable, kind, and courteous to strangers.' Combe Royal undoubtedly was so named because part of the King's demesne, but it also merits the distinguishing epithet, as one of the kings of the wooded valleys of the country.

The entrance lodge is at one extremity of the valley, the house is at the other end; and the approach is by a road winding along the valley between the well-planted hills which border each side. Its situation is peculiarly adapted to the growth of exotic plants, as it is two hundred and eighty feet above the sea level, and screened by hills from the prevailing south-west winds, and also from the north and east.

The successful culture of the trees of the Citrus family is a peculiarity of Combe Royal, as it is believed that the luxuriance and fruitfulness of the trees cannot be equalled in England, when it is remembered that no protection is afforded them beyond the walls on which they are trained, and the frames of wood or reed with which they are covered by night, and partially by day, when needful, in the winter. One Seville Orange tree, from which vast quantities of fruit are annually gathered, is traditionally known to be 250 years old, from the fact that the grandmother of the present proprietor was told when a child by

---

* "It is believed that the Combe Royal family branched from the parent stock more than three centuries ago, and after residing at Scobbahul and Wood, settled in their present home."—J. L.

her grandfather, John Luscombe, Esq., that it was more than a century old when he became the possessor of the place.

The Citron trees often produce enormous fruit, several having attained seventeen, eighteen, and even nineteen inches in circumference. The Shaddocks, Lemons, and Limes are fine in proportion.

No permanent injury has ever been done to the trees by the severest winters, except in 1859-60, when a vigorous Bergamot Lemon was killed, which at the time bore a fine crop of fruit, averaging twelve inches in circumference. A magnificent basket of Citrus fruit was in 1850 presented to the Queen, who, through Sir Charles Phipps, graciously expressed her surprise and admiration of their size and beauty, and sent Mr. Toward from Osborne to inspect the trees. The Orangery, or, as it might more justly be entitled, the Citrusry, for it includes the best fruit-bearers of the genus, is on the side of the valley, has nearly a southern aspect, and is a recessed wall. * * * The recesses are all eleven feet high, but vary in width. That in which the Lemon is growing is fifteen feet, that of the Citron sixteen feet, and the six other recesses are twelve feet: all of them are fifteen inches deep. The occupants of these eight recesses are the Lemon, Bergamot, Citron, Seville Orange, Shaddock, Orange, Lime, and Mandarin Orange. Although the thermometer fell to zero last winter no injury was caused to any one of the trees, although their only protection was reed panels. When we saw them, ripening fruit was on all of them, and the healthy luxuriance of their foliage was most striking. Anyone about to erect such recesses for the culture of the Citrus genus would do well to have each eighteen feet wide, for the need to prune back the branches in the Combe Royal

recesses must increase the difficulty of securing the fruitfulness of the trees by avoiding over luxuriance.

Perhaps one of the largest specimens of Acacia dealbata
in England once ornamented the grounds. It was, unfor-
tunately, broken down and uprooted by the weight of
snow in an unusually heavy fall in December, 1859. It
measured fifty-four feet in height, and the trunk was more
than five feet in circumference. From the heart timber
an ornamental drawing-room chair has been manufactured.
A very large species of Eucalyptus, a native of Tasmania,
has stood the last winter well, and bloomed profusely in
the spring of the present year, while Embothriums coccineum
and lanceolatum have been gorgeous with their scarlet
flowers, and Camellias prodigal of bloom. Desfontainea
spinosa has done well, and Opuntia Rafinesquiana grows
and blooms in the open air. Many more plants, shrubs,
and trees, deserving notice must be omitted, but we will
observe that the Datura arborea in the conservatory had four
hundred of its noble flowers open simultaneously. In the
open ground we saw specimens of Cycas, huge bushes of
Camellias, species of Aralia, Bamboos from the Himalaya,
Abutilon vitifolium, all of which endure the winter unprotected. We also noticed a deciduous Conifer, the name
of which is doubtful. We think it is the Glyptostrobus
pendulus, a native of China; at all events it is hardy at
Combe Royal, and we should like to be certified of its
name. We must note one bed of Phlox Drummondi in
front of the conservatory. We never saw a bed of crimson,
scarlet, purple, and pink flowers so brilliant. Beds of
verbenas on each side looked poor and paltry in comparison.

Almost equalling the orangery in interest is the American
garden, formed by the present proprietor in a branch of

this 'happy valley.' Among a collection of other trees and shrubs, it includes the Sikkim Rhododendrons received from Kew through the kindness of the late Sir William Hooker. Many of them are doing well. The strongest and most floriferous are Thomsoni, niveum, and Blandfordiæflorum; the latter produces its gay and peculiar blossoms in the greatest profusion, and the bushes of Thomsoni are gorgeous with their wax-like bells of the richest crimson. Being seedling plants they vary much, and several cannot be identified when compared with Dr. Hooker's exquisite drawings, or rather the plates from his drawings. This year the beautiful yellow Rhododendron Wightii flowered for the first time, but the blossoms were pure white; its foliage, however, is unmistakable. Some of the more tender sorts, Dalhousiæ, Edgworthii, Aucklandii, Falconeri, and one or two others, will not endure the winter even at Combe Royal. The Japanese Rhododendron Metternichii has borne the severity of the last two winters well, as have five plants of the Himalayan R. cinnamomeum. The preceding winters have proved fatal to many large specimens of the true R. arboreum, two only having survived. The trunk of one of the defunct trees was measured recently, and found to be, a short distance above the earth, three feet one inch in circumference.

The recent proprietors of Combe Royal have been gardeners as well. As far back as 1812 a practice of J. L. Luscombe, Esq., for successfully raising cuttings of the Citrus genus was made known to the Royal Horticultural Society, and approved by the then President T. A. Knight, Esq. The same Society awarded him a Banksian medal for Oranges, Lemons, and Citrons, exhibited in the April of 1827."

We may add that J. Luscombe, Esq., says, "Wood in
Woodleigh, where the family also lived was a very large,
low, Tudor mansion, originally the seat of one of the
many branches of the Fortescue family. During the
minority of the late John Luscombe Luscombe, Esq., a
great portion of the house was taken down, the porch and
two or three gables only remaining: one of the wings is
used as a barn, and still goes by the name of 'the dining
parlour,' and on the walls of which fresco paintings might,
a few years since, be here and there discerned: the chapel
stood on the opposite side of the enclosed court-yard:
the andirons of the hall chimney, three feet high, form
the stand of a marble table at Combe Royal."

In this parish is also Bowringsleigh; a large and
ancient Tudor mansion, recently restored, but admirably
retaining its former character. It lies in a beautiful valley
below West Alvington.

Sir William Pole says of this place, "Bowrings Legh was
th'ancient dwellinge of the name of Bowringe; the last of
which name, called Thomas, had issue Alis married unto
William Pike of Pike's Ash, in Somersetshire, and had
issue Robert Pike, which had issue Thomas, which by
Mary, daughter of John Stowell, of Cotheston, had issue
Elizabeth, married unto one James Leghe, called Reynolds,
sometyme a singing boy in the church of St. Peter, in
Exon, a man of great baseness, which hath sold a great
estate, which he had by the said Elisabeth, and this unto
Nicholas Webber, alias Gilbard Esq., who now dwelleth
theire. Theire is now a tytle sett on foote, that the said
Thomas Pike should have a sonne called Stephan, long
tyme concealed, and never known unto his supposed father,
or publickly unto any other, before all Pike's land was sold."

This fine old mansion was purchased of the Gilberts in the reign of William III., by William Ilbert, Esq., of Rill, (of which place there is a picture over one of the mantlepieces at Bowringsleigh). Since that time Bowringsleigh has continued in this family, and it is now the residence of W. R. Ilbert, Esq.

An old picture of Bowringsleigh represents it after undergoing a restoration, when the roofs were replaced by others in the Dutch style, and the gardens were laid out in the same formal manner; but the present possessor has adopted the *original* style of architecture in carrying out the recent restorations.

Many years ago the chapel and some other parts of the building were accidentally burnt, many of the old family portraits and other valuable paintings were destroyed, besides the tapestry which hung on the walls; but there are still paintings of value remaining; amongst them is a portrait of Queen Anne, which was given, we believe, by that Queen herself to Mr. Ilbert's great grandmother, to whom her Majesty had performed the office of god-mother.

The chapel, which abuts from the south front is a faithful restoration of the original chapel: a magnificent screen, (which was formerly in South Huish Church), admirably restored and gilded, adorns the interior.

In one of the rooms there is a grand old ceiling, with emblematic figures moulded in plaster, in high relief. In the centre is Fame, blowing her trumpet, while in various compartments around there are warlike implements and instruments of music; the whole of the figures so raised as to appear as if clinging by magnetism to the ceiling.

There is a very curious clock in one of the rooms, the

date 1702.   The present writer cannot attempt to recapitu-
late all the wonderful things it undertakes to perform.
A clock on the tower roof is dated, we believe, 1717; its
bell might be made to sound, in case of need, for some
miles around.

Bowringsleigh has not been without its traditionary ghost,
and haunted room.   The "singing boy," "the man of
great baseness" (according to Sir William Pole) was said
to have been murdered on the premises, which dreadful
event coming to the ears of his wife "Elisabeth," she
rushed, shrieking wildly, into the room where the tragedy
occurred; never again to be seen or heard of, save as a
haunting ghost, occasionally wandering about the house in
her rustling silk attire!   How much, or how little of truth
there may be in this story "deponent sayeth not."

However, the ghost seems to have been summarily ejected,
for the room, which was for many years closed up, and
specially devoted to its ghostly inhabitant, has been converted into a dressing room, into which she certainly
never intrudes her presence.

One of the curiosities at Bowringsleigh is an ancient
bed, with hangings of needlework, the laborious production
of a lady-ancestor of the family.   Many other things
of interest might be mentioned, but we must retrace our
steps down the noble avenue of lime trees, and across
the wooded meadows, through which passes the "private
road" to Bowringsleigh, and also to Norden, the residence
of Mrs. Ilbert, mother of W. R. Ilbert, Esq.

Although South Milton is situated not far from the shore
of Bigbury Bay, being within an easy distance of Thurlestone Sands, yet this seems the most fitting place to
introduce a few words respecting it, seeing that it is

included in the vicarage of West Alvington; and that Horswell House, the residence for many years of W. Ilbert, Esq., is in this parish. Of South Milton Sir William Pole says, "Midleton, or South Milton, anno 24 of Kinge Ed. 1, James de Mohun held; and anno 19 of Kinge Ed. 3, Sir William Pipard Kt. held the same. Hee died anno Domini 1349, and left issue Margaret, wief of Sir Gerard de Lisle, and Matild, wief of Sir Osbert Hameley. This mannor came afterwarde unto Carew of Haccomb; and is lately sold unto Sir James Bagge, of Plymouth, by Carew, of Haccomb." White said in 1850," Mrs. Prideaux is lady of the manor." We believe it has descended to her daughter, Mrs. Douglass.

South Milton Church "is a fine ancient edifice in the perpendicular style, with a noble embattled tower, containing six bells."

The old stone font is surmounted by a high, conical carved wood cover, which is much admired. There is also a carved screen. On the walls are tablets recording the names of Elliot, Prideaux, &c.; and on the pavement, that of Roope, accompanied by coats of arms.

Very many tomb-stones in the churchyard bear the name of Elliot. There is also a vault of the Ilbert family distinguished by a yew tree within iron railings. Milton is now (like Thurlestone and Buckland) noteworthy from the absence of a public house! The one which formerly existed there was converted, some time since, into school-rooms, where considerable numbers of children are now educated. Some of the farm houses in this neighbourhood bear evident traces of a somewhat aristocratic origin, such as Higher and Lower Sutton, Callicott, &c.

CHAPTER VIII.

With ceaseless motion comes and goes the tide,
Flowing it fills the channel vast and wide;
Then back to sea, with strong majestic sweep
It rolls, in ebb yet terrible and deep.

Crabbe.

RETURNING to Dodbrooke Quay, and passing the house, with timber and coal stores, (once the property of the late Joseph Hingston, who was a deservedly respected and valued resident for many years; and afterwards belonging to F. H. Fox & Co., who sold it to Messrs. Beer & Trant) we come to Pindar Lodge, which now stands on the site of the "smart little mansion," where John Wolcot, M.D., was born (an account of whom is given in the fourth chapter).

Almost, if not quite, the only *mile* of level road adjacent to the town, is that which runs from Dodbrooke Quay down by the side of the Estuary. This is a very pleasant promenade, especially when the tide is in.

After passing Pindar Lodge, as well as a pretty cottage which was built in 1816 by Mr. John Lidstone, and Victoria Place, and Glenâ, pleasant looking modern houses, we reach Boxhill, a substantial mansion, with a verandah in front. Part of it was built on the site of the old Dodbrooke Poor-house; indeed, until rather recently, a small portion of that ancient erection might still be found somewhere on its back premises.

Then comes Foxhole, or as it now called, Vauxhall, and behind it is Garden Mill, overlooked by Buttville, the property of the late Admiral Hawkins, and now of his son, C. S. Hawkins, Esq.

A quarter of a mile below Dodbrooke Quay is Saltmill Quay, on the same side of the Estuary. Here stood some corn mills until the middle of the eighteenth century, driven by the water secured by flood gates at the flowing of the tide, in an enclosure at the side of the Quay, but which about the year 1800 was turned into a meadow.

A lime kiln just here was for a long time noticeable on account of a noble Wych elm, growing quite through a side wall, and spreading its graceful branches all over the front of the kiln. It was the only specimen of this particular kind of elm that we knew of anywhere in the neighbourhood, but it was laid low by a fearful gale which occurred in January, 1866, and did much damage in this vicinity. At Wallingford, the gale seems to have been felt in its greatest force—the wind taking the line of the valley. There are, or rather were, in that valley, several hedges full of fine elm trees, and one after another of these were completely swept away, the trees lying along in regular rows, as if they had been felled with an axe. There were altogether one hundred and four trees prostrated in this valley alone.

About the end of the last century, a wall was commenced by Edward Hodges, Esq., at Salt Mill Quay, in order to form a public walk, to be planted with trees, which would make a pleasant communication, secure from the flowing tide, between the wharf and Dodbrooke Quay;

but when this design had been partially effected, a dispute arose as to the freehold right, and the work remained unfinished till 1816, when it was completed by a public subscription.

In the year 1804, a spot of ground on the east side of the Estuary was selected by the late Lieutenant-General Simcoe, and temporary barracks were erected thereon to contain six hundred men. Various regiments occupied them during the war : the materials of these structures, however, were disposed of by auction in the spring of 1815, but some of the buildings, particularly the hospital, having been purchased by the owner of the land, are yet suffered to remain, and are occupied by different families. We have been told that the bakehouse which belonged to the barracks now forms part of the house once known as Ivy Cottage. Winsor Lodge was erected in one of the fields, by Mr. Andrew Winsor, in 1818. High-house, a seat situated on these lands, is about half a mile to the east, but not in sight of the water.

We must not omit to notice the Shipwright's Yard, where many a well-built vessel is constructed, to be employed in the foreign fruit trade, or some other branch of commerce. Date's yard presents a busy scene, and is especially attractive to the population of Kingsbridge and Dodbrooke when it becomes known that a launch is to take place. There is generally, at such times, a large gathering assembled to watch the new vessel make her first plunge into the tide. This yard was first established in 1837. Vessels are there built of from one hundred to five hundred tons burden; the *largest*, as yet, five hundred and fifty tons; and the average number of men employed, forty.

Complaints having been made that the public path

beneath the cliff was much interfered with by the lodgment
of timber, the Harbour Commissioners requested the owner
to remove the obstruction, which was effected; but only
for a time. He was therefore requested to make a new
and good road, as an approach to the steamer landing-
place at High-house Point. This has been done, and it is
much used, instead of the steep and narrow path some
time since cut in the cliff.

A field at High-house Point has recently been purchased
from the Rev. P. A. Ilbert, for the purpose of forming a
new cemetery for Kingsbridge. This being considered a
larger piece of ground than would be required, a portion
of it was again sold, and the remainder retained for the
cemetery. It was expected that the ground would be ready
for use about the end of last year (1873); but it is not
yet available.

Nearly opposite the shipwright's yard, on the other side
of the estuary, is Tacket (or Ticket) Wood, where there
are a few houses and a slate quarry. There is a bridge
near by, bearing the same name, crossed by the old road
to Salcombe. It was erected by the county in 1768.

Ticket Wood is supposed to have derived its name from
the circumstance that, in the days of Nonconformist persecution, *tickets* were here given to all who were in the
habit of attending the meetings, probably as a precaution
against the admission of spies amongst them.

On a hill, between Ticket Wood and Kingsbridge, there
is a large rope-walk, which was established by Mr. Thomas
about fifty years ago. This rope-walk was burnt down
on the 14th of August, 1868, and re-built early in 1869.
Since that time, it has been lengthened very considerably,
necessitated from the increased demand for the cordage made

here. Large quantities are sent off to the North of England;
also to Quebec and the Labrador fisheries. About eighteen
men and nine boys are usually employed here.

To return to the east side of the estuary. Rather
beyond the first mile-stone on this, the "new road" to
Dartmouth, is Charleton Bridge, crossing a creek, near the
head of which is Shindle mill. This bridge possesses some
peculiarities of construction, probably not to be found elsewhere. The following particulars were kindly furnished,
in 1864, by Mr. Joseph Pulliblank, builder, and son-in-law
of Mr. John Eddy, therein mentioned:—"The present horizontal swing-bridge over the Bowcombe creek was erected
in the year 1815. The contract for its erection was taken
on the 1st of January in that year by Mr. A. Saunders, of
Kingsbridge, millwright and engineer, and the work was
carried out under the superintendence of Mr. John Eddy,
surveyor. The principle of the bridge (being required to
open to allow of the navigation of the creek) is a strong
horizontal framework of wood, about forty-five feet long
by sixteen feet wide, resting on a strong fulcrum of timber,
built into a solid mass of masonry, and shod with tempered
iron at its upper end—the weight resting on twelve cannon
balls, which play freely in two grooved pieces of cast-iron,
one of which is fixed to the movable framework, and the
other to the solid masonry below. This application of
cannon balls excited the admiration of a very worthy
member of the Society of Friends, since deceased, who
observed that it was such an use of cannon balls as he
could approve of, and he wished they were always as well
employed."

Since the foregoing was written, the bridge being much
out of repair, it was rebuilt. Mr. Pulliblank says: "The

plans for the present bridge were prepared by Mr. W. Symons, who was also the contractor for its erection. There are a few unimportant alterations of detail in construction, but the *principle* is the same, and I believe the *cannon balls* remain where the good Joseph Hingston was *pleased* to see them."

From the Bowcombe quarry, on the Charleton side of the inlet, is drawn a large quantity of good building stone. Descending a little further, you get a pretty near view of Charleton church (St. Mary), which is an ancient structure, but it was thoroughly renovated in 1849-50, when the nave and aisles were mostly re-built, and new windows were inserted, with mullions of Caen stone. "The lordship of Charleton was, amongst other lands, granted by Henry VIII., in the thirty-fifth year of his reign, to Catherine, Queen of England, for her dower. On the death of Catherine, in the second year of the reign of Edward VI., it reverted to that king, on whose death it descended to, and became the property of, his sister Queen Mary, who by letters patent of the 22nd of June, in the first year of her reign, granted the same unto Francis, then Earl of Huntingdon." It was afterwards held by Lord Borringdon; and is now the property of Lady Ashburton. As lately as the year 1753 the Hundred Court was regularly held, presentments were made, and the different parishes in the Hundred paid small chief-rents to the lord of the manor. The original grant conveyed most extensive privileges, but many of them are no longer exercised. The rectory house, which was spoken of by Polwhele as an "uncouth structure," was mostly taken down by William Tickell, L.B., at that time the Incumbent, and re-built; and it is now said to be one of the "best parsonage houses in the county." The Rev. Thomas Twysden, M.A., is the present Rector.

Charleton is divided into two portions, so that it appears like two separate villages; these are known as East Charleton and West Charleton. The hamlets of Goveton and Lidstone, as well as part of Frogmore, are in this parish; as also is Slade, the residence of the late Fortescue Wells, Esq., and now of his son-in-law, Edward Arthur, Esq.

Across the estuary, and nearly opposite High-house Point, is Park, a very pleasant house, overlooking the water, and further on are the remains of a decoy, commonly called Coypool, which, in the beginning of the last century, was much used for taking wild fowl.

Gerston, or Garston, the ancient seat of the Bastard family, lies just above, but is not visible from the water. During the eighteenth century, the gardens at this place were famed for producing oranges and lemons, trained against the walls in the manner of peach trees, and sheltered only with mats of straw in winter. Some of the fruit, said to be "as large and fair as any from Portugal," was presented to the king by Lady Bridget Bastard's brother, Vere, the third Earl Poulett, about the year 1770. Here the noble family of Bastard resided from the days of William the Conqueror till the year 1773. William Bastard, Esq., having, however, fixed his abode at Kitley, the ancient mansion was deserted. When the French fleet menaced Plymouth in the summer of 1779, this gentleman raised a large force of yeomanry and peasants, and repaired to the scene of alarm. For his exertions on this occasion he was created a baronet on the 19th of October in that year. However, although the dignity conferred was gazetted, yet neither he nor his descendants have thought proper to use the title.

After passing Gerston Point there is a creek which leads to Collapit. Besides the farm-house, there is a bridge of the same name in the road to Salcombe. Then comes Rowden Point, and a creek runs thence to Blanks' or Alston Mill, also headed by a bridge. On the left side of the estuary there is a piece of land now used by the Volunteers as a "rifle range," which is usually denominated "Charleton Marshes." In 1805 Earl Morley here formed an embankment, by which between thirty and forty acres were reclaimed from the tide, and in a couple of years this land began to vegetate.

You now enter an extensive breadth of water, called Wide-gates, where, in a high wind, it is occasionally a little hazardous to small boats; for instances have occurred now and then of a capsize.

Upon the high land overlooking the little port of Salcombe, and about four miles from Kingsbridge, stands "All Saints'," the church of the parish of Malborough, one of the four included in the West Alvington Vicarage, and (as elsewhere stated) this church has undergone a thorough restoration, through the exertions of the Vicar, the Ven. Archdeacon Earle. Decayed as many parts of the building were, the masonry is remarkably substantial; so far, therefore, as the walls were concerned, little was required to be done; but new roofs have been constructed, the windows re-filled with stone mullions and tracery, the pews cleared away and replaced by open benches, and the tower-arch thrown open, by the removal of the gallery, so that the bells are now rung from the ground. Of these bells, Polwhele says "they are much esteemed by those who like such ding-dong sounds." The building is chiefly of the Late Perpendicular period; but the tower and chancel

exhibit indications of Early Decorated work; and the font
is Early English.

Within the church is a handsome white marble monument,
erected to the memory of the 28th Baron Kingsale. This
will be referred to in the account of Ringrone.

A memorial window was placed in the church by —
Pinwell, Esq., of Salcombe; and there is another, the history
of which is unknown to the writer. Both of these are
modern.

In the month of August, 1829, this spire was struck by
lightning in a very similar manner to that which injured
the Kingsbridge spire in the previous year. At the time
of the occurrence the minister was reading the burial service
in the church, while the relations and friends of a deceased
parishioner were assembled for the funeral. The sudden
flashes of lightning, and the tremendous peals of thunder,
caused such an alarm, that the clergyman, as well as all
the people, rushed out of the church, and did not return
until the storm was over. The spire was so much injured
that it had to be taken down and re-built.

Some new school-rooms having been erected in Malborough, they were opened, in May, 1873, by Dr. Temple,
Bishop of the Diocese.

A Baptist chapel was built in this place in 1815. This
was enlarged and repaired in 1872. A new school-room
was also built in 1872; and much has been done this
year (1874). The names of successive pastors are

   Rev. John Nicholson,
    ,, W. H. Evans,
    ,, H. Crossman,
    ,, E. Tamsett Davis (the present pastor).

A Wesleyan chapel, of very neat design, has also recently
been erected in Malborough.

This place stands on very elevated ground, and commands an extensive prospect, bounded on the south by the open sea, in the direction of Bolt Head and Bolt Tail.

Some of the inhabitants used to say, no moon ever shone so brightly as "Marber moon," and perhaps this is not altogether imaginary, for, being raised so far above the mists and fogs of the valleys, there may be less vapour to intercept the light which shines down upon them.

Batson, Bolberry, Collaton, Combe, Rew, and Shadycombe, are hamlets forming part of the parish of Malborough.

At Batson (where some of the most productive cider orchards in the kingdom are situated) there is an old ruin, partially covered with ivy, which is still known by the name of "Batson Hall." Tradition says that it was formerly a prison. Bit by bit, the materials which composed this, evidently, at one time fine old place, are removed, to serve as repairs for the adjoining farm-house, which was doubtless a part of the same mansion. There is little now remaining save a window or two, where the fine carved work may still be seen, and a stone mantlepiece, on which a very early date may be deciphered. This place is the property of Mr. Bastard, of Kitley.

At the upper part of Blanks' Mill Creek is seen Alston, the seat of the late Abraham Hawkins, Esq., author of the "History of Kingsbridge" which was published in 1819. This gentleman was a descendant of Sir John Hawkins, who, as well as his son, Sir Richard, were both celebrated navigators and naval commanders in the reign of Queen Elizabeth. On the south of Alston, but scarcely to be seen from the water, is Yarde House, in the parish of Malborough. This is on the barton of Yarde, and was formerly the residence of the family of that name, to whom, according

to Prince, it belonged for twenty generations. In the reign
of Richard II., a Yarde having married the heiress of Bussel,
their posterity changed their dwelling to Bradley. It then
came to the Dyers, in whose family it remained until the
male heirs became extinct. In 1765, Samuel Savery, Esq.,
succeeded to it, with other estates, in right of his great-
grandmother, whose maiden name was Dyer, from whom
it descended to Miss Burnell.* The name of Yarde still
continues in the Buller and other families.

In the middle of Wide-gates is an islet, or rock, called
the Salt-stone, about a hundred feet in length, and more
than fifty in breadth. "As it is extra-parochial," says
Hawkins, "and perhaps doubtful to whom it belongs, lying
nearly equi-distant from the parishes of Charleton, South
Pool, and Malborough, it is surprising that no one has
taken possession of it, to erect some building thereon for
speculative purposes." This remark leads some to think
that formerly the Salt-stone must have been considerably
more raised above high-water mark than it is at present;
others do not suppose this to be the case.

"The Earl of Devon claims to hold a Court of Admiralty
—a royal privilege granted by the Crown to his ancestors,
extending from this islet on the east to a place called
Shaggy Rock, in the river Aune, or Avon, which empties
itself into Bigbury Bay on the west, including the sea
coast between these limits, *as far off as a man on horseback
can see an umber barrel;* and by a jury of thirteen respectable men, settles matters respecting salvage, pays the
amount, and preserves the property for the owners till

* It is now the property, by purchase, of T. W. Weymouth, Esq.

claimed, when the same is delivered over, deducting only what has been paid the salvors."*

It is traditional that in the old days of persecution, the Nonconformists took advantage of the fact of this rock being a sort of "no man's land," and accordingly resorted thither at low water, in order to hold their meetings, seeing that the "justices" could not legally interfere with them there; not that these justices were always very particular as to the lawfulness of their proceedings. These meetings appear to have been associated with the name of Flavel rather more than that of John Hicks.

The Salt-stone is mentioned by Colonel Montagu in his "Testacea Britannica," as the locality in which he procured several marine animals; amongst others, the Amphitrite infundibundum, one of the molluscous tribe, which he describes in the Transactions of the Linnæan Society; and amongst the crustacea he particularises Cancer astacus subterraneus (we give the Colonel's own nomenclature, though many changes have taken place in this respect since his time). "This crab," he says, "is a new and curious species, discovered in digging for Solen vagina." Of the Solen vagina he remarks, "this shell has been usually considered as rare in a living or recent state, but we have lately had the good fortune to discover it in its native bed. In a sand bank, near the Salt-stone, in the Estuary of Kingsbridge, it is by no means uncommon at the depth of two feet or more beneath the surface." Montagu also says, that by far the finest specimens he ever saw of Bulla hydatis were found on the south side of the Salt-stone. The Turbo clathrus is found in the same locality. He

* Hawkins.

says, "as the animal becomes sickly by keeping for some days in sea water, it frequently discharges a most beautiful purple liquor. This circumstance was known to Plancus, who observes that it is *one* of those shells which yields the purple dye of the Mediterranean."

Kingsbridge Estuary is full of interest to the student in natural history. Amongst the feathered tribes almost every genus has its representative, either as an inhabitant, or an occasional visitant. In winter these sheltered waters become the rendezvous of a great variety of birds.

Many different kinds of gulls may be seen, preening their delicate plumage, and enjoying the still, cold water, or standing in groups on the shore, making the most entertaining noises. Did you ever listen to them holding forth in one of their conventicles? (for they, too, frequent the Salt-stone). If not, you have missed one of the most amusing sounds of the sea shore. Frequently, herons are seen, stalking silently about in search of their slippery prey; while flocks of tringa are coursing over the mud when the tide is low, industriously foraging for their daily food; streams of wild ducks vary the scene; and to crown all (if the weather is very severe) the Hooper, or wild swan, with its snow-white plumage, and its gracefully-arching neck, may be seen sailing along.*

Various sorts of fish are caught in the estuary, such as millet, bass, eels, dabs, smelts, and mackerel. About sixty years since, a large shoal of porpoises were seen rolling up past Salcombe, apparently in hot pursuit of some of their favourite prey (probably mackerel). It was about

* Mr. Henry Nicholls has kindly furnished a list of birds which have been found in the neighbourhood; and also of butterflies. Both will be found at the end of this book.

half-tide, and it was ebbing rapidly. The fish passed over what is called the "four hours' mud" into the shallow water, the porpoises still pursuing, and intent on their anticipated feast. At last they were seen to be flapping and floundering about in a distressed manner, until it became evident that sixteen of them were completely left by the tide, and were stranded on the mud. The whole of them were secured, and became a profitable speculation to their captors.

Passing Wareham Point, and just at the mouth of the Frogmore Creek, Halwell Wood rises from the water's edge. Halwell House lies about half-a-mile from thence; it is in the parish of South Pool. In Domesday Book, Halwell is spelt Halgewelle, which is nearly the correct Saxon spelling of Holywell. The wood used to be a favourite resort for pleasure parties from Kingsbridge on a fine summer's evening; and frequently a thin column of smoke might be seen rising in the vicinity of the shed which was erected for their accommodation; for a fire was sometimes extemporised, and the kettle boiled amongst the trees. But since the *Queen* steamer has been available, the North and South Sands have almost entirely superseded the wood in the matter of picnics.

A murder was suspected to have been committed near this spot many years ago. Nicholas Wood and another man, who both lived at Kingsbridge, and worked at Salcombe for Mr. Strong, maltster, went down together in a boat. They were apparently on good terms, but on returning it appeared that, although both sober, they must have disagreed about something, as Wood's companion was overheard saying, "I'll settle thee before we get back to Kingsbridge;" but this was thought nothing of at the

time.   It was nearly dark when they returned, or rather
when *one* of them returned, for Wood was never more
seen alive.   Several persons bore witness to the fact of
having heard cries of murder in the direction of the water,
but being dark they did not ascertain the exact spot from
whence they proceeded; it was thought, however, that
some withheld their testimony lest through their means the
man's life would be forfeited; and so the affair remained
a mystery; but sixteen years afterwards, a human skeleton
was found buried beneath the beach on one of the points
of land, and kept down by large stones.

The village of Frogmore (which is partly in Charleton
and partly in Sherford parish) is situated at the head of
a navigable creek.   Vessels of one hundred tons here load
and unload their cargoes; and there are lime kilns, coal
wharfs, and corn stores.   There was formerly an extensive
flour mill in this village, but it was destroyed by fire about
the year 1845, and it has never been re-built, which is
somewhat surprising, considering the amount of water power
which would be available for working it.   The ruins of
the mill, although gradually crumbling away, have been so
beautifully covered with ivy, and look so picturesque, that
strangers very commonly suppose them to be the remains
of an old monastery, which they closely resemble.*

There are some valuable slate quarries in the neighbourhood of Frogmore.   The Molescombe quarries were
first opened in the reign of Henry VIII.   The Winslade
quarries were very old workings re-opened a few years
ago, but from repeatedly falling in, are, we believe, again

---

* " The Thames to the Tamar " has the following remark :—"At Frogmore a decayed flour mill, covered with ivy, has received a kind of counterfeit
dignity, being generally taken for a ruined castle."

abandoned. The watchful care of a superintending Providence was remarkably exemplified on the occasion of one these fallings-in, and ought to be recorded. About thirty men, we believe, were assembled by appointment, in order to work at one particular spot, when it was discovered that the man who had the key of the powder store was absent; and after waiting some time for his return, they dispersed, being unable to proceed with their work without the blasting powder. In a very short time that part of the quarry in which they *would* have been, but for this *disappointment*, fell in, and entombed the two men who alone were there, instead of the large number who were thus providentially prevented from going. Although great exertions were made at the time, yet the bodies of these two poor fellows were not recovered for two or three years. We should like to know that the men who experienced this remarkable preservation were duly sensible of the great mercy shewn them, and that thanksgivings arose in every heart.

And now leaving the Frogmore creek, we are advancing towards another, which soon divides into two branches, or, as Hawkins expresses it, "with a bifurcated continuation;" that to the left leading to South Pool, while that towards the right runs up to Waterhead, and almost to Chivelstone. South Pool is said to have been formerly a part of the parish of Stokenham. The church, which is dedicated to St. Syriac, is a fine specimen of the perpendicular style, with a lofty tower. The interior has transepts; the screen is elaborately carved; and in the chancel is a handsome altar tomb, or Easter Sepulchre, with a representation in the front of the Resurrection. In this church there are many handsome antique monuments.

The Rev. R. D. Alexander, the Incumbent of South Pool,
says (April 7th, 1873) :—"The church is mainly of fifteenth
century work.   Our school, which everybody said was
absurdly large, &c., has proved a great success.   Indeed,
the only mistake I made was that I did not build it large
enough; H. M. Inspector having twice told us he shall
expect to see a class-room built soon."

Risdon says, that "South Pole was the lands of the
Lord Nicholas de Pola in the time of King Henry I.,
whose son, the Lord William, went with King Richard I.
into the Holy Land: after whom Maurice de Pola held
this land.   In South Pole is Scobbahull, and Chivelstone
the ancient inheritance of Scobbahull, which, from Robert,
in the reign of King Henry III., unto Robert, in King
Henry IV.'s time, remained in that name."   Scobbahull,
or as it is now called Scobell, is not within sight from
the Estuary.   Chivelstone is a small village, but the parish
extends southwards to the romantic sea cliffs between Start
and Prawle Points; it includes the fishing village of Prawle,
and the hamlets of Ford and South Allington.   The church
at Chivelstone is an ancient one, dedicated to St. Silvester;
this is the only church named in his honour in all England.
The old rood loft remains, and the pulpit is formed of a
solid block of wood.

"South Pole, in Kinge Henry I. tyme, the Lo. Nicolas
de Pola held; and Will^am Pomeray held it anno 27 of
Kinge Henry III.; anno 24 of Kinge Edwd I., John de Cirencester was lorde thereof; anno 8 of Kinge Edw. II., Thomas
de Cirencester held the same; afterward, anno 19 of Kinge
Edw. III., Sr Thomas Courtenay was Lord of South Pole,
from whom, by Peverell and Hungerford, it descended unto
Henry Hastings, Erle of Huntingdon, wch sold this mannor

unto Walter Hele, of Gnawton; from hym it descended unto Samson Hele, the now lorde thereof."*

"Scobhull and Chevilston lieth in the parish of South Pole, anciently Scobbahull, and belonginge unto y^t name, wch I finde to have contynewed their possession their from Kinge Henry III. tyme unto Kinge Henry V. tyme. * * * This land came wholly unto Speccot, and is linealhy descended unto Sir John Speccot."†

The rectory house of Portlemouth stands near the entrance of this creek; it is a pleasant looking dwelling, surrounded by trees, and overlooking the water.

Parts of the building are very ancient. An archway, without a key-stone, the Rev. T. B. Wells says, is of the time of Henry VII. or VIII. On the premises there is a granary, which once formed a part of the old Kingsbridge Barracks. At the time they were taken down, this portion was purchased by Mr. Wells' father, and re-erected in his yard. A few years ago a swarm of bees took possession of part of the wood-work, and since then two other swarms have migrated there also; endeavours have been made to eject them, but unsuccessfully, and the three separate families are still occupying this "Timber House."

The following account of a son of the rector of Portlemouth, is copied from the "*Illustrated London News*" of December 27th, 1873.

"Lieutenant Lewis Fortescue Wells, R.N., late of H.M.S. *Barracouta*, died at sea, on board the *Biafra*, on the 26th ult. This gallant young officer, whose demise occurred

---

* Sir William Pole.

† Sir William Pole.

K

on his return from the West Coast of Africa, entered
the Navy in 1861, and since that period has been successively employed in the allied expedition to Mexico,
for nearly four years on the China station (where he was
present at the bombardment of Kagosina and Simonassaki)
and afterwards on the North American station, as Sub-
Lieutenant in H.M.S. *Royal Alfred.* He became a Lieutenant
June 1st, 1869, and was subsequently appointed to the
training ship *Indefatigable,* and then to the *Volage.* In
March last Mr. Wells was made First Lieutenant of H.M.S.
Barracouta, which proceeded to the West Coast on the affairs
of the Ashantee expedition. While crossing the Bay of
Biscay the Lieutenant courageously leaped overboard, and
saved a man of his ship. On June 13th, at the action
at Elmina, he greatly distinguished himself by leading
a small body of *Barracouta* men against the Ashantees,
receiving the thanks of his commanding officers upon
the field for his great skill and decision.

He was subsequently thanked by the Commander-in-
Chief for gallantly landing despatches through a heavy
surf, and was afterwards left in command of a small naval
brigade at Abrakrampa, where, too, he rendered effective
service. The fatal fever of that region was the cause of
his untimely death. Lieutenant Wells was the second
son of the Rev. Thomas Bury Wells, rector of Portlemouth,
Devon, (formerly in the navy) by Catherine Frances, his
wife, eldest daughter of the Rev. William Stockdale, rector
of Wilby, Northamptonshire. His ancestors in the female
line were the old Devon race, the Fortescues of Fallapit."

In addition to the foregoing, it may be mentioned, that
at the time of his death, Lieutenant Wells was on his
way home, in order to take the command of Her Majesty's

yacht, the *Victoria and Albert,* to which important post he had just been appointed. A portrait of this gentleman appears in the " *Graphic* " of December 27th, 1873.

The Church at Portlemouth, which is dedicated to St. Onolaus, stands on very high ground, and commands extensive views of the neighbourhood. It is an ancient cruciform edifice, somewhat dilapidated, but contains a very beautifully carved oak screen. The stone font is also very ancient; but we could not learn the probable date of either font or screen. At the west end of the churchyard there is a lych-gate, not uncommon in Devonshire, but seldom seen elsewhere. ? Some of the inscriptions on the tombstones are becoming almost obliterated by time and exposure to the weather—indeed we looked in vain for some of the old epitaphs which were legible a few years ago, and failed altogether to discover a curious one which we copied not many years since, respecting a master who had been poisoned by his servant girl. It was as follows:—

> " Through poison strong he was cut off,
> And brought to death at last;
> It was by his apprentice girl,
> On whom there's sentence past.
> O may all people warning take,
> For she was burned to a stake ! "

The tombstone bears date May 25th, 1782, and the execution of the criminal was performed at Exeter; but in her case the burning did not take place until after death by hanging. This is the last recorded instance in the country, it is believed, of the infliction of burning as a punishment for poisoning.

Very different are the relations between master and servant recorded in the following inscription:—

" To
The Memory of
James Wood,
Who departed this life
On the 25th Jan^r 1835 ;
Aged 26 years.
.   Erected
by Mr. Jackson, of the Moult, as a testimony of his sincere regret for the loss of a most valuable servant, whose many excellent qualities caused him to be respected and lamented by all who knew him."

On another stone, over the remains of a child, aged two years, we read these lines :—

"Death takes the good,
Too good on earth to stay,
And leaves the bad,
Too bad to take away."

(A sentiment, by the way, not particularly gratifying to *survivors*).

A white stone cross (on which, for a considerable time, hung a wreath of "immortelles") bears the following inscription :—

"In memory of
John Dyker, eldest son
of John Dyker and Jane Thew,
of Kings Lynn, Norfolk,
.   who was drowned
off Prawle Point, Decr 10th,
1868; aged 16 years."

Many are the tombstones in this churchyard, overlooking the sea, on which is inscribed the mournful word *drowned*.

Jewitt, in his History of Plymouth, says—"When a sea-port from which a ship was required for the King's service was too poor to furnish it, the neighbouring towns were ordered to contribute for the purpose. Thus in 1310, when the inhabitants of Dartmouth declared that they were unable to maintain a ship and its crew, orders were sent to the people of Totnes, Brixham, Portlemouth, and Kingsbridge, to assist those of Dartmouth, on the occasion."

The mention of *Portlemouth*, rather than Salcombe, has been suggested as "strongly indicative that Portlemouth was more important than Salcombe, in the time of Edward II., and probably the harbour was Portlemouth Harbour rather than Salcombe Harbour at that time."*

Taking the lane on the right hand of the church at Portlemouth, you pass through the little village of Rickham, and about three-quarters of a mile further on reach the coast-guard station, situated near the top of the fine bold cliffs. The row of houses presents a neat and substantial appearance, and attached to each one is a well-cultivated little plot of garden ground. The rocket apparatus, for saving life from shipwrecks, occupies a detached building close to the flag-staff.

From the look-out rock a fine sea view is obtained: the Start on the left, and the Bolt Head on the right.

Iron mines have, until lately, been worked by a company, just beneath the station, the quality of the ore being better than at other portions of the coast. Some little distance on the left is a bold arched rock, always called by the coast-guard "Temple Bar:" it is not approachable by land at any tide. From this rock the jagged outline of the point on

---

* So also, Kingswear is said to be of greater antiquity than even Dartmouth.

which the Start Lighthouse is built may be seen. Rickham was one of the Fitzroy storm-signal stations.

An amusing circumstance is narrated of a party of excursionists, who a few years since were rounding the point from whence the flag-staff came in view, and they imagined the collapsed drum (signifying "fine weather") hoisted on the mast to have been a *teakettle*, which some of the party had thus hoisted as a sort of telegraphic intimation that *tea was ready*.

It appears by the Domesday survey, that not long before that survey was taken, Thurlestone, Portlemouth, West Alvington, Collaton-Prawle, East Sewer, and other manors on the southern coast, were laid waste by the Irish.

In King's "Dartmoor," we find it stated that Godwin and Edmund, the sons of King Harold, fled into Ireland with the greater part of the Saxon fleet; that in the spring of 1068 they landed on the coast of Somersetshire, where they were met by Ednoth, who had been a "leader of the army," under their father Harold, but who had now become the liege man of the Conqueror. A battle took place in which many fell on both sides, amongst whom was Ednoth: and the sons of Harold, having plundered the coasts of Devon and Cornwall, returned again to Ireland. Here they received fresh assistance from Dermot, King of Dublin: and in the following year again appeared off Exeter, with a fleet of sixty-six ships, and a numerous army. From Exeter they plundered along the southern coasts; and the line of their ravages may be traced from the Domesday survey, which tells us how the manors lying along the coast from Dartmouth to Kingsbridge were "laid waste by the Irishmen."

The little seaport town of Salcombe is seen to the greatest advantage from the Portlemouth side of the harbour; indeed, Ringrone, Woodcot, and some other villas, are so embosomed in trees, that they are scarcely discoverable to a passer-by on the *same* side of the water.

Strangers who are desirous of obtaining the view in question, (if they are going from Kingsbridge to Salcombe by the *Queen* Steamer), can be landed at "Dutch End," and after spending a little time in a ramble on the Portlemouth shore, they can proceed to the Ferry House, from whence the boat will readily convey them across to Salcombe.

SALCOMBE.

CHAPTER ~~XI.~~ IX.

"Silvery bays
Are seen, where commerce lifts the peaceful sail;
The indented coast
Frowns with wave-breasting rocks, and cliffs high crowned,
And flags that wave in the fresh ocean gale."

Carrington.

In Leland's Itinerary (temp. Hen. VII.) Salcombe is thus described:—"Saultcombe Haven sumwhat barrid, and having a Rok at the entering into it, is about a vij miles by West South West from Dertmouth; and aboute half a mile within the mouth of this Haven, longing to the Privileges of Dertmouth, is Saultcombe, a fishar towne and a three miles upper at this Haven Hedde is Kingesbridg, sumtyme a praty Town. The Est Point of Saultcombe Haven is a great Foreland into the Se, caulled the Sterte."

Salcombe is a port under Dartmouth, and the out-port of Kingsbridge. Foreign vessels sometimes land their mails here, when prevented by stress of weather from proceeding to their usual ports. It is often used as a harbour of refuge, and has safe anchorage for about two hundred ships.

Hawkins thus describes the situation of this place:—
"Salcombe lies between those two well-known points of land, the Prawle and the Bolt Head, the former on the oriental,

the latter on the occidental side, which last, rising to a tremendous height, discloses the resemblance of a human profile, while the projection immediately opposite, and nearly two miles within the Prawle, called Peartree Point (being part of Rickham Common), is low and flat."

The town of Salcombe does not present a very attractive appearance on first entering it. The streets are narrow and ill-paved, and the shops by no means first-rate, but great improvements have taken place of late years; many new houses have been built, and there is a prospect of its becoming a place of much more importance than it has hitherto been, especially if the Kingsbridge Railway should ever be opened, and the proposed extension to Salcombe carried out.

The coast scenery around is very fine, and the climate exceedingly mild; indeed, it is considered the warmest place on the south-west coast. The celebrated Dr. John Huxham, who practised at Plymouth in the reign of George II., used to call it "the Montpellier of England;" and Humboldt says "its mean temperature is but 2°-4 Farht. below that of Montpellier and of Florence." Invalids resort thither for shelter during the winter months, and doubtless will do so to a much greater extent when there is more accommodation provided for them than is to be found there at present.

The manor of Salcombe belongs to the Earl of Devon, whose steward holds a court leet and court baron here, and appoints the constables. He is also Lord of the Manors of Malborough, Ilton,* East Sewer, Bolbury, Batson, Collaton-Prawle, Hope, &c.

---

* "Ilton, or Ithelstone Castle, was the ancient dwelling of Bozun, in King Henry II.'s time, whose inheritance after some descents, was divided between two daughters; the one married Sir Hugh Ferrers, and the other

The old Salcombe *chapel,* which had gone to decay for some centuries (it was licensed by Bishop Stafford in 1401), was re-built, partly by subscription, but chiefly at the expense of James Yates, Esq., formerly of Woodville. It was afterwards augmented with Queen Anne's Bounty, but being too small for the greatly increased population, it has given place to *Salcombe District Church,* dedicated to the "Holy Trinity," erected by subscription and grants in 1843, at the cost of £2,605.

The east window is enriched with stained glass, given by Viscount Courtenay (now Earl of Devon). The perpetual curacy is in the patronage of the Vicar of West Alvington.

The present incumbent has a handsome modern residence, a little out of the town.

Until rather recently almost all funerals took place at Malborough; consequently there are no tombstones of ancient date to be found in Salcombe Churchyard. This yard is planted with aloes, yuccas, myrtles, and other flowering shrubs.

The Wesleyan minister at present stationed at Salcombe has kindly furnished the following facts relative to the commencement of Methodism in that place:—

"Methodism was introduced into Salcombe shortly after its appearance at Kingsbridge, I think about the year 1809 or 1811, but it is impossible on this point to be strictly accurate, as I find no documents that throw any light upon

---

Sir John Chiverstone, who had this house. Two Knights of this tribe succeeded, the son and grandson of Sir John, who dying without issue, settled this land on his father-in-law, Hugh Courtenay, Earl of Devon, to which family it now belongs." Ilton Castle has so long been in ruins, that in the middle of the eighteenth century nothing was to be seen except a heap of brambles, which having been cleared away about the year 1780, the traces of the foundation of a square building, flanked with turrets, were perceptible.

the subject. A room near the present Market Hall was first used for Divine worship, and afterwards the Infant Society removed to another in Buckley. The next migration was to the site of the present chapel at the Island; then occupied by a pretty looking cottage. This was bought and turned into a preaching house, which soon became too small for the worshippers. At this early stage a Sunday School had been commenced, and was in so flourishing a condition as to call for some special accommodation for the children, beyond what the already enlarged structure would afford.

After successive alterations and enlargements the house was taken down, and, in 1824, a chapel was built, which in its turn gave place to the present much larger edifice, which consists of a fair–sized, substantially-built chapel, with school room and vestries on the ground floor. This was in 1849, since which date the gallery has been extended along each side, an organ has been introduced, and the accommodation from time to time improved. The present congregation is large enough on ordinary occasions comfortably to fill the chapel, and the Sunday School, consisting of nearly two hundred children, loudly calls for some further addition to the premises."

The "Plymouth Brethren" have a *Room* at Salcombe, in which their meetings' are held; and we believe there is also a small gathering of the body calling themselves the " Catholic Apostolic Church." In August, 1866, the Baptists commenced holding their services in the Town Hall at Salcombe, and in April, 1868, the Earl of Devon was applied to, and granted a site on which they might build a chapel. The foundation stone was laid on June 24th, 1869, by Mr. Peter Adams, of Plymouth, and the chapel was opened June 22nd, 1871. At the evening meeting, after the opening, the pastor, the Rev.

F. Pugh, on behalf of his late wife's mother, presented for the use of the church, a silver communion service, engraved with the following inscription :—" Presented to the Trustees for the use of the church worshipping in Courtenay Park Chapel, Salcombe, June 22nd, 1871, by E. W., Mother of Eliza, the beloved wife of Frederic Pugh, first pastor of the said church, who departed this life, November 29th, 1870, aged 29."

The National School at Salcombe was built in 1847; and there is, besides, a flourishing Infant School.*

There are Shipwrights' yards from which many fine clipper-built vessels are turned out; indeed this may be considered the principal trade of the place. The facilities for launching vessels, of almost any burden, are great; and of subsequently fitting them up, without leaving the port.

You will find at Salcombe those usual accompaniments of a sea-port town, viz., a Custom House, and a Coast-guard station. Among the various societies and institutions, an important one is that of the Salcombe Shipping Association.

The Gas-works, which were erected in the little creek, almost close to Salcombe, called Shadycombe, were opened in December, 1866.

"The new Pier, or landing place at Orestone,† Salcombe, was built in the summer of 1871, by public subscription, to which the Harbour Commissioners, the Earl of Devon, and the shareholders of the *Queen* steamer Co., were the chief subscribers. The stones used for the work were taken from Limebury, with the exception of the steps which are Cornish granite. The whole is covered with a thick coat of Portland cement, and fenced with a stout fence of

---

* A new National school-room for girls is about to be built in the town.

† Hawkins calls this place "Hoar, or Old Stone."

iron tubing. The work was very satisfactorily executed by Messrs. George Stear & Sons, of Salcombe, under the superintendence and from the designs of Mr. John Wills, of Dodbrooke. While this erection facilitates the landing from boats at low water, it is a matter for regret that its length was curtailed in deference to the wish of some of the leading shipowners of Salcombe, who apprehended a danger to sailing vessels in tacking. It is admitted, however, on all hands, that the original design, which was twenty feet longer, might have been carried out with the greatest possible advantage."*

This new pier is a great accommodation to passengers in the ferry-boat which plies between Salcombe and the Portlemouth shore, being exactly opposite the ferry-house.

The following report respecting a proposed "Oyster and Mussel Fishery" is extracted from a more lengthy account which appeared in the *Kingsbridge Journal* of October 7th, 1871, and of May 4th, 1872.

"A meeting of the inhabitants of Salcombe and neighbourhood was held in the Town Hall on Friday afternoon last, for the purpose of considering the application made by Capt. Russell, of Gillingham, Kent, to the Board of Trade, for permission to lay down oyster and mussel beds in the river, from Keeve Mud to the Ferry. Capt. W. H. Webb presided.

Capt. Hill pointed out the importance of the issues involved. He stated that if Mr. Russell obtained the permission he sought from the Board of Trade, and laid down the oyster beds he contemplated, the harbour and immediate approaches to the port of Salcombe would be practically

---

* Information from Mr. J. Wills.

under his control, and mariners would be legally compelled to ask his permission before anchoring their ships, or to enter over his ground. Such an assumption of authority would prevent dredging for scallops and netting by the fishermen of Salcombe, and a very large number of them would thus be thrown out of employment, especially in winter. Capt. Hill having pointed out the disastrous consequences of the granting of the application, proposed the following resolution: 'That, having regard to the commercial and shipping interests of the port of Salcombe, this meeting considers that the application of Captain Jonathan Russell to the Board of Trade for an oyster and mussel fishery, from Keeve Mud to Salcombe Ferry, would be most injurious to those having charge of the harbour, as well as to the inhabitants of the neighbourhood.'

Rev. T. B. Wells remarked that it had been an uninterrupted privilege throughout generations for the inhabitants to dredge in the river for oysters and scallops. £500 worth of scallops were caught during the winter of 1869. He proposed 'That this meeting uses every legitimate means to oppose the establishment of oyster and mussel fisheries in Salcombe river.'

Capt. Sladen moved 'That a memorial be prepared, petitioning against the grant, that the memorial be taken round to the inhabitants of the district for their signatures, and then forwarded to the Board of Trade; also, that a copy be sent to Capt. Russell.'

These resolutions were seconded and carried."

Notwithstanding the universal feeling against this measure, and the general belief that, if carried out, it would be a serious injury to the neighbourhood, the Board of Trade decided on "granting to Mr. Russell a several oyster and mussel fishery, from Snapes Point to Salt-stone Rock, instead of from the Passage-way to Keeve Mud, as applied for. Mr. Russell will not be allowed to interfere in any manner with any persons using seine, tuck, or other nets, which do not fish for or take oysters. This order will continue in operation for sixty years from its confirmation by Act of Parliament."

Ringrone House, a little out of Salcombe, is a handsome marine villa, with terraced gardens extending quite to the water's edge. Until his lamented death, which took place in April of this year (1874), it was the residence of the Right Honourable Michael Conrade de Courcy, Lord Kingsale, respecting whom the following account appeared in the *Illustrated London News* of April 25th, 1874:—

"The Right Honourable Michael Conrade de Courcy, thirtieth Lord Kingsale, Baron Courcy of Courcy, and Baron of Ringrone, Premier Baron in the Peerage of Ireland, died at Salcombe on the 15th instant. His Lordship was born December 21st, 1828 ; the second son of John Stapleton, twenty-eighth Lord Kingsale, by Sarah his wife, second daughter of Joseph Chadder, Esq.; and inherited the title at the decease of his brother, June 15th, 1865. He was not married, and is succeeded by his cousin, John Fitzroy de Courcy, born March 30th, 1821, now thirty-first Baron, who is son of the late Lieutenant-Colonel, the Honourable Gerald de Courcy, fourth son of John, twenty-sixth Lord Kingsale. The historic and very ancient family of which the deceased lord was the representative, was founded in Ireland by the famous soldier Sir John de Courcy, created Earl of Ulster in 1181, and granted the privilege that he and his successors (after first obeisance being paid) should remain covered in the presence of the King and all future Sovereigns of

England. The privilege is still enjoyed by the Lords
Kingsale, whose right to it was confirmed by William III.,
George I., and Queen Victoria."

Ringrone was built on the site of a former house by the
twenty-eighth Baron, John Stapleton de Courcy, who died
in 1847, and was buried in Malborough church, where there
is a monument to his memory, of white marble, surmounted
by the arms of the family, and motto, "Vincit omnia
veritas" (Truth conquers all things). It bears the following inscription :—

"This Monument is erected to perpetuate the memory
of the Right Honourable John Stapleton de Courcy, 28th
Baron Kingsale, and Premier Baron of Ireland, whose
ancestors have obtained for themselves laurels which time
can never wither. He died at Ringrone House, in this
Parish, justly lamented, on the 7th day of January, 1847;
aged 42 years.

Also the Honourable William Everard de Courcy, third
son of the above, who was born the 11th day of January,
1832, and died the 25th day of May in the same year."

The particulars respecting the De Courcy family were
mostly gathered from a work on the "Aristocracy of the
Empire," by Richard Sprye.

"The family of Courcy claims alliance with most of
the royal houses of Europe, paternally through the Dukes
of Lorraine, and maternally through the ducal house of
Normandy. Louis IV., King of France, born in 920, married
in 939, Gerberga, daughter of Henry I., Emperor of Germany, by whom he had two sons, Lotharius, who succeeded to the French throne (and with whose son, Louis
V., the race of monarchs descended from Charlemagne

ceased,) and Charles Duke of Lorraine whose immediate descendant, Robert de Courcy, was Lord of Courcy, in Normandy, in 1006,* and was succeeded by his eldest son Richard de Courcy, who accompanied his sovereign William into England, and distinguished himself at the battle of Hastings, participated largely in the Conqueror's .spoil, having been allotted numerous lordships, amongst which was that of Stoke, County Somerset, and thence denominated Stoke Courcy." (Passing over four descents, we reach the name of) " Sir John Courcy, who having distinguished himself temp. Henry II., in that monarch's wars in England and Gascony, was sent into Ireland, in the year 1177, as an assistant to William Fitz-Adelm, in the government of that kingdom. Sir John having prevailed upon some of the veteran soldiery to accompany him, invaded the province of Ulster with twenty-two knights, fifty esquires, and about three hundred foot soldiers; and after many hard-fought battles, succeeded in attaching that quarter of the kingdom to the English monarchy — for which important service he was created, in 1181 (being the first Englishman dignified with an Irish title of honour), Earl of Ulster. His lordship continued in high favour during the remainder of the reign of his royal master, and performed prodigies of valour in Ireland; but upon the accession of King John, his splendour and rank having excited the envy of Hugh de Lacie, appointed Governor of Ireland by that monarch, the Earl of Ulster was treacherously

---

* About midway between Amiens and Laon in France, stands Courcy castle, a great object of attraction to visitors, and among the finest of the kind in France or Western Europe. The most conspicuous remains are one entire wing, with great corner towers, and, rising above all, the massive circular keep, a solid machicolated pile, 100 feet high, and 30 to 32 feet thick."

seized (while performing penance) unarmed and barefooted,
in the churchyard of Down-Patrick, on Good Friday, anno
1203, and sent over to England, where the King condemned
him to perpetual imprisonment in the tower, and granted
to Lacie all the Earl's possessions in Ireland.

After his lordship had been in confinement about a year,
a dispute happening to arise between King John and Philip.
Augustus of France, concerning the Duchy of Normandy,
the decision of which being referred to single combat, King
John (more hasty than advised) appointed the day, against
which the King of France provided his champion; but the
King of England, less fortunate, could find no one of his
subjects willing to take up the gauntlet, until his captive in
the tower, the gallant Earl of Ulster, was prevailed upon to
accept the challenge. But when everything was prepared
for the contest, and the champions had entered the lists, in
presence of the monarchs of England, France, and Spain,
the opponent of the Earl, seized with a sudden panic, put
spurs to his horse, and fled the arena; whereupon the victory
was adjudged with acclamation to the champion of England.

The French King being informed, however, of the Earl's
powerful strength, and wishing to witness some exhibition
of it, his lordship, at the desire of King John, cleft a massive
helmet in twain at a single blow. The King was so well
satisfied with this signal performance, that he not only
restored the earl to his estates and effects, but desired him to
ask anything within his gift, and it should be granted. To
which Ulster replied, that having estates and titles enough,
he desired that his successors might have the privilege (their
first obeisance being paid) to remain covered in the presence
of his majesty, and all future Kings of England; which
request was immediately conceded. This heroic warrior and

able statesman died in France, about the year 1210, and was succeeded by his only son, Miles, upon whom Henry III. conferred the Barony of Kinsale,* in Ireland, as a compensation for the Earldom of Ulster, which was retained by Hugo de Lacie.

For five centuries afterwards the honours descended regularly. (But we pass on to) "Almericus, twenty-third baron, outlawed in 1691 for his adhesion to the fortunes of James II., but the outlawry was very soon removed, and his lordship took his seat in the parliament of Ireland, in 1692. This nobleman, in observance of the ancient privilege of his house, appeared in the presence of King William, covered, and explained to that monarch, when his majesty expressed surprise at the circumstance, the reason thus :—' Sire, my name is Courcy. I am Lord of Kinsale, in your majesty's kingdom of Ireland; and the reason of my appearing covered in your majesty's presence is to assert the ancient privilege of my family, granted to Sir John de Courcy, Earl of Ulster, and his heirs, by John, King of England.' The King acknowledged the privilege, and giving the baron his hand to kiss, his lordship paid his obeisance, and continued covered." He died in 1719, and was buried in Westminster Abbey, where his tomb may be seen.

It is left on record that his successors, Gerald, twenty-fourth baron ; John, twenty-sixth baron ; and John Constantine, twenty-ninth baron ; on different occasions " exercised this ancient privilege of their ancestors."

A fine specimen of the American Aloe flowered last year (1873) in the grounds at Ringrone House. The continuance of a colder atmosphere than is usually experienced here, just

---

* We know not when the family of De Courcy first adopted the present mode of spelling the name *Kingsale* : it was clearly not so at first.

at the time that heat was desirable, probably prevented this
noble plant from attaining the height it would otherwise
have done. Twenty-six feet was about the length of the
flower stem. The photograph accompanying these pages
was taken from *this* plant.

The *Journal of Horticulture* of September 5th, 1872,
says — " The first of our herbalists who mentions the
American Aloe is Parkinson. In his 'Theatrum Botanicum,'
published in 1640, he says—' It grew first in America,
which being brought into Spaine, was from thence spread
into all quarters.' He also observes on its early flowering
in the hotter countries, ' but never in these colder,' so that
at that time we may conclude it had not flowered in
England, although we know that it had flowered in France
and Italy. ⁂ This Agave is not merely an orna-
ment, for, as stated by Dr. Hogg, in his ' Vegetable
Kingdom,' the root as well as the leaves yield excellent
fibre, called Pita fibre, which is separated by bruising and
steeping them in water. The Mexicans make their paper
of this fibre."

The following paper, which was contributed to the
Gardeners' Chronicle, in October, 1842, by John Luscombe, Esq., of Combe Royal, will doubtless be read with
interest. It was kindly lent by the author, with permission
to copy.

THE SALCOMBE ALOES.

" Believing that there is no part of England, where so
many plants of the Agave Americana have grown to maturity
in the open ground, without the slightest protection, I am
induced to send you a brief statement of the specimens that
have flowered at Salcombe, a small seaport near Kingsbridge, in the South of Devon. The first on record bloomed

in 1774,* being then only twenty-eight years old: it grew in the garden of Cliff House, a residence (as its name implies) within a few yards of the sea. In the middle of June the plant was first observed to have shot forth a flower-stem, which grew rapidly, and advanced about nine inches daily, until at the end of September it had attained the height of twenty-eight feet, bearing innumerable flowers on forty-two branches: its leaves were nine feet long and six inches wide. In 1820 a second Aloe flowered at Woodville, the seat of the late James Yates, Esq., which attained the height of twenty-seven feet, and produced forty flowering branches, bearing sixteen thousand flowers: this plant is fully described in the fifth volume of the 'Transactions of the Horticultural Society.' In 1832 a third flowered at the Moult, the seat of W. Jackson, Esq., which was twenty-eight feet high. The lawn at Woodville was again ornamented in 1835 with the almost countless blossoms of this most stately exotic: the stem of this specimen was twenty-four feet nine inches in height, forming the fourth Aloe that had flowered here. In the Autumn of 1840 a fifth flowered at the Moult, and was

* Hawkins gives a copy of a handbill which was printed and circulated at the time this Aloe was flowering. It is as follows:—

"Now to be seen at SALCOMBE, near
KINGSBRIDGE, in full blow,
A Remarkable ALLOE,

Supposed to be the largest ever seen in this kingdom; and although continually exposed to the Weather, it hath grown to the following Dementions:—

	feet.	inches.
In height	20	0†
Length of the leaf	9	0
Thickness of ditto	0	6

As the Proprietor hath been at great expenses to keep it for the Inspection of the Curious, the Terms of admission are, for Ladies and Gentlemen 2s. 6d. each; all others at one shilling each person, and to be paid at the Door."

† It afterwards grew eight feet more.

twenty-seven feet in height: this plant was transplanted the
previous year, which perhaps threw it into bloom, as the
leaves were not quite so large as those of its predecessors.
At the present time (1842) a sixth Aloe is coming into bloom
at Cliff House, the residence of Mrs. Prideaux. This plant
is between thirty and thirty-five years of age, and is inferior
in beauty to the others that have bloomed at Salcombe, as
instead of sending up a central flower-stem, seven stalks
have protruded themselves from different parts, the principal
of which are about ten feet high. From this circumstance
the peculiar character of the plant is lost, and it is at present
a mass of stems and flower-stalks, upon which only one or
two blossoms have yet expanded. At each of the places
mentioned, many fine young Aloes, of large size, are growing
luxuriantly; and in another small garden, overhanging the
sea, and constantly exposed in stormy weather to the spray,
five magnificent specimens are manifesting more than ordinary vigour.

It may not, perhaps, be out of place to speak of Salcombe
itself, and the other tender plants that flourish there. It is
a populous village,* carrying on a considerable trade, and
situated between Torquay and Plymouth. At the west end
are Cliff House, and the mansion of Lord Kingsale, with
other respectable abodes, and towards the entrance of the
harbour, which is about a mile from the village, are placed
in their wooded grounds the delightful residences of Woodville and the Moult. From the south-west gales, which in
this part of Devon blow with such resistless violence, the
harbour is entirely protected by the magnificent head-land,
called the Bolt Head, and from the storms from other
quarters by lofty hills on almost every side. In point of

* So denominated when this paper was written, but decidedly a *town* now

picturesque scenery, there are few portions of the coast that exceed it, while the various tender plants which it displays render it a spot of no ordinary interest to the horticulturist.

At Woodville there is a wall of thriving Orange, Lemon, and Citron trees, protected only by temporary frames of reed. Near them stood, a few years since, a large Olive tree, trained also against a wall, but wholly unprotected, and there is still a specimen in the grounds. The luxuriance of the New Zealand Flax is remarkable, some immense masses being more than seven feet high. The beauty of these plants is great, as they evince the strongest health, and are uninjured by the severest Devonshire winters. Two smaller plants have blossomed, the flower-stalks being between two and three feet higher than the leaves.

At the Moult, a great number of exotics have been planted in the open air, and the grounds at the present moment are gay with Dahlias, Salvias, Petunias, Seneceos, Sollyas, Bouvardias, Pelargoniums, and Brugmassias. The last-named shrubs stand the winters well; and though often cut down to the ground, form strong plants by the end of the summer. There are also some fine specimens of Cassias, New Holland Acacias, an interesting species of Eucalyptus (raised from seed) marked 'White Gum.' A still finer species, called the 'Blue Gum,' (the fragrance of which was very perceptible after rain) was killed by the severity of the winter of 1840-1. Various herbaceous plants from Mexico, particularly Stevias, are perfectly acclimatized; and a species of Phytolacca is conspicuous from its numerous spikes of deep purple berries. Until the intense cold we experienced a few years since, the varieties of Cape Pelargonium had formed immense bushes, and were everywhere rising from self-sown seeds. A

splendid Ipomœa, apparently allied to, if not identical
with, I. Tyrianthina, raised from South American seeds,
flourished for several years at the foot of a wall, but
was destroyed by the incessant rain of last winter. It
had a fleshy root, and its twining stems, which perished
in December, bore an abundance of rich purple flowers,
of large size." * * *

Some few years after this paper was written, four Aloes
were in flower at one time at Salcombe, in different gardens
there; and last year (1873) a fine one flowered in the
grounds at Ringrone, as we have previously stated. .

There are many good and attractive residences in and
around Salcombe, but we cannot attempt to mention them
all. Adjoining the Ringrone grounds (on the Salcombe
side) are the terraced gardens belonging to Cliff House;
one way of approach to them from the house being by a
bridge thrown across the road.

Woodville, now called Woodcot, was built in the year
1797, by James Yates, Esq. It is now the property and
residence of Major-General Birdwood. The windows of
the villa, which are shaded by a colonade, command a
fine view of the Bolt Head, and the rocks and high hills
of Portlemouth. The grounds are tastefully laid out, and
abound with evergreens and flowering shrubs. Oranges,
Lemons, and Citrons, are produced here in great luxuriance.
Hawkins, when referring to this place, speaks of "a large
camera obscura, fixed on a perpendicular rock"; of "a sort
of quay, with a mock parapet, and small swivels to fire a
royal salute"; and of "a sinuous enclosure for retaining
and preserving fish in their natural element." All these,
excepting the small quay with the mock parapet, are now
things of the past.

FORT CHARLES.[*]

CHAPTER X.

"One lonely turret, shattered and out-worn,
Stands venerably proud—too proud to mourn
Its long-lost grandeur."

PERHAPS no period of English history is more momentous than that of the Civil Wars, in the time of Charles I.; nor was the share which this neighbourhood and the adjacent towns had in these events of inferior importance.

Long before the rebuilding of the castle at Salcombe, collisions took place between the forces of the King and the Parliament in this neighbourhood. The Royalists were quartered at Tavistock, Plympton, and Modbury.[†] Plymouth seems to have supported the Parliament throughout, and shewed a remarkable spirit of disaffection; and being strong, often sallied out to the Royalists at Plympton, Modbury, and elsewhere, generally bringing back prisoners, and arms, and also cattle.[‡]

In 1642, Sir Edmund Fortescue was High Sheriff of Devon. He has been known to us mostly as being Governor

* Although this chapter is headed "Fort Charles," yet it includes many particulars respecting the Civil Wars, as affecting this neighbourhood generally.

† Moore.

‡ Whitelocke.

of Salcombe Castle, and maintaining a gallant resistance for a lengthened period; but it seems this was far from being all he did for the Royalist cause. From the first, he had shewn great activity on behalf of the King, and his bravery and daring were known to his opponents, insomuch that they speak of him at this date as "a very great malignant."

Early in February, 1642, Sir Edmund's head quarters being at Plympton, he had gone over to Modbury to meet other gentlemen of distinction in the county, and the trained bands, when they were attacked suddenly by a party of five hundred horse from the garrison at Plymouth; and the men being seized with a sudden panic, under the impression that the forces of the enemy were more numerous, took flight, and Sir Edmund Fortescue and the other gentlemen were taken prisoners. The particulars are found in the following quotation.

"The Commanders of the garison at Plymouth having had intelligence that the High Sheriffe of that Shire, by name Sir Edmund Fortescue, a very great malignant, lay at Modburie, where the trained bands, by virtue of his '*Posse comitatus*,' met also with him that day, the Cavaliers' chief quarters being then at Plympton, which was within three miles of them; hereupon they thus formed their designs. Very early in the morning, Capt. Thompson, Capt. Pym, Capt. Gould, and some others, with five hundred horse and dragooners, marched to go away privately northward towards Rowbardown, as if they meant to go to Tavistock; but suddenly wheeling about, they came secretly to Modburie, where, in Master Champnon's house,* they found

---

* This was Modbury House, the residence of the Champernowne family from the time of Edward II. to the end of the seventeenth century. The

the High Sheriffe, with divers other gentlemen of quality, and two thousand trained souldiers and voluntcers, who presently, on their approach, crying out 'The Troopers are come,' most swiftly all ran away, many of them leaving their arms behind them. The house fore-mentioned was instantly beset, where the High Sheriffe stood stoutly on his defence, till the house was fired, and the assailants breaking in upon them, possessed the house, and took there divers prisoners, to the number of twenty eminent persons of those parts, among whom were Sir Edmund Fortescue, High Sheriffe of the County, Sir Ed. Seimour, Baronet, Mr. Ed. Seimour, Mr. Basset, Capt. Champnoon, Capt. Pomeroy, Capt. Bidlock, Capt. Peter Fortescue, Mr. Barnes, Mr. Shipton, Clerk of the Peace, and others. After this, they marched with their prisoners towards Dartmouth."*

The following extracts are from an old pamphlet of the same month and year, bearing the date, Plymouth, Feb. 24th, 1642.

"On Tuesday last all the Devonshire forces met at Kingsbridge, and marched towards Modbury—they were in all, as is supposed, eight or nine thousand, at the least—and came to Modbury about noon, where the Cavaliers had strongly fortified themselves with brest Workes, and laid all the hedges round about the Towne, for half a mile's compasse, with Musquetiers. There went from hence the London Gray-coats and about four hundred Horse and Dragooners, who came time enough to doe good service. But the Bastable

site was sold in 1705, and the family seat is now at Dartington, near Totnes. One of the Champernownes was the mother of Sir Humphrey Gilbert, and, by a second marriage, the mother also of Sir Walter Raleigh. Sir Edmund Fortescue was descended from the Champernownes through his grandmother.

* For this account, obtained at the British Museum, and for many particulars of the siege of Fort Charles, from the same source, we are indebted to Mr. John Hooper.

and Biddeford men were the first that came on, before
they were aware, about halfe a mile ere they came to the
Towne, not expecting to be charged by the enemy so soone,
yet so forward and desperate were the Cavalliers that they
let flye amaine upon them, but did little or no execution,
nor did abate the courage of their assailants; but the
Bastable men went on with such abundance of resolution
as if they feared not bullets, and the whole Army comming
up, and our men joyning with them, they beate the Cavalliers from hedge to hedge.   The fight beganne about one
of the clocke at noone; and towards night they drave
most of them into the Towne, and to their Works, where
they made a very hot defense, and had many men slaine,
which they perceiving, and our Forces having beaten them
out of their Works, the chiefe of them privately stole away
about three of the clock in the morning (the fight continuing
all night), and by degrees drew away all their Forces by a
way which the Easterne Army supposed was kept by our
men, but in truth neglected by both, onely their haste
forced them to leave their Armes behind them, and some
threescore of their Dragooners, to keepe our men in sus-
pense, with command to keepe shooting continually until
the day appeared, and then to take their horses and to
follow them.   But when the day came on, our men found
out their drift, how they were deluded, and pursued them,
took fourscore prisoners and many horse, much armes
scattered in the way, which they were faine to cast off
that they might flye the faster.

Our Horse and Foot, on Munday night last, visited Fleete
House, where Baronet Heale dwels, and there tooke about
twenty Horse, with some Prisoners.   Our army have taken
in all above a thousand armes, double the number they

tooke from us at Liskerd. We lost seven men that were slaine, and Sergeant-Major Herbert's Lieutenant and six others, that were taken prisoners by adventuring too farre. It is supposed that they have a hundred men slaine, besides abundance hurt: we have three or four hurt, but not dangerously.

This evening, Captaine Boskowen, with a partie of Horse, hath brought in twelve prisoners, of which there are two Captaines, viz., Captaine Nevill Blight (a furious malignant), and one Captaine Pomroye, that was sent to London by water, with the Sheriffe, but escaped thence."*

By this pamphlet we see that the Sheriff, Sir Edmund Fortescue, Captain Pomeroy, and others, who were taken prisoners at Modbury, were marched towards Dartmouth for the purpose of " *sending them to London by water.*" And we are also told that Captain Pomeroy (and probably the others) " *escaped thence.*" The manner of this escape is not known, but that they did escape accounts for their being so soon again at their old posts of duty for the King.

About three quarters of a mile beyond Salcombe, towards the harbour, are the remains of Fort Charles, built on a rock, and insulated at high water.

There had been an ancient castle, called the Old Bulwark, standing on this site for ages before the time of the civil war, (Hawkins says it was attributed to the Saxons) but which was in 1643 " *utterly ruined and decayed.*" It is not improbable that Sir Edmund Fortescue suggested the importance of its restoration. He certainly made known his willingness to undertake to reconstruct and re-fortify it, and

---

* This very rare old pamphlet was in the possession of the late George Prideaux, Esq., of Plymouth. It is also among the King's pamphlets in the British Museum.

received an order for that purpose from Prince Maurice, the King's nephew, by whom he was also appointed Governor. The following is a copy of his commission.

"Prince Maurice, Count Palatine of the Rhine, Duke of Bavaria, to Sir Edmund Fortescue, Kt. Forasmuch as I have received very good satisfaction that the fort, called the Old Bullworke, near Salcombe, now utterly ruined and decayed, which being well fortified and manned may much conduce to y^e advancement of his Ma^{ts} service in annoying the rebells, and securing those partes from their incursions; and whereas you the said S_r Edmond Fortescue, have given mee assurance of your readyness and diligence in refortifying and manning y^e said fort; These are to will and require you, hereby giving you full power and authority, by all possible ways and means, to refortify and man the same, willing and requiring the Sheriffe of the county of Devon, and all other his Ma^{ts} officers and loving subjects, to ayde and assist you in perfecting of the said fortification, which fort with the officers and souldiers you shall for his Ma^{ts} service by virtue of this commission receive into your charge and command, requiring all officers, souldiers, and others belonging thereunto, you to obey readily, to receive and accomplish your directions and commands, and you yourselfe in all things well and duely to acquit yourself for the best advancement of his Ma^{ts} service, for which this shall be your warrant. Given at Whitley under my hand and seale att armes this 9th of December, 1643.   MAURICE."

Sir Edmund immediately set about repairing this fortress, which by the 15th day of January, 1646, he had completely provisioned and fortified with great guns and muskets, the expense of which, as appears by the Knight's daily account, amounted to the sum of £3,196 14s. 6d., exclusive, as he remarks, of a single penny being charged for furniture. The provisions laid in for the siege amounted to £740 1s. 6d. The wages paid in the rebuilding of the castle were, for masons, quarry men, and carpenters, a shilling a day each; plasterers, one shilling and two pence each; joiners, one shilling and eight pence each. The attendants (which it is supposed means labourers) ten pence; and lime was at six shillings a hogshead.

The garrison consisted of SIR EDMUND FORTESCUE, *Governor*, SIR CHRISTOPHER LUCKNOR, MR. THOMAS FORTESCUE, CAPTAIN PETER FORTESCUE,* MAJOR SYMS, MAJOR STEPHENSON, CAPTAIN ROCH, CAPTAIN KINGSTON, CAPTAIN POWETT, CAPTAIN PETERFIELD, CAPTAIN DOUES, MR. SNELL, *Chaplain*, and the men, in all numbering sixty-six. The names of all the men are on record, together with a few notes respecting some of them; such as that Lieut. John Ford, William Cookworthy, and Stephen Goss, *ran away*, and that Thomas Quarme, *being sick, went by leave.*

Everything was now ready, and the little garrison only waited the attack. They would know that Sir Thomas Fairfax had arrived at Totnes, and an eager watch would be kept for the first sign of his coming, but Fairfax had decided first to reduce Dartmouth. On the 12th January, 1646, he sent his regiments with orders to besiege the garrison of Dartmouth, and on the 18th followed them himself with his army, and the summons to surrender being refused, commenced storming the town the same night. "Every commander was assigned to his post, and to fall on upon the word of command given. The contest was vigorous and severe, but short. Col. Hammond entered the west gate,

---

* Captain Peter Fortescue was uncle to Sir Edmund. He married Elizabeth, daughter of John Bastard, Esq., of Gerston.

where four guns were placed, and two by the Mill-pool, but
the great guns were fired but once. Hammond's men went
freely on, and possessed one fort after another, from the West
Gate to Little Dartmouth, while Col. Pride took the north
part of the town called Hardness, unto the Drawbridge.
Townstal Church, which was manned with above a hundred
men, and had in it ten guns, was next taken, so that now
there only remained the great fort, and the castle, into which
the Governor, with the Earl of Newport, and as many as
escaped, did flye."

"Sir Thomas Fairfax's Dragoons, with two companys of
Firelocks and some seamen, were ordered to alarm the great
fort, wherein was Sir Henry Carey with his regiment,
twelve guns, and store of amunition, but they came willingly
to terms, and Sir Thomas Fairfax agreed that Sir Henry
Carey should march away with the rest, leaving the arms,
ordnance, ammunition, and provisions, in the fort, and
engaging never to take up arms against the parliament, which
was done by them, and the next morning the Governor
yielded the castle."*

An extract from a letter of the period shows that Fairfax
now turned his attention to Salcombe.

"The General then sent for five hundred men from Plymouth, that he might employ those of his own in reducing
other places which was not then resolved, only a party was
sent to fall upon a fort near Salcombe, a harbour that lies
between Dartmouth and Plymouth, which hath Frigots in it
that much infest the seas.†"

These Salcombe frigates had made themselves a name, and

---

* Whitelocke's Memorials.

† "The Moderate Intelligencer impartially communicating Martial Affairs
to the Kingdom of England."

sad stories were told of their deeds in the Channel; for, during the re-building of the fort, they had been ever on the watch, to pursue and harass the vessels of the enemy.

Another letter says—"The General having left at present the care of Dartmouth to Col. Lambert, went on Wednesday to Totnes. We go on to attempt Fort Charles, near Salcombe. It is commanded by Sir Edmund Fortescue. There must be ordnance to batter it, which are coming; likewise some addition of forces to Col. Inglesby's* regiment, now before it, are to be raised and gathered out of the country, which they do willingly."†

The commencement of the siege is said by some authorities to be January 15th, while others say January 23rd. It is probable [that Col. Inglesby commenced proceedings on January 15th (the siege of Dartmouth was on the 18th), and that General Fairfax, having with him the additional force and the ordnance to batter it, which was said to be coming, summoned it to surrender on the 23rd. The General was, however, unable to produce much effect upo n it.

"When Fairfax entered Devonshire the Royalists had most of the garrisons in the county in their possession, as Tiverton, Exeter, Dartmouth, Barnstaple, Torrington; but he speedily reduced one garrison after another."‡ It must have been mortifying therefore to Fairfax to have to leave the little garrison at Salcombe unsubdued, as well as to Col. Inglesby, who had been so successful elsewhere.

It is probable the situation of Fort Charles was a difficulty, but may it not have been that the Governor and his garrison

---

* Col. Inglesby was killed soon afterwards, at the siege of Pendennis.

† Martial Affairs.

‡ Moore.

were also difficult, and not so easily made to yield as they
had found those at Dartmouth and elsewhere to be?

There is no doubt Fairfax recognised the Governor's
qualities, and the determined stand which he took in his fort,
and endorsed the opinion of those who, so long before, had
called him "a very great malignant."

Among some notes left by Sir Edmund Fortescue is the
following : "Item, For great shot and musket shot when
Fort Charles was formerly twice besieged, £15 17s. 0d."
This alludes to the two short sieges before the last. The last
siege which necessitated capitulation is said to have been a
lengthened one, and there is no doubt "Sprigge" refers to
this last siege, when he says, "Salcombe Fort yielded in 50
daies. 8 pieces of ordnance taken."*

On the 25th March, a week after the commencement of the
last siege, Colonel Weldon no doubt perceiving how little he
would be able to accomplish, made offers to Sir Ed. Fortescue
to surrender, which are called by the writer "very faire,"
and were somewhat similar to the articles afterwards signed.
It was supposed, on the side of the besiegers, that Sir
Edmund intended to yield, and premature news to this effect
was sent to Plymouth, and from Plymouth to the "Diurnall
of Parliament." What was the motive of the Governor in
this feint, does not appear; but it is unlikely that he intended
any thing of the kind, well knowing, as he did, that the
enemy could produce but little effect upon the fortress, and
that he could hold out until May. We at least know, that he
did not yield, that the siege went on, that certain men of
the garrison were shot after this date, and that at length,
articles of capitulation were signed "ye 7th of May, 1646."

Tradition has handed it down, that the Parliament forces

* Sprigge's Anglia Rediviva.

attacked the castle from Rickham Common, on the opposite side of the harbour, and a half-moon trench with a mound, and places for guns, is shown on the hill-side exactly facing the castle, where they erected a battery. They must, however, have had other positions also. Be this as it may, on the 7th of May, 1646, a little less than four months after the commencement of the siege, the garrison was obliged to capitulate, which they did upon honourable terms.

One account says, "For a period of nearly four months, the retired inlet of Salcombe was a scene of incessant uproar. The batteries thundered from each side of the harbour, but at the end of that time, the garrison capitulated. For this spirited resistance, Sir Edmund Fortescue was allowed to march with the honours of war to his mansion, Falapit House."

A letter to the "Diurnall of Parliament" says, "Charles Fort, sometimes called Salcombe, is surrendered to us, to the obedience and use of the Parliament, which is the only considerable place that the enemy has lately held, in all the west parts, except the strong garrison of Pendennis Castle."

This ruined fort, therefore, although regarded by many as of no particular historic interest, may at least boast that it held out for the King until almost every fortress in Devonshire had succumbed.

The articles signed were ten in number. It was agreed first, "That the Governor and all the garrison, in their several and respective places, capacities, and degrees, should have full liberty in thire profession of the true Protestant religion, professed and vowed by both houses of this present Parliament, &c." Also, "That the said fort may not bee knowne by ancy other name than Fort Charles, as now itt is, or any coate of arames in y⁰ dininge rume defaced; or any-

thing belonging to ye said fort." The eighth article in the
agreement runs thus—"That the Governor, with Sir Ch^r·
Luckner, thire servants, and all officers and souldiers in the
fort, have free liberty to march from hence to Fallowpit with
there usuall armes, drums beating, and collars flyinge, with
boundelars full of powder, and muskets apertinable, and
after three valines to yield up theire armes to those whome
Corronell Welldon shall appoint to receive them—the Governor, Sir Ch^r· Luckner, with both thire servants, likewayse y^e
officers in common, excepted."

When the tide is particularly low, numbers of bullets,
large clumsy pieces of metal, are found.

"A large key, said to have belonged to this fort, is
preserved by the representatives of the Governor's family.
It is sixteen inches long, and two-and-half inches wide at
the bit or ward."*

For the expenses of the garrison, Sir Ed. Fortescue had
an order from the Commissioners of the County of Devon,
dated from the Charter House, Exeter, the 12th day of
August, 1644, assigning him the weekly contributions of
the parishes of Malborough and Portlemouth—the former
amounting to £11 15s., and the latter to £6, making
together £17 15s. weekly: and this he continued to receive
till the first day of November in the same year, when it was
further ordered by the said Commissioners that he should be
paid £14 weekly by Mr. Geo. Potter, supposed to be the
receiver-general for the county. This, perhaps, proceeded
from the Parliament army having by that time possessed
themselves of the neighbouring district, so as to prevent
these payments from being made by the parishes to the
royal party. It appears that the Governor received also a

* Hawkins.

weekly contribution of £7 1s. 8d. for some time from West Alvington, and that he was paid by them to the amount of £245 16s. 10d. The Knight seems to have kept a very regular account of his receipts and disbursements. At the end of the account he observes that he has not taken a single penny for himself as Governor.

The question arises, how has this fort, rebuilt, and restored in 1644-5, at a large cost, become an utter ruin, although not destroyed in the siege? Many buildings, less substantial, and of greater age, remain. There seems little doubt that the articles agreed upon were broken, viz., " that not any coate of armes in yᵉ dininge rume should be defaced, nor anything belonging to yᵒ said fort." Perhaps the Parliament feared to allow a fort to remain intact which had for nearly four months resisted all the attempts of the enemy; and probably an order was sent down for its destruction, which may have been effected by its own gunpowder, after its "*eight pieces of ordnance were taken.*"

Sir ·Edmund Fortescue married a daughter of Lord Sandys. He was created a Baronet by Charles II., in 1664. He lies buried at Delft, in Holland, where a monument is erected to his memory. He was succeeded by his son Sir Sandys, at whose death, without issue, the title became extinct.

THE SANDS, BOLT HEAD,
AND BOLT TAIL.

CHAPTER XI.

" Old majestic sea !
Ever love I from shore to look on thee,
And sometimes on thy billowy back to ride,
And sometimes o'er thy summer breast to glide ;
But let me *live* on shore."

Barry Cornwall.

"THE field above the Castle is called the Gore, or Gutter ;
and tradition points it out as the scene of a bloody
affray. The summit of the hill is known as the Bury,
or Berry, and it is said to be marked with an old circular entrenchment."* A little below this spot a battery
has been constructed, mounting two pieces of ordnance,
and used by the Salcombe Volunteers for artillery practice ;
the target being ,moored off the bar at the entrance of
the harbour ; and on the other side, at Limebury Point,
a battery of much older date, mounting two smaller
pieces, points its guns at patches of white paint on the
cliffs, a little beyond Splat Cove. During their practice,
the concussion amongst the rocks is far from pleasant to
those who may be sauntering along the walks just above ;
the first notice of anything taking place being announced

* Murray.

by the puff of smoke in the distance, and the reverberation of the explosion.

Not far from the castle there is a beach called North Sands. A wood is believed to have been here overwhelmed by the waves in times remote, · and the stumps of a number of large trees, discernible some years ago, strengthen the supposition; some of these may yet be seen at the low ebb of spring tides. These relics may also be found in Millbay, on the opposite shore. Three kinds of Pholas, the dactylus, candidus, and parvus, are found burrowing in these old stumps. The animals belonging to all these shells are luminous in the dark, even while living. That fan-like shell, the Pinna ingens, is found in Salcombe Bay, where it has been known to fishermen as the *French mussel*. These creatures lie on a gravelly bottom, covered with mud and long sea weeds, and are only to be got at when the sea recedes further than usual. They stand upright, with the large end about an inch above the surface; the lower end fixed by a very large, strong *byssus*, or beard, so firmly attached to the gravel, that much force is required to draw them up, and most commonly the beard is left behind. This is composed of numerous fine, silk-like fibres, of a dark purplish brown, two or three inches in length. Some of these shells were taken occasionally for many years, the animals having been accounted very good food, but they require five or six hours stewing, to render them eatable; if this is properly attended to, they are said to be nearly as palatable as scallops, but never so tender. The Pinna has been long celebrated for giving protection to a small species of crab, which was supposed to be of great use to the animal, by giving it notice either of approaching danger, or of its

prey. Montagu says it *does* occasionally become the habitation of a small crab, which seems to live in harmony
with it, but that in not less than fifty of the Pinna ingens
which he opened, not a single crab was found; yet in
the only specimen of Mytilus modiolus, taken in the same
place, three crabs were found within the shell. The ancients
used to make costly vestments from the silky byssus of
this animal, and modern travellers assert that gloves and
stockings are still manufactured from it at Palermo, Naples,
and one or two other places.

We have been furnished with a few particulars respecting
the laying of the telegraph cable at Salcombe : they are here
given.

"In order to effect a direct communication between the
French-Atlantic telegraph cable and London, a sub-marine
cable between Salcombe and Brest has been laid. The
steamer *William Cory*, having the cable on board, under the
superintendence of Captain Mayne, R.N., C.B., arrived off
Salcombe on the 27th, and the shore end was landed on the
28th of May, 1870—the point selected being a sandy beach
at Starehole Bottom, under the Bolt Head. It was then
conveyed about two hundred and fifty yards, to the top of
the adjacent cliff. The temporary testing house into which
the cable was carried was, in the course of a few months,
dismantled, and a more substantial erection of stone received
the instruments, so as to test at intervals the state of the
insulation and continuity of the submerged portions of the
cable. Subsequently, the Anglo-American Cable Steam-ship
Robert Lowe was engaged off the coast, raising the shore
end and making a fresh splice, so as to bring it into the
instrument house built for the purpose on the North Sands.
This was effected on the 15th of October, 1871; the wires

also being connected at the same time with the Salcombe receiving office.* Some of the leading telegraph gentlemen of the day were engaged in testing the cable at this building, by forwarding and receiving messages from very distant parts of the world; the long ribbons of communication uncoiling from the beautiful instruments in a marvellous manner, and displaying their hieroglyphic dots and strokes to the amazement of the uninitiated.

In these times of rapid telegraphic or railway communication, one is rather inclined to smile at the primitive style of postal arrangements at Salcombe in days gone by, for Hawkins, who wrote in 1819, says — "No regular mail reaches this place; but a woman on foot (reversing the order of expediency) proceeds daily to Kingsbridge, where she arrives long after the letters are sorted, executes numerous petty missions, and returns to Salcombe, heavily loaded, at night, charging a penny for each letter conveyed to or from the office."

Between the North and South Sands, stands the Moult, the property of the Earl of Devon, but for many years it was the summer residence of the late Lord Justice Sir George Turner. Lady Turner continued to reside there until her death, when her daughters removed from the Moult to another house at Salcombe. The Moult was built in the year 1764, by the late John Hawkins, Esq., as "a mere pleasure box," but he did not live to finish it. He left it to his widow, who in 1780 sold it to the late Henry Whorwood, Esq., of Holton

---

* The *Robert Lowe* was lost, November 20th, 1873, having struck on the "Shotts," near St. John's, Newfoundland. She filled and settled down a few minutes afterwards. The commander, Capt. Tidmarsh (who remained on the bridge to the last), and sixteen of the crew, were lost, some of them having been washed overboard by the heavy seas which struck the vessel; thirty-three others were saved in three of the boats which got clear of the sinking ship.

Park, Oxford. The grounds were laid out under his directions, the trees planted, and the house fitted up as a decorated
cottage. Since then it has changed hands, until it came into
the possession of the respected nobleman who now owns it.
The gardens and conservatories contain plants and shrubs
rarely to be seen elsewhere, many of which are referred to
in Mr. Luscombe's paper, already given.

Although the Moult stands in such a sheltered spot, yet
in some winds the waves have been known even to surmount
the barrier at the bottom of the garden, but this is of rare
occurrence.

The South Sands, which are in the manor of Batson, have
been for many years a favourite place for pic-nic parties.
Boats laden with pleasure seekers flock to this delightful
locality, and the *Queen* steamer also makes periodical trips
to the Sands during the summer months.

A shed, known by the name of the *Boat-house*, is the
frequent rendezvous of luncheon and tea-parties; that
essential element, hot water, being procurable from the
cottage on the opposite bank; or if you prefer it, a fire may
be made, gipsy fashion, close at hand, and water brought
from a little nearly hidden stream which comes down on the
rocks from the Moult grounds.

In 1869, R. Durant, Esq., of Sharpham, near Totnes,
presented Salcombe with a life-boat and its accompaniments, at a cost of £700, in connection with the Life-boat
Institution.

It was arranged that Miss Durant should " christen" the
boat : she therefore said, " May this life-boat realize the
object of its institution. I send it forth on its mission of
mercy, to save the tempest-driven and shipwrecked mariner,
under the name of the " Rescue ;" and I ask you all to join
with me in the prayer, " God bless the Rescue."

A house for the reception of the life-boat was built by subscription, on the South Sands. This situation being chosen was a matter of regret to many, who feel some doubt, whether, in case of a violent storm (when its services are the most likely to be needed) it would be possible to get the boat over the Bar.

"There is," says Hawkins, " a large and dangerous knot of rocks, about a furlong within the Bar, and rather on the east side, called Blackstone, rarely covered at flood tide; and a smaller rock named the Wolf, towards the west shore. Some are of opinion that if these were blown up, the harbour would be greatly improved; while others as confidently pronounce, that the removing of these obstructions would cause the port to fill with sand."

In June, 1869, H.M.S. *Cadmus*, Capt. Gibbs, 1,466 tons burden, in running down the Channel from Portsmouth to Devonport, whilst going eight knots an hour, struck on the Hillstone, close under the Bolt. There was a very dense fog, and the vessel was carried by the strong current peculiar to that coast out of her course. No suspicion seems to have been entertained that she was so near the shore. The Salcombe fishermen, who were pursuing their avocations at the time, witnessed her perilous position, and warned them to back off at once, so as to ground on the Bar, otherwise, owing to the injury she had sustained from her plates being broken in, she would have sunk in deep water. Telegrams were forwarded from Kingsbridge to the naval authorities at Devonport, who at once despatched a tug and other assistance. The position of the leak was soon discovered by the divers, and temporary repairs effected by patching the plates. By means of constant pumping and lightening the ship, she was at last floated off, and

was taken in tow by the *Scotia* and *Trusty*, and brought
to Devonport, where she was docked for repairs.   At a
Court-martial subsequently held it was proved that every
care had been taken, but, owing to the denseness of the
fog, the captain was unaware that the ship had approached
so near to the shore.*

From the South Sands we commence the ascent of a hill,
and after passing through some fields, we reach a pathway,
called "Courtenay Walk," cut about half way down the
magnificent cliffs, for the accommodation and gratification
of the public, through the liberality of Lord Courtenay, now
Earl of Devon.   This pathway is bordered by ferns, fox-
gloves, purple heath, and yellow broom; in fact, with a
great variety of such plants as will thrive with but little
soil to support them.   The lovely little Burnet rose, with
its deliciously scented cream-coloured blossoms; the dwarf
scabious tinting the banks with its blue flowers; various
orchises; the delicate pink convolvulus, with the woodbine
and briar rose, are mingled with the dark-green glossy ivy,
which is wrapped around the overhanging rocks, while the
purple iris, and the butcher's broom, with its bright
scarlet berries, in the *winter season*, diversify the scene.
The furze bushes are plentifully covered, in some places,
with the long tangled crimson threads of the parasitic
dodder, sometimes sprinkled with pink-white blossoms.
Suddenly the path becomes obstructed by rocks, which allow
only a narrow egress, and on turning a corner, we find
ourselves in a most exposed situation, the path strewn with
fragments which have fallen from the sharp tors, now towering above our heads, like ruined castles.   Although the road

---

* The *Illustrated London News* of the day contained an account, accompanied by a pictorial representation, of the grounding of the *Cadmus*.

is rugged you should still push on, for the Bolt Head is a noble pile of rocks, and should be viewed from either side. Be cautious, however; for a high wind sometimes renders it a "pursuit of *scenery* under difficulties;" but if you prudently can do so, by all means go on, and then look *back*. The Bolt Head seen from that side is a magnificent object, towering high above us, and extending to the sea, down far below. There is a curious hole, all through these rocks, which, seen from either side, has a very peculiar effect. From this point may be seen the whole of the bay, shut in by the opposite headland.

It is to be feared that the frost and rains of another winter or two will render a portion of this pathway impassable, as slips have already taken place in different parts, and there is a feeling of insecurity even now, when passing over cracks, and sunken bits of ground, when you remember that the sea is a hundred feet or more below.

In clear weather, the double peak of Heytor, on Dartmoor, and also the Eddystone Lighthouse, can be distinctly seen from the Bolt Head.

The larger rocks, out of the reach of the spray, are ornamented with lichens of a deep golden colour, while the little Sedum Anglicum, inserting itself into the crevices, and reddened by exposure to the wind, adds greatly to the beautiful colouring around you.

It may not be altogether unacceptable to botanists if we give a short list of plants and flowers (with both their English and Latin names) which have been found in this immediate neighbourhood. We shall only mention those which, in botanical works, are denominated *rare*. It is scarcely worth while to insert the names of such as are common to almost every locality.

Burnet Rose	*(Rosa spinocissima.)*
Yellow-horned Poppy	*(Glaucium luteum.)*
Stinking Iris	*(Iris fœtidissima.)*
Climbing Corydalis	*(Corydalis claviculata.)*
Sea-side Everlasting Pea	*(Lathrus maritimus.)*
Sea Holly	*(Eryngium maritimum.)*
Lesser Dodder	*(Cuscuta epithymum.)*
Bird's-nest Orchis	*(Listera nidus avis.)*
Butcher's Broom	*(Ruscus aculeata.)*
Vernal Squill	*(Scilla verna.)*
Autumnal Squill	*(Scilla autumnalis.)*
Bloody Crane's-bill	*(Geranium sanguineum.)*

A lady named Acton, who was staying at Salcombe awhile since, writes, " The lichen I got on the rock beyond Bolt Head is such a wonder. Dr. Moore, of Glasnevin botanic gardens, has written to me for a good handful of it for his museum. He congratulates me for being so happy as to find this brocella—the rarest and most valuable of lichens. * * * The only place in the United Kingdom where it had been previously found was in the Isle of Wight."

A scramble around the point leading towards Splat Cove (notwithstanding the difficulty from slippery rocks), will be amply repaid by a sight of the entrance to an old iron mine, which appears to have been worked for some fathoms into the schistus rock, and has much the appearance of a natural cavern. For several feet the walls are studded with patches of a most brilliant, soft, emerald-green moss, which, reflecting the light, almost rivals in splendour the gorgeous tints of the humming-bird, or the elytra of some of the foreign beetles. It is seen to the greatest advantage at the distance of a few yards, especially when it meets the eye in one particular direction. Upon detaching some portions of the moss from the disintegrating stone, and removing it to a full light, its resplendent character nearly, if not quite, disappears, and nothing is visible on the surface of the stone but a filmy, irregular network of green, and extremely short moss. In the "*Magazine of Natural History,*" vols. ii. and iii., there are notices of the discovery of a similar "shining moss." In one of these papers, signed J. E. Bowman, the Court, near Wrexham, June 3rd, 1830, he says, "I have no hesitation in referring this beautiful moss to the order of Algæ, of which it will probably be found to belong to the tribe of Confervöideœ, but I must leave it to those who are better acquainted with this obscure family to decide whether it has yet obtained a name and place in the system of modern cryptogamic botanists."

In the *Gardeners' Magazine* of February 3rd, 1872, there is an interesting paper, from which we extract a portion.

"In 1843, the luminosity of plants was recorded in the Proceedings of the British Association. [Dr. Allman had expressed an opinion respecting a plant, that the phenomenon was not due to phosphorescence, but was referable to the state of the visual organs, that is, an optical delusion.] This led Mr. Babington to mention that he had seen, in the West of England, a peculiar bright appearance, produced by the presence of the Schistostega pennata, a little moss which inhabited caverns and dark places; but this, too, was objected to by a member present, who stated that Professor Lloyd had examined the Schistostega, and had found that the peculiar luminous appearance of that moss arose from the presence of small crystals in its structure, which reflected the smallest portion of the rays of light.

These remarks having been published in the *Gardeners' Chronicle,*[*] Dr. Lankester, in a succeeding number, said, 'The light from the moss, mentioned by Mr. Babington, has also been observed in Germany on another species

---

[*] 1843, page 691.

N

(Schistostega osmundacea). It has been observed by Funk, Brandenberg, Nees Von Esenbeck, Hornschuh, and Struve. Bridel-Brideri and Agardh attributed this light to a small Alga, which the former called Catoptridium smaragdinum, and the latter Protococcus smaragdinus, which they supposed occupied the moss. Unger, however, has examined the moss accurately, and finds that at certain seasons the peculiar utricles of this moss assume a globular form, and, being partially transparent, the light is refracted and reflected in such a way as to present a luminosity on the surface of the vesicles. Meyen says he has confirmed Unger's observations.' "

Whether the *Salcombe* shining moss is identical with either of those above described, we do not know; but there is sufficient similarity to render the extracts interesting and valuable. It should, however, be stated that in this instance the *luminosity* does not vary in intensity, but is precisely the same at all seasons of the year.

The entrance to the cave where this beautiful moss may be seen is decked with that pretty fern, the Asplenium marinum.

Hawkins says that "just within the Splat Cove rocks (towards the South Sands) is a subterraneous passage called Bull-hole, which the common people have an idea runs quite under the earth to another such place, of similar name, in a creek of the sea called Sewer Mill, about three miles distance to the west." An absurd story is told of a bull which entered it, and came out at the opposite end with its coat changed from black to white; and it is curious enough to find a similar legend current near Corunna, on the coast of Spain. "Whether," continues Hawkins, "these two cavities be really the same continuous aperture from one extremity to the other, has never been fully identified; none of those who have entered the respective openings having had the resolution to proceed sufficiently far to ascertain the fact."

A little beyond the Bolt Head is a small cove, called Stare-hole Bay. Stare (or Stair) Hole is supposed by some to derive its name from a steep roadway by which sea-weed is carried up from the beach.

This bay is remarkable (again we quote from Hawkins) "for a cavern that is reported (or, rather, imagined) to terminate near Malborough Church, which stands three miles off. The dripping of water, however, by extinguishing the torches, added to the fear of otters, which resort thither, has hitherto compelled the curious to abandon every design of penetrating to the end, few having advanced above a hundred yards. On the left of the bay, and near the mouth of the cave, is an excavated rock, eight or nine feet high and about five broad, forming a natural arch, opening towards the sea. It is not improbable that Bull-hole and the interior of Stare-hole cavern form a junction."

The neighbourhood of Salcombe, and of the Bolt Head, are peculiarly rich in the variety of animal life existing there. While strolling along the cliffs near the signal house on a fine summer's day, you may see in the waters below, shoals of porpoises, tumbling and rolling about, and searching in the creeks for the fishes, of which they consume great quantities. In the caverns of the rocks close to the sea there are numbers of otters, who take an early bath and a breakfast at the same time. They may be heard whistling and calling to their mates and young ones. After their repast they return to their caverns, and remain in sleep and solitude until hunger again drives them forth in search of food. A little higher up in the cliffs there are rabbits in abundance, and occasionally a wily fox makes his presence known in the neighbouring poultry yards. That much-persecuted creature, the badger, has sometimes been captured here. He is very harmless, unless when attacked by men or dogs, but then he becomes formidable and ferocious. The chief food of these animals consists of insects and roots, though when driven by hunger, they are *occasionally* obliged to be satisfied with a duck or a chicken. What a pity it is they are so seldom allowed to enjoy, in peace and quietness, the life which was given by the Creator, on purpose, doubtless, for their enjoyment.

In the clefts of the rocks may be seen an almost incredible number of herring and kittiwake gulls, sitting on their eggs in the bare hollows, without any materials used for making a nest. In the most inaccessible part of the cliff, and under some projecting rock, the peregrine falcon is snug in its eyrie. On leaving the nest (which usually contains two or three eggs, of a red-brown colour), it will drop almost perpendicularly down to the surface of the water, and then sail off in majestic style, in search of some poor stray gull, which becomes an easy prey. Next you may see, peering over the narrow ledges of rock, a number of heads and necks of snake-like appearance; they belong to the shags, or green cormorants; birds which weigh about four pounds, and whose plumage is of a fine metallic green, while the male has a fan-like crest. In close proximity to these are the nests of birds of the same genus, but much larger size—the great cormorant, which weighs about nine pounds. These birds sally forth during the day, and levy contributions from the ocean storehouse beneath, from which they collect their whole subsistence.

In the sheltered hollows, which are covered with short grass and furze, the place seems teeming with animal life: rabbits burrowing in the ground; and polecats, stoats, and weasels, skulking and hunting them from burrow to burrow; vipers, slow-worms, snakes, and lizards, writhing in the grass, and basking in the sun; beetles of brilliant hues; butterflies of the rarest kinds alighting on the blossoms, and spreading their beautiful wings; amongst them is the large blue butterfly (Polyomatus arion) which is quite a local fly, being found only in a very few places in England.*

Now look upwards—that kestrel is hovering above our heads, intent on the capture of an unsuspecting mouse or mole, who may be enjoying himself amongst the herbage below.

Soaring aloft over the sea, at an altitude of some hundreds of feet, the solan goose, or gannet (who looks as if he had on a pair of spectacles), is surveying the surface of the waters, on the look-out for a passing fish. Suddenly his wings are closed, and he plunges down, head foremost, into the deep; in a few seconds he is seen struggling with the prey, which he quickly dispatches, and then away he soars again to watch for more.

Sometimes, while rambling on the cliffs, a sound strikes the ear as of horses and dogs rapidly approaching, and a poor timid hare, almost black with perspiration and terror, passes before you. He stops a moment, raises his ears, and then dashes on again. Poor hapless creature, our heart aches for thee! oh, if the huntsman could only exchange places with his victim for one short hour, we think he would never again have the least desire to pursue this cruel

* For Mr. H. Nicholls' list of butterflies found in the district, see end of the book.

sport. We knew a dear lady who never would willingly partake of a *hunted hare*—she always said it had "*the cruelty taste.*" How we wish other people had palates as sensitive!

Underneath the cliffs, in the pools left by the ebbing tide, sea anemonies of the most brilliant colours are expanding their tentacles, and enjoying the rays of the summer sun; and in the same pools prawns are darting about, and various kinds of shell fish are clinging to the sides.

Navigation along this rock-bound coast is attended with many perils, and numerous are the disasters to shipping left on record from time to time.

In July, 1871, during a very dense fog, the barque *Westmoreland*, 250 tons register, belonging to Messrs. Andrews, Andrews, & Co., of London, for which port she was bound from Jamaica, went ashore about two miles west of Bolt Head. No land had been sighted since the vessel (which was laden with sugar, rum, cocoanuts, walking-sticks, &c.) had entered the English Channel, and she now stood in for the land, in order to make the Start light, which the captain believed was not far distant. About half-an-hour after midnight the master saw land on the port bow, and directed the helm to be put down, in order to go about. The ship was brought up to the wind, but missing stays, fell off, and went ashore. Rockets and blue lights were burned, but no assistance arrived. When daylight shewed them their situation, the captain directed the boat to be got out, and he and the crew (in all, sixteen persons) got safely to land. They lost everything but the clothes they were wearing.

Between the two headlands known as the Bolt Head and the Bolt Tail, almost every rock and cove seems to have its own peculiar name and distinguishing characteristic. At Stare-hole Bottom, there was, a few years ago, a straight rampart, or barrow, in perfect preservation, fifty-six paces in length. It was commonly called the *Giant's Grave*, though the popular tradition is equally strong that the whole bottom is the site of a Danish encampment, or settlement: to use the language of the tradition itself, as recited by a guide, " by the records of England, it was a Danish town, and had sixty dwellers." It is said that brass coins have been found by some labourers on this spot. In a field just below this there was formerly a quadrangular tumulus, but it has long been destroyed by agricultural operations.

At Roden or Randon Cove, about the middle of the eighteenth century, a foreign vessel was wrecked, which had some marble statues on board.

There were several mounds about that part of the coast, which had all the appearance of tumuli, but many of them have been levelled in the process of farming the ground. A considerable portion of this district is called "The Sewers," divided into east, west, middle, lower, &c., and there are farm-houses bearing these names. The whole neighbourhood is described as being strikingly fine and beautiful.

Dragon Bay was so called from the wreck of a ship belonging to London, bearing that name, which was lost here in the year 1757, in which wreck perished a family called Chambers. Their remains were buried in Malborough Churchyard, where a headstone, over-run with yellow lichen, bore this inscription :—

" Here lye the bodies of Rhodes, Daniel, Mary, and Joseph Chambers, sons and daughters of Edward Chambers, of Jamaica, who were shipwrecked at Cat-hole, within this parish, August 22nd, 1757."

Nearly at the top of the almost perpendicular cliffs of
Bolberry Down is a cavern, called Ralph's Hole, about
twenty feet long, six or seven broad, and eight high. It
is directly facing the sea, which is between four and five
hundred feet below. The rock at the corner of the entrance,
by doubling which this cavern is alone approached, projects
to within two or three feet of the precipice, in such a
manner that a single person from within might easily defend
his habitation from a host of foes; for only one being able
to pass at a time, they might successively be tumbled
headlong down the steep. "There is a tradition," says
Hawkins, "that one *Ralph*, in order to avoid the bailiffs
or the constables, made this his abode for many years;
and, with a prong for his weapon of protection, kept his
pursuers constantly at bay." [Others say Ralph was a
noted smuggler, which seems, of the two, the more likely
account.] "On Sundays he was accustomed to wander
abroad, and his wife assisted him through the rest of the
week in getting provisions. At what period this happened
does not appear, but certainly it is of very old date."

Some terrible inundation of the sea, or it may have been
an earthquake, has divided the cliffs about here into deep
fissures, and shattered immense rocks to pieces. At Ouse-hole
Cove there is a noble view of Bigbury Bay, the Rame Head,
the Eddystone, and the Cornish coast. A mine was commenced in 1770, by John Easton, of Dodbrooke, in a part of
the cliffs of Bolberry Down, not far from Ralph's Hole; but
it was soon abandoned on submitting the spangled produce
to the test of the assayer, who pronounced it to be mundic
instead of copper; and the adventurer gained nothing save
the empty honour of leaving the shaft his name. It lies
about three or four hundred feet down a declivity, so steep
as to be scarcely accessible.

Mr. John Cranch, when investigating the neighbourhood many years ago, said, "About twenty yards from Easton's mine is a most admirable and abundant chalybeate spring, very pure, and grateful to the taste. In combination with the advantages of marine air and water, sea bathing, the fisheries, &c., &c., this spring I consider as inestimable, and that it will one day be the means of drawing to the vicinity a great resort of wealthy invalids and others, and make the neighbourhood of Hope and Salcombe rich and prosperous." This expectation, however, has not yet been realised. Hope, although it possesses much to attract in the surrounding scenery, still continues to offer scarcely any accommodation for visitors beyond what is to be found at the two small inns.; which is certainly much to be regretted. In the cliffs, under-neath the Greystone, which is a very lofty rock rising high above this village, an iron mine was opened some years since, but it did not produce sufficient ore to pay the cost of work-ing; and moreover the access to it was so dangerous for vessels, that one was wrecked there with its cargo of ore on board. It was therefore discontinued. There are veins of iron in many parts of the coast, and several attempts at mining have been made, but ere long relinquished. Just about here begins Bolt Down, where the Kingsbridge races used to be held. The remains of two barrows are mentioned as having been found on this spot.

In the hurricane of 15th February, 1760, so dreadful both by sea and on shore, the *Ramilies*, a fine ship of seventy-four guns, and seven hundred and thirty-four men, com-manded by Captain Taylor, was lost near this promontory, where she was embayed in consequence of mistaking the Bolt Tail for the Rame Head, and erroneously supposing they were driving into Plymouth Sound. Having let go their anchor close upon the rocks, and cut away all their masts, they rode safely till evening, when the gale increased to such a degree that the hull parted; and only one midshipman and twenty-five men, out of the whole number, jumping off the stern upon the rocks, were saved. This fatal spot is near the cove and village of Inner Hope, and it has ever since been known as "Ramilies Hole." It is so peculiarly situated that it can only be entered by boats at certain tides and winds, in very calm, still weather, and when there is no swell of the sea. It cannot even be seen from any part of the cliffs. It is said that some of the guns of the ship may yet be perceived in six or seven fathoms of water, near the mouth of the cavern.*

Close to the flagstaff, on the cliff which rises just above the coast-guard station at Hope, there is an old cannon, which was recovered from this wreck. The present writer also possesses a memento of the *Ramilies*: it is a small instrument, which appears to have been a guinea-weigher. There is a thin rod of ivory, with graduated marks on it; a brass saucer hangs at one end, and the weight is to be suspended to the rod, on the steelyard principle. The whole is enclosed in a small, dark wooden case, in shape not very unlike a fiddle.

The following paper was contributed by Robert Dymond, Esq., F.S.A., to a local newspaper, some years since. He kindly permits its insertion here.

"A FRAGMENT OF LOCAL HISTORY.

The appearance of Miss S. P. Fox's book on Kingsbridge, its Estuary, and Neighbourhood, has doubtless rekindled the interest excited nearly half a century ago by Mr. Abraham

* Mostly from Hawkins.

Hawkins' History. Any additional particulars relating to a locality so rich in historical incidents may, therefore, be acceptable to the readers of a local journal.

Stories of shipwreck and maritime adventure can hardly fail to be prominent amongst these incidents. Standing far out into the English Channel, the rocky coast of South Devon has witnessed the loss of but too many gallant ships. The wreck of the *Ramilies* man-of-war in 1760, and that of the *Chantaloupe* twelve years later, have been well described by the writers above-named; but I am not aware that the story has yet been told in print of an earlier shipwreck, that may as worthily fill a page of local history.

Let the reader carry back his thoughts to the reign of Elizabeth, and to the year of grace 1588—the most eventful of that remarkable era. Early in the month of May the long-expected Armada, fitted out with vast and careful preparation by Philip of Spain, had entered the Channel to fulfil his long-cherished plan for restoring heretic England to the bosom of the Church of Rome. No sooner was the Spanish fleet descried off the Lizard than the ready beacon fires carried the news from headland to headland, all along the southern coast to the capital. On the morning of Saturday, the 20th of May, thousands of eager spectators crowded on the Start, on Bolt Head, and upon every cliff from which a seaward view could be obtained, to look upon a sight, the like of which had never before been witnessed from those grim rocks. One hundred and forty ships, most of them of unwieldy bulk and strange form, were moving slowly up Channel in crescent-shaped array, closely beset by the smaller and less numerous, though nimbler, vessels, in which Drake and Hawkins, and many more renowned sea captains, had issued the night before

from Plymouth Sound, under the command of the Lord
High Admiral Howard, of Effingham.

The reader of English history needs not to be reminded
how, in spite of isolated captures, the Spanish fleet held
its course through the narrow seas, with purpose to form in
Calais roads a junction with the land forces of Alexander
Farnese, Duke of Parma, Philip's astute general in the
Netherlands; how this purpose was frustrated by the com-
bined agency of the weather, the confusion resulting from
the attacks of the English ships, and the blockade of Farnese
by the Dutch in their own harbours; and how, scattered
by a storm, the remnants of the great Armada staggered
northwards through the German Ocean. The great heart of
England again beat freely, for the disaster which had well
nigh changed her history was providentially averted. The
comparatively few vessels that escaped loss on the perilous
shores of Norway, and the equally inhospitable Hebrides,
sought to beat their way homewards by the western coasts
of Britain and Ireland, till of all that splendid fleet of
gilded and turreted ships, scarce fifty returned to bear the
tidings to King Philip of the lamentable end of the mightiest
of his great enterprises.

One of the two hospital ships appointed for the Spanish
navy was named the *St. Peter the Great*. She was upwards
of 500 tons burden, and was laden with drugs and medical
stores. Either the adverse gales of November had driven
the ship from its course, after completing the entire circuit
of Great Britain, or her commander had made for the
enemy's land as the only chance of saving his sinking
vessel. Certain it is that she came ashore in Hope Bay,
near Salcombe. Manned by a thoroughly dispirited crew,
the ill-fated *St. Peter* was set upon and plundered by the

country people, before the authorities could take measures for securing the prize in the name of the Queen.

George Cary, of Cockington,* one of the Deputy Lieutenants of the county, received intelligence of the wreck at Plymouth, and immediately rode across the country to Hope, where he took order for the disposal of the crew, and the recovery of the remnants of the cargo. Mr. Cary found the hulk lying, full of water, on a rock, where she soon fell in pieces. He gathered from the sailors that at their departure from Spain they had numbered thirty mariners, a hundred soldiers of various nations, and about fifty persons attached to the duties of the hospital. Out of these, one hundred and forty succeeded in reaching the shore in safety. Of the drugs and 'potecary stuff' of six thousand ducats value which had been on board, the greater part was spoiled by water. The plate and treasure had already been carried off, and even the seamen's chests had been plundered by the wreckers. The ordnance, which was all of iron, appears to have been secured; but of the tackling only one cable remained.

Twenty of the Spanish officers were separated from the rest : eight of these were left to the charge of Sir William Courtenay, at Ilton Castle, near Kingsbridge, the wreck having occurred on that good knight's property. Mr. Cary undertook the custody of the apothecary and the surgeon, and having caused the remainder to be guarded by day

---

* This gentleman was an ancestor of the present R. S. S. Cary, Esq., of Torre Abbey. A member of one of the most ancient and distinguished of our county families, he himself became one of the most illustrious of his race. He had already done the state good service in the measures taken for the defence of the coast, and shortly after received the honour of knighthood at the hands of his kinswoman, Queen Elizabeth. He was a friend of the great Secretary Walsingham, and in later years was successively Lord Treasurer and Lord Deputy, or Viceroy of Ireland. His biography will be found in Prince's "Worthies of Devon."

and night, he assigned for each prisoner's subsistence an allowance of one penny per diem out of his private means, until the pleasure of Her Majesty's Privy Council should be made known. His report to their Lordships of these proceedings is dated 5th November, 1588, from his house at Cockington, near Torbay, whither he had retired after leaving the further care of the matter to Anthony Ashley, the Clerk of the Council, who took up his abode with Sir William Courtenay, at Ilton Castle. The orders received for the execution of the prisoners having been countermanded, Ashley proceeded in a business-like way to make a careful inventory of their names, offices, and quality, distinguishing such as made offers of ransom, from those who were unable to purchase their liberty. In his report to the Council, bearing date the 12th of November, he refers to the wholesale rifling of the cargo, and the injury sustained by the drugs; and adds,

'By late examinations taken of the Spaniardes, I fynde that certain besar stones and other simples was purloyned out of the shippe, of which besar stones I hope to recouer the most of them. I have been bould to staie this messenger hitherto, thinking I should have been able to have advertised some certaintie of them, but must now leave the same to my return, wch shall be as speedilie as I maie.'

As to the prisoners, he writes,

'X. or XII. of the best sorte are placed in a towne called Kingsbridge, where order is taken for the provision of their wants, and accompt kept of their expence. The rest, untill yor Lpps. further pleasure knowen, are remaining together in one house, whither they were first committed, where they are safe kept, and provided of necessarie food.'

With what eager curiosity must the good townsfolk of

Kingsbridge have regarded the ten or twelve olive-complexioned gentlemen of Spain, whom Anthony Ashley had sent over to their keeping. A good idea of the aspect of Kingsbridge at that period may be formed from an examination of the quaint frontispiece to Mr. Hawkins' History. It is a kind of picture-plan, bearing the date 1586, or only two years before the wreck of the *St. Peter the Great.* People the scene here depicted with the Jarvises, the Adamses, and the Lidstones, who then, as now, thronged to their market town from the neighbouring South Hams. Imagine groups of these countrymen and countrywomen gathering round the foreigners, who lounged in strange costumes about the 'Cheap House,' which then encumbered the centre of the Fore Street, near the Church. Being, as Ashley says, 'of the best sorte,' these Spaniards most likely had their liberty on parole, and could regale their hosts with many a story of proud endurance of the hardships of their luckless voyage. Some could doubtless recount tales of personal adventure in the golden colonies of their royal master in the Indies. They may have stirred the blood of these men of Devon by glowing narratives of encounters on the Spanish main, with Raleigh and Drake, and their bold west-country seamen.

But my present concern is with historical facts, and these conjectures must, therefore, be left with the novelist. The presence of the foreigners could hardly have failed to leave a deep impression on the inhabitants of the district, and possibly some of your readers, possessing, like the author of 'Kingsbridge Estuary,' the advantages of good local sources of information, may find, still lingering in the neighbourhood, traditions whose origin may be traced to the wreck of the *St. Peter the Great.*

It only remains for me to direct those who may desire
to verify the strict historical accuracy of these particulars
to the Domestic Series of State Papers of the reign of
Elizabeth, preserved in the Record Office in London, and
to which ready access may be obtained for literary purposes.
The original letters of George Cary and Anthony Ashley
to the Privy Council will be found in vol. ccxviii. of the
series 1581—1590.

Exeter, December, 1865."

CHAPTER XII.

"There is a rapture on the lonely shore;
There is society where none intrudes,
By the deep sea, and music in its roar."

SNUGLY ensconced within a beautiful cove are the two
fishing villages of Inner and Outer Hope, from whence
the neighbourhood derives its chief supply of lobsters and
crabs.

From the flag-staff, just above the coast-guard station,
there is a charming look-out; indeed, it is marvellous that
this part of the coast has not become the resort of a greater
number of visitors. This usually quiet little cove sometimes
presents a curious spectacle, from its being a sheltered
retreat for wind-bound vessels, which occasionally lie there
for a week or more, at least, until the breeze is a favourable
one. We have seen between fifty and sixty vessels lying
at anchor, at the same time, within a limited space; and
then the villages presented a very animated scene, from
the influx of sailors, both foreign and English, who came
ashore, and caused great demand for provisions of various
kinds. Cart after cart arrived with butchers' meat and
loaves of bread, and were as speedily emptied of their loads,

o

with much laughter and vociferation. Then came the filling of water casks from the clear spring just in front of one of the inns; and then the discovery of water-cresses in an adjoining meadow. How they raced and chased, and vaulted over the stone hedge, and then came back again with caps, and handkerchiefs, and *arms* full of this wholesome and pleasant vegetable.

"About the time the restoration of West Alvington Church was completed, South Huish Church had become so dilapidated that one Sunday, while the resident clergyman (the Rev. F. R. Hole) was preaching, a large window was blown in, and it was impossible that Divine service could be any longer conducted there. It was, therefore, determined to build a new church at once. But as the bulk of the parishioners resided at Galmpton and Hope, it was desirable that the new building should be erected amongst the population; and a site close to the former village was given by the Earl of Devon, where a commodious and neat church has been raised. The site of the building is all that could be desired—on a slight elevation, and with a large yard surrounding it. The church is dedicated to the Holy Trinity. It is of the style of the fourteenth century."* The consecration took place in July, 1869, by the Bishop of Exeter, Dr. Temple. Upon this new church, about £2000 has been expended; and the little chapel within sight of it, at Hope Cove, erected at the expense of the Earl of Devon and the late Sir George Turner, has been converted into a school.

At Inner Hope there is a small chapel belonging to the Wesleyan Methodists; and the Plymouth Brethren have a meeting-house at Galmpton.

* From the *Kingsbridge Gazette* of July, 1869.

Unless your walking powers are very small, we would advise a ramble over the cliffs between Hope and Thurlestone, for carriages have to make a considerable détour inland, through the village of Galmpton; consequently you would miss a sight of the rocks and white pebbly beaches along the coast.

Thurlestone is a village and parish, about four miles west of Kingsbridge, and near the junction of the Avon with Bigbury Bay. The village is situated on high ground, about half a mile from the sea. It is a straggling place, with pretty rural cottages, the fronts of which are, many of them, covered with roses, woodbine, and fuschias.

It is worthy of remark that neither in Thurlestone nor Buckland (as is the case with South Milton) can you find a single public house. The Rector has, so far, been successful in his determination to prevent the opening of any place for the sale of strong drink; knowing well its demoralizing effect on a rural population.

"This parish is called Torleston in Domesday Survey, and is there described as having 'two meadows and two pasture lands; it seems to have been, about the time of Edward the Confessor, the property of Ordgar, or Algar, the Saxon Earl of Devon. About the thirteenth or fourteenth century, it appears to have passed into the possession of Courtenay, the Norman Earl of Devon, from whose family it has but recently passed away.

Thurlestone, (or Torleston, *Saxon*) takes its name from a curiously arched rock of conglomerate, of so hard a character, that while all the other rocks around, being of clay slate, have been washed away by the violence of the waves, this arch which is a small isolated portion of the ~~Devonian, or old~~ red formation, still stands erect, and

"Tried, or new"

//

has given rise to the well-known saying of the neighbourhood,

> 'Brave every shock
> Like Thurlestone's Rock.' "*

The noise made by the wind rushing through the archway
is sometimes heard many miles away, and when it is
perceptible at Kingsbridge it is regarded as the fore-runner
of storms of rain.

"An eminent geological authority considers that the sea,
in the course of many centuries, has effected strange changes
here, and that there are manifest proofs that there was
once a forest where Thurlestone Sands are now. There
is perhaps no healthier locality in the kingdom than
this, owing to its enjoyment of the full, pure, bracing,
though comparatively warm, breeze that from the Atlantic
accompanies the course of the Gulf Stream, a portion of
which appears from the character of the shells and
debris frequently cast into the little bays, to flow straight
in here, more particularly than elsewhere, before making
its bend more directly eastward.

At the mouth of the Avon, which bounds this parish
westward, stands Burrow Island (or Burr Island) where
the waves in a storm appear so grandly wild, that it is
reported to have been the spot chosen by the celebrated
marine artist, Turner, as the best he could select for the
study of such a scene.†

Doubtless when modern facilities for approaching it render
this neighbourhood, with its picturesque valley of Buckland,
its fine sands and cliffs, beautiful coast scenery, its bathing

---

* Morris's " Devonshire."

† Mr. Cyrus Redding describes Turner at a pic-nic on Burr Island, watching the long dark Bolt, under the varying changes of a stormy day.

and other advantages, more known, it will be far better appreciated than it is at present. The Rectory is in the incumbency of the Rev. Peregrine A. Ilbert, M.A."*

The church is an ancient edifice, not long ago restored at considerable expense, and there is a good school for children of both sexes.

Some time since there were seen on Thurlestone beach several specimens of that curious creature called the "Portuguese Man-of-war" (Physalia pelagica). They are abundant in tropical seas, and especially so on the vast shores of Australia, but it is a very unusual circumstance to see them on our own coast, whither they were probably driven by stormy weather. After being beaten about by the waves, much of the beauty of the creature was destroyed; but in its natural condition it has been described as "an inflated oblong bladder, glowing in delicate crimson tints, as it floats on the waves; and not only with crimson, but with veinings of rich purple, and opaline flashes of azure, orange, and green, changing in position at every movement; with long dependent tentacles of the deepest purple, the rich tone of which is seen even beneath the water." The earliest modern name of this zoophyte, Acalepha pelagica, or Sea-nettle, was given it in consequence of the venomous sting caused by the tentacles, a sting which leaves after it a white pimple, precisely similar in appearance to that caused by a nettle.

"Strange traditionary tales of the practice of 'wrecking' or plundering the cargoes of lost ships are rife all round the extensive coast line of Devon and Cornwall. It cannot be denied that the spectacle of a homeward-bound Indiaman, or richly-freighted trader from the Mediterranean, drifting

* Morris's " Devonshire."

disabled towards their shores, was openly rejoiced over by
the half-seafaring, half-agricultural population of the more
secluded cliffs and beaches of these two counties. The
rifling of the cargo was the first object, and it is even
said that sailors whom the waves had spared sometimes
encountered a worse fate than mere neglect."*

"About the year 1772, a vessel returning from the West
Indies, called the *Chantiloupe*, was wrecked in Bigbury
Bay; all on board perished, with the exception of *one* man,
who was rescued by the humanity of a farmer, who lived
in the neighbourhood, of the name of Hannaford. Amongst
the other passengers there was a lady, who it is supposed,
seeing the desperate state of the vessel, put on her richest
gems and apparel, with the hope that if she were washed
towards the shore, those who found her might be induced
to save her. She *was* thrown by the sea on to the beach,
and they say that life was not extinct when she reached
it, but the savage people (from the adjacent villages) who
were anxiously waiting for the wreck, seized and stripped
her of her clothes; they even cut off some of her fingers,
and mangled her ears in their impatience to secure her
jewels, and then left her miserably to perish! A lady in
the neighbourhood, hearing the frightful tale, sent and had
the body removed from the sands where it was left, and
decently buried. It was supposed that the unfortunate lady
was married, and that she had attendants on board the
wrecked vessel, but her name was never known. The men
who were principally concerned in plundering, and most
likely *murdering* her, seemed from that time *marked men*,
even in the rude neighbourhood in which they lived, and
what is singular, they all three came to awful and untimely
deaths."

* Dymond's "Early Records."

There is in the possession of Miss J. B. Cranch a corner of the ill-fated lady's apron, which was secured by a man (doubtless one of the wreckers), and given on the evening following the wreck to her grandmother, who preserved it as a relic of the sad fate of its unfortunate wearer. The fragment is a beautiful specimen of finely embroidered muslin. The account goes on to say that "the celebrated Edmund Burke came down at that time, fearing some relatives or friends of his whom he expected from abroad might be on board the wrecked vessel. He stayed some days at Bowringsleigh House."

After receiving this deplorable history, we had its truth confirmed by a gentleman to whom application had been made on the subject. He says "The tradition here is that the vessel was called the *Chantiloupe*. The old man who seemed to know most about it said, 'the lady *was* a-murdered, he believed—'cause the doctors said so, for the blood that was about the fingers and the ears *proved* it. All hands were lost except one man. Jan Whiddon's father's dog found this here lady buried in the sand: he scratched up the hand. 'Twas never found out who murdered her; but *one thing* was *know'd*—which was this—that when the wreck was about to take place, this here lady had put on her best clothes, and all her jewels, in order that *if* she was drownded, she might be buried *decent*. However, (he added) all who were concerned in it, or supposed to be, came to a bad end.' I have looked in the register (of Thurlestone church) but can find no entry of about 1772 respecting the burial, but I *hear* she was buried here, and then exhumed and taken to London, and that her name was Burke, or Birt, or some name like it."

It would appear from the book entitled "A dreadful

Alarm," which has been already spoken of as written by
Henry Hingeston about the year 1700, that in his day
wrecks were much more frequent on the neighbouring
coast than is the case now (which, without lighthouses,
and with inferior vessels and seamanship, would be likely),
and wrecking was carried on in the most hard-hearted and
barbarous manner. The following are Henry Hingeston's
remarks on this subject.

"I have been deeply affected to see and feel how sweet
the report of a *shipwreck* is to the inhabitants of this
country, as well professors as profane, and what running
there is on such occasions, all other business thrown aside,
and away to wreck. * * * I am verily persuaded
that it hath been more sweet to hear that all the men
are drowned, and so a proper wreck, than that any are
saved, and by that means hinder their more public appearance on that stage for getting money. O! the cruelty
that hath been acted by many. My heart hath been often
heavy to consider it, insomuch that I verily think multitudes
of heathen are nothing near so bad. Remember the broad-
cloth slupe, stranded in Bigbury Bay, richly laden. O!
for shame, for shame, I am really vext that ever my countrymen should be guilty of such devilish actions."

Is it not sickening to think that such scenes ever were
enacted in this professedly Christian country? But the
days of these savage deeds are long past away, and now
instead of the greedy wrecker, we may picture the life-boat
launched, and manned by a brave and honest crew, eager
to risk their own lives in the endeavour to save those of
their fellow-men.

The most *recent* wreck which we have to record as having
occurred in Bigbury Bay is that of the brigantine *Theodore,*

of Hamburgh, which came ashore at Thurlestone Sands, in February of this year (1874). She was laden with cotton seed and dye woods. During a heavy gale, a few days previously, she was struck by a heavy sea, which swept off the captain and two men, and damaged the vessel. The mate then took the command, and having been at the wheel for several days, got out of his reckoning, and the vessel became embayed. The brigantine was then off Hope, and the officer of the coast-guard, seeing she must come ashore, got out a small life-boat, and took off the mate and two lads before she struck, and landed them at Hope.

Many years ago, some young people were amusing themselves by digging in the sand just under Bantham Ham, and to their astonishment they came upon a *human skull*. It was apparently that of a negro—certainly not that of an Englishman. Afterwards several other skulls were disinterred near the same spot, and it seems probable that they were relics of those who perished either in the wreck of the *Ramilies*, or of the *Chantiloupe*.

When the valley between Bantham and Thurlestone was in process of being drained some years ago, the workmen stumbled upon a *mass* of bones, which were at first supposed to be human remains; they were, however, afterwards discovered to be those of various animals, but how they came there remains a mystery. Many cartloads of bones were carried away to be used as manure. This draining altered the course of a stream which ran all through the valley, and after a while a beautiful bubbling spring burst up through the sand of the beach, where it remains a great boon to thirsty picnic-ers.

Thurlestone parish includes the hamlets of Buckland,

Bantham, and Avon-mouth. Buckland is in a warm sheltered valley, studded with orchards, and presents such an
old-world appearance that it called forth the remark from
a working man, when he saw it for the first time, that he
thought "it must have been built when *Adam and Eve
were little.*"

A short distance from the village of Buckland is Clan-
nacombe—a fine Elizabethan mansion, but much modernised.
It is approached, from the gateway, through a short avenue
of elms. In one of the gardens is a fine specimen of the
old dovecote—a circular, domed building, in a good state
of preservation. Access to the interior is obtained by a
small square doorway at the base, when upon looking up
you will see a great number of square "pigeon holes,"
arranged in circular tiers, one above another. There is no
projecting alighting place for the birds, and the only place
of ingress and egress is a circular aperture at the top of the
dome. No safer home could have been designed for the
feathered inmates, as it would be impossible for either
quadruped or biped to obtain access to the nests, except
by the proper doorway, and then by a long ladder.

Bantham is built almost close to the mouth of the Avon,
where there is a harbour for sloops and barges. There is
here a salmon-pool; and at low water the fine flat sands,
which extend some way up the creek, are much frequented
by cockle-boys. The Ham, which is a piece of turfy land,
of considerable extent, is used for sheep grazing: it is a fine
breezy down, frequented by rabbits, who burrow in the
banks; while the joyous songs of hosts of skylarks may be
heard high over head. Oh, who that has ever heard the
song of the *free* skylark, could think of making him a
captive within the bars of a *cage!* Truly we believe these

poor prisoners often sing for sorrow of heart, and we miss the exulting, gleeful strains of the free "bird of the wilderness."

The sands on the beach at Bantham are the firmest for walking on of any we know in the neighbourhood, and a great variety of shells (some of them rare ones) may be collected here. The rocks are capital for a scramble, and the deep rock pools, fringed with beautiful sea-weeds and corallines, and tenanted by prawns, periwinkles, hermit crabs, sea anemonies, and many another creature, most tempting to the collector for a marine aquarium, may occupy the attention very pleasantly on a long summer's day. In the village of Bantham there is what may be termed an out-station belonging to the coastguard, in connection with the larger station at Challaborough. Avon-mouth, or as it is generally called, Onnamouth, consists of only a very few houses, higher up the creek than Bantham.

The Avon divides the parish of Thurlestone from that of Bigbury.

"Where Avon's waters with the sea are mix'd,
Saint Michael firmly on a rock is fix'd."

St. Michael's rook, now called Burrow, or Burr Island, belongs to Bigbury parish. The sands that connect it with the mainland are passable at half tide : in these sands may sometimes be found beautiful microscopic shells, which can be scooped up by handsful in some states of the wind and tide. A very elegant shell, supposed to be a nautilus, was found here by the late C. Prideaux, Esq., and given to Colonel Montagu. He describes it as "minute, with sides perfectly equal, and very much resembling the cornu-ammonis, transparent, and strongly ribbed." Of this shell he found three specimens.

Camden mentions the ruins of an old chapel as existing somewhere here, but there is no appearance of such now. On the summit of the island there *is* a ruin, and some time ago we were informed by a Coastguard that he supposed it to be the remains of an observatory that had been erected in war time. He was rather surprised at receiving the counter information that it had been built by the writer's grandfather, for the accommodation of pic-nic parties at the island. The short turf here affords about ten acres of sheep pasture. It is *riddled* with rabbit burrows, so as to render it quite a perilous feat to ascend to the top on horseback. The wild squill is so abundant, that in the season of flowering, the ground has the appearance of being overspread with patches of blue carpet. There is a fine archway of rock at the base of the island, and deep fissures in the cliffs tenanted by innumerable sea gulls.

Large quantities of pilchards are taken in Bigbury Bay. These fish annually assemble in millions, and perform a stately march through the sea, generally in the same direction, and within certain limits.

Mr. Couch, in his Report of the Penzance Nat. Hist. and Antiq. Soc., 1847, says, "The main body retires for the winter into deep water, to the westward of the Scilly Islands. About the middle of spring they rise from the depths of the ocean, and consort together in small shoals, which, as the season advances, unite into larger ones, and towards the end of July or beginning of August combine in one mighty host, and advance towards the land in such amazing numbers as to discolour the water as far as the eye can reach. They strike the land generally to the north of Cape Cornwall, where a detachment turns to the N. E., and constitutes the summer fishery of St. Ives; but the bulk of the fish passes between Scilly and the Land's End, and entering the British Channel, follows the windings of the shore as far as Bigbury Bay and the Start."

It is said in Moore's "Devon" that "many years since a quantity of pilchards large enough to produce about £7000 were taken in Bigbury Bay; but of late years the fishing seasons have been less successful."

"There is a Bigbury Bay Company, possessing the necessary boats and nets, &c., for the pilchard fishery, and cellars for the cure of the fish at Challaborough and at the Warren, from whence they are shipped in hogsheads for the Mediterranean market."

Pilchards constitute an important article of food to the poorer classes in all the villages and towns surrounding Bigbury Bay.

The Avon (which is navigable for barges as far as Aveton Gifford only) rises in Dartmoor, a short distance north of Brent Beacon. It flows through a fertile country, rich in interesting views Immediately before it passes under Brent or Leedy Bridge, it pours down a ledge of rocks, not much higher, indeed, than a common weir; but the height of the arch of the bridge, beautifully covered with ivy, and the waterfall seen through the arch, together with the picturesque approach of the stream towards the bridge, afford an assemblage of romantic objects, so finely harmonised, that Polwhele says it has been preferred even to Becky Fall, and considered superior to the cataract at Lydford Bridge.

Passing Brent, the Avon runs between Diptford and North Huish; there it is crossed by two or three bridges, besides that at Loddiswell and Aveton Gifford, and discharges itself into the sea near Bantham.

Sir William Pole says, " Bigbery (anciently, Bikabiry) th' ancient dwelling of y^t name. John de Bikabiry, in Kinge John's tyme, dwelled in this place. * * *"

In Billing's " Devonshire," we find " Bigbury, anciently *Bikaberry,* was held by a family of this name for nine generations. * * * The village is very pleasantly situated, on the west side of the Avon valley, about a mile and a half from Bigbury Bay, and three and a half miles from Modbury. The navigation of the bay is very dangerous, on account of its rocky nature; the coast is here indented with several coves, affording convenient retreats for smugglers; there is a coast-guard station here. The bay commands a magnificent view of the ocean."

" Bigbury, Prall, Yarde, Toutsaints, Huish, Bolberry, &c., are the names of ancient families of importance who once resided at these places, or to whom they belonged. The Bigburys lived in this neighbourhood from the Conquest to the time of Edward III."

Bigbury Church, dedicated to St. Lawrence, has a handsome tower, surmounted by a spire. There are, or were, some remains of paintings in the windows, and armorial bearings of the Champernowne and Drake families.

This church has recently undergone a complete restoration, at a cost of about £1,200. It was re-opened in May, 1873, by Dr. Temple, Bishop of Exeter. It contains a fine brass for a lady of the Bigbury family, 1440. There is also a brass for Robert Burton (effigy gone) and wife, Elizabeth de Bigbury, 1460.

CHAPTER XIII.

"Ever varied, too,
Is the rich prospect : valleys softly sink,
And uplands swell—no level sameness tires ;
While in the distance, happily disposed,
Sweeps round the bold blue moor."
Carrington.

LELAND says, "Arme Haven is a . . . miles from Saultcombe Haven. The mouth of this lyith full of Flattes and Rokkes, and no shippe cummith in tempest hither, but in desperation. Two of Philip, King of Castille, shippes, fell to wrack in this haven, when he was driven into England by tempeste. Arme river cummith to this haven; and, as I have hard say, Aune river likewise."

Neither Bigbury nor Aveton Gifford are strictly within our limits, both these places being in the hundred of Ermington; but the latter is in the picturesque valley of the Avon, and therefore must have a passing notice. The Giffords were anciently Lords of the Manor of Aveton—hence the name. Sir William Pole says "William Gifford held the same anno 27 of Kinge Hen. III.

In Morris's "Devonshire," we find the following :—
"The church is a fine ancient cruciform edifice, in the Perpendicular style, dedicated to St. Andrew, with a tower

containing six bells. It has been thoroughly restored, at
an expense of £2,003, and was re-opened for Divine service
in October, 1869." The Rectory is a large and handsome
modern residence, built in Elizabethan style, in 1842.9.

The Baptists, Bible Christians, and Wesleyans, have
places of worship here, and there is a National School for
the children of both sexes, with house for the master,
which was erected in 1857.

The Avon (which is here crossed by a bridge, and is
navigable thus far, and no further) abounds in salmon and
trout, and at the hatch is a salmon weir. Three brooks,
which form feeders of the river, can be crossed at low
tide at a place called 'The Stakes,' which gives a shorter
route to Bigbury."

At one time salmon were much more plentiful here than
they are at present. Of late years they had so materially
decreased that a society was formed for their preservation,
and no one is now permitted to fish in the river for them
without a ticket.

In Domesday Book, among the sources of revenue of the
Manor of Loddiswell, the salmon of the river are mentioned.
It is said of this, as of some other places, that the indentures
by which apprentices were bound in the valley of the Avon
contained the provision that they should not be fed on
salmon more than three times a week.

Loddiswell is a large village, situated on rising ground,
at the western side of the Avon vale, and about three
miles from Kingsbridge.

Risdon's account of this place is as follows:—"Loddiswell was held by Heath in the Saxons' time, and Judael de
Totnes was owner thereof the twentieth year of William
the Conqueror. William de Brays had this Manor given to

him by King Henry II., whose grandchild Eva was mother unto the Lady Millicent de Montacute, of whom Gilbert Knovill, Knight, held this land. Near about the same time, Adam de Hatch was Lord of Hatch, which formerly belonged to the Arundells of Sampford, in Somersetshire. About the time of King Henry IV., the family of Karswill came to be Lords of this land."

Sir William Pole says, "Hach Arondell belonged unto the famyly of Arondell, of Sandford Arondell, in Somersetshire; and in Kinge Edw. I. tyme, Adam de Hach held the same, and John de Hach, anno 19 of Kinge Edw. III.; afterward, in Kinge Henry IV. tyme, Walter Carswell had the same." * * *

From Prince's "Worthies," we extract the following:—
"Sir William Karswill, Knight, was a native of Devon, and the second son of Walter Karswill, of Hach, Esq., in the parish of Loddiswell. A descendant of an ancient and worshipful family of great estate and honour heretofore in these parts, as most others in its time. Their most ancient habitation was also Carswell, in the parish of Holberton, near the town of Modbury, from whence they took their name. In process of time they removed to Hach, called Hach Arrondel, as belonging to a noble tribe so surnamed. More anciently this place had owners denominated from their seat, as Adam de Hach in King Edward I. time, and John de Hach in the nineteenth year of King Edward III." Elsewhere it is recorded that "in 1463, Thomas Gyll had license to castellate his house of Hach Arundell, and enclose a park;" but the place has long been reduced to a farm-house.

In this parish is situated Hazelwood, the residence of the late Richard Peck, Esq., the "Devonshire magistrate,"

of whose career Mrs. Balfour gives a little sketch in her
work entitled "Moral Heroism."

An interesting notice of this gentleman appeared in the
Kingsbridge Gazette of March 16th, 1867, from which we
extract largely.

"The career of Mr. Peek, of Hazelwood, affords an example
of how a man in this country may raise himself if he has
the spirit and industry which are requisite to success in
most undertakings. Few have begun life under more un-
promising circumstances, and yet raised themselves to a
position of affluence in less time than did the subject of
this brief memoir. Some strange and contradictory accounts
of the business history of this remarkable man are current;
and we have been favoured with some information from
one of his nearest relatives, which enables us to correct
them.

Richard Peek was born at Hazelwood in 1782, of parents
in a very humble position of life. When a young man, in
the service of Mr. Lampin, a large grocer at Plymouth or
Devonport, he was balloted for the militia; but not liking
to be a soldier, and suspecting he was drawn, he went off
suddenly to London, where he was a perfect stranger, and
with very little money in his pocket. When crossing
London Bridge, he saw a benevolent-looking Quaker [John
Hamilton], whom he accosted, and to whom he told his
simple tale. This gentleman mentioned his case to a large
wholesale tea dealer, who happened at that time to have
a subordinate situation vacant in his warehouse, which was
offered to the young man. No false pride deterred him
from earning an honest livelihood, and he gratefully accepted the situation, feeling sure he could work his way
upwards. In two years he got promoted, and introduced

his brother to his own place. In seven years he rose to be traveller, and his brother to be head warehouseman. After being a few years in this position, his brother determined to commence business on his own account. The great risk attendant upon the long credit (five months) then given to grocers, considerably enhanced the prices of their goods. William Peek (the brother referred to) thought that by buying through the brokers at one month's credit, and selling for ready money to dealers who could pay cash, a good and safe trade might be done. The system succeeded admirably, with perseverance and application, and in about eighteen months the prosperous state of the business induced Richard to relinquish his situation, and join his brother as partner, when the style of the firm was altered from William Peek & Co. to Peek Brothers & Co., and a younger brother was taken into partnership as soon as he came of age. Soon after this, a large broker offered them a permanent loan of £1500, which enabled them to buy direct from the East India Company, for cash, and spread their trade amongst a higher class of town and country dealers. Since that time the business has been steadily increasing, and is now divided into three large wholesale houses, carried on by the sons of the original partners and young men brought up in the house. .

Mr. Richard Peek early devoted much of his time to public business and various charitable and religious objects. He filled the offices of Common Councilman and Sheriff of the City of London, having in the latter position been the first returning officer after the passing of the Reform Bill. Having been made a magistrate for his native county, he retired to the residence he had built at Hazelwood, and employed the remainder of his life in works of philanthropy and beneficence. * * * Among other good works in which he took a prominent part, we may mention the British School-house in Dodbrooke, the ground for which was given by him; and shortly before his death he contributed handsomely towards the erection of a chapel for the Bible Christians in the same parish. A pretty chapel on his estate at Hazelwood was erected at his sole expense, while chapels and school-rooms at Loddiswell, Ugborough, Staunton, and East Allington, have been built chiefly by his instrumentality.

Mr. Peek warmly advocated the Temperance cause, and was, during a large portion of his life, a consistent tee-totaller. Of late years he took great interest in the spread of Peace principles, and warmly supported the plan of arbitration between contending nations, in aid of which he spent both time and money.

The remains of the deceased gentleman were interred in the catacombs at the new cemetery at Hazelwood, the funeral service being conducted by the Rev. J. C. Postans; and notwithstanding the very unfavourable weather, there was a large concourse of people, anxious to pay the last tribute of respect to the departed gentleman."

For many years the Sunday School children of this neighbourhood have enjoyed annually "the Hazelwood Treat." The last time this took place before the death of Mr. Peek was in July of 1866. Tried as Mr. Peek had been by a recent illness, he appeared to enjoy this festal day as much as any present, though he expressed a belief that this was the last time he should witness the annual gathering. After singing the hymn "Shall we meet beyond the River?" the benediction was given, and the large party broke up, and thus ended the *last* "Hazelwood Treat."

The following information has been kindly furnished for insertion :—

"The Hazelwood Chapel Trust has been founded by James Peek, Esq., to perpetuate the memory of his brother, the late Richard Peek, Esq., of Hazelwood, by placing in trust the sum of £11,000, which amount is to be supplemented at some future time by other sums from other branches of the Peek family. The objects of the Trust are—to support an Evangelistic Agent at Hazelwood, whose duty it is to conduct Divine worship in the chapel there on the Sabbath, and in the immediate neighbourhood during the evenings of the week, as opportunities offer; to superintend a Sunday School at Hazelwood, and to distribute religious tracts, &c., in the neighbourhood around it; to visit and minister to the sick poor in the same locality, by supplying them with medical comforts and small gifts in money, at the discretion of the visitor; to support either wholly or partially, by payments not exceeding thirty-two shillings per month, eight incurable invalids, and to give annuities of twelve pounds to each of four blind persons, who, as well as the invalids, must be resident within six miles of Hazelwood."

The amount of good effected by the "Hazelwood Chapel Trust," and also by the "Kingsbridge Invalid Trust," is incalculable. Truly this whole neighbourhood has cause to hold in high esteem the names and memories of these benevolent gentlemen, who have done so much for the temporal and spiritual necessities of their fellow men.

The following is copied from the *Western Times*, of April 24th, 1874 :—

"Sir Henry William Peek, M.P., who is one of the first of Mr. Disraeli's new Baronets, is son of James Peek, Esq.,

of Watcombe, near Torquay, and nephew of the late Richard
Peek, Esq., of Hazlewood, South Devon. This latter gentleman was founder of the mercantile house which has
enriched all the family. The father of Richard Peek was
an agricultural labourer, and when Richard served the
office of Sheriff of London and Middlesex he had his aged
father up to town to see his 'brave' equipage. There was
settled in business in London the son of a Devonshire
yeoman, who had employed the father in husbandry in
Devon, and the old man went to him and described, in
ecstatic terms, the wonderment of the finery in which he
saw his prosperous son arrayed. 'Lor a' massy—zilver
harness and goold lace, and sich cattle, and sich a bootiful
coach!' The worthy old rustic was only restrained by the
slenderness of his vocabulary from doing justice to his
feelings. We had the story from a gentleman well known
in Devonshire, and who is a brother of the merchant in
London to whom the old man delivered his mind on the
subject. Richard Peek was a rigid Nonconformist, and was
the life and soul of 'the cause' in his district. He went to
London an unfriended youth, with nothing but good principles and a sound constitution to stay him—and they
brought him to a first-rate position in London. The new
Baronet became a Churchman and a Tory. He has used
his great wealth freely in 'helping' churches and Tory
candidates. Restoration of fabrics, ornamenting interiors,
giving new organs, have all been described as modes by
which he has shown his zeal for religion."

The village of Woodleigh, which gives its name to a
Deanery, is in the Avon Valley. The manor belonged at
an early period to the Damerells, but now, we believe,
it is the joint property of three or four families. The small

antique Church belonging to Woodleigh was renovated a few years ago, and a new east window inserted. The interior has several handsome mural tablets belonging to the Luscombe, Cornish, Edmonds, and other families. There is a silver flagon here, which was given by Lady Amy Fortescue in 1686; it weighs 4lbs. 12oz., and is emblazoned with the Fortescue and Courtenay arms.

"Woodlegh was aunciently thenheritane of Damerell; anno 27 of Kinge Henry III., Raph Damerell was lord thereof; anno 24 of Kinge Edw. 1, John Damerell held it, and after him Rose, his wief, whom Henry de Rohant tooke unto his wief; Roger de Rohant, Kt. was lord of this mannor; by his daughter Elinor it descended to Sr Richard Chambernon, which gave this mannor, wi$_{th}$ other lands, unto Richard, his eldest sonne, by his 2 wief Katerine, y^e daughter of Sr Giles Dawbeney; and soe it descended unto Sir Richard Chambernon, of Modbiry.

Therle of Devonshire had also his mannor of Woodlegh."*

Wood Barton is referred to when speaking of the Luscombes, of Coombe Royal, it having been at one time their family residence.

Woodleigh Woods are a favourite resort for pic-nic parties: the rocky river and overhanging trees are very beautiful.

There is a singular history connected with the parish Church of Morleigh (which formerly belonged to the parish of Woodleigh). In Prince's "Worthies" we read that Sir Martin Fishacre had two sons, "Sir William Fishacre, of Coombe Fishacre, and Sir Peter Fishacre, of Morlegh, which lies about five miles to the south-west from Totnes, in the Road to King's-bridg, of which last knight, Sir Peter, tradition hath handed down unto us this remarkable

* Sir William Pole.

passage :—That upon some controversy between him and the Parson of Woodlegh about tythes, the matter grew so high that the Knight in his fury slew the Parson. Which abominable fact was so eagerly followed against him, that he was constrained to answer the same at Rome, where he could not be dismissed until he had submitted unto this penance, enjoyn'd upon him by the Pope—*to build a church at Morlegh;* which accordingly he did, and lies buried under an arch in the wall thereof."

Four miles north of Kingsbridge, in the parish of Loddiswell, is Bleak, or Black-down, commonly called Blakey-down, which commands a fine prospect. Here are (or were) the remains of an encampment of large extent. Lyson's account is this :—"Blackadon Camp is an irregular oval, the extreme length being above 1,000 feet, and in the broadest part about 500. The whole is said to contain about eleven acres. The keep at the north-west corner is about ten feet higher than the vallum. On the south and east of it the vallum is double and irregular."

The ancient fortress of Stanborough, which gives name to the Hundred, is similar, but of smaller dimensions.

Several barrows were examined in this district many years ago, some of them containing fragments of human bones.

Near the Blackdown entrenchment is a copper mine, but it is not now worked.

About two miles from Kingsbridge, on the road leading towards Plymouth, is the village of Churchstow, which has already been mentioned as belonging to the same vicarage as Kingsbridge. The earliest document known to be in existence in reference to Churchstow, under the deanery of Woodleigh, bears date 1291. It appears by the Hundred

Roll that the Abbots of Buckfast, and also the Lord of the Manor of Churchstow, formerly had the power of inflicting capital punishment. The church of St. Mary has a lofty tower, and Polwhele says " *Four bad bells.*" The church was restored in 1849. The east window is enriched with stained glass, and the whole interior has now a handsome appearance. The Rev. John Wilcocks lies buried in this cemetery. The following inscription is on his tomb:—

" In memory of the Rev. John Wilcocks, A.B., vicar of this parish, and during thirty years, master of the endowed grammar school at Kingsbridge, who died on the 27th of August, 1809, aged 66 years. In every station of his life he executed its respective duties with judgment, diligence, and fidelity. To great and various intellectual acquirements, he added universal candour of mind and primitive simplicity of manners, which conciliated the esteem and regard of all who knew him. This humble testimony of her most affectionate remembrance was placed here by his widow."

[The widow afterwards married Major Bennett, of the Cornwall Militia, who had been one of her late husband's pupils.]

In the valley below Churchstow is Leigh, once a cell belonging to Buckfast Abbey. The whole place has an aspect of great antiquity: the walls are composed of large and beautifully-chiseled stones of blue schist—in many parts in excellent preservation, but in others crumbling, and clothed with ferns and ivy. The entrance archway is a fine specimen of the less acute gothic order. Although the walls are in many places cracked and shaken, particularly those of the room above the archway, yet care appears to have been taken, by iron stays, and other means, to prevent further dilapidation. In one part of the building there are steps (containing some unusually massive hewn stones) which lead to an open balcony, the pillars of which remain, but the rails and open work which probably at one time existed, have disappeared. This balcony opens into two large well-proportioned rooms. Some of the original oak beams, supporting the roof, remain, but are grey with age and incrusted with lichen. A narrow doorway in one corner looks down into a deep well, or pit, which is considered to have been a place of confinement. This, as well as other parts of the rooms, is almost full of rubbish.

Leigh, being at present a farm-house, agricultural implements and such matters are here stowed away; and sundry wooden partitions having been erected, the extent and symmetry of these fine apartments has been sadly marred. At different periods Leigh has been the property of the the Hayes family, the Aldams, and the Bickfords.

Norton farm lies a little off the road between Churchstow and Kingsbridge; it is a fine specimen of an old Devonshire mansion, with its stone gate posts, surmounted by large balls. It was formerly the seat of a branch of the Hawkins family. From some high ground belonging to this estate, and known by the name of Norton Ball, there is a good view of the estuary, which, from thence, looks almost like a lake, shut in, as it is apparently, by the Portlemouth Hills at the lower end. It is considered that Norton and Norden (pronounced Norn) are only two forms of one name, common to the slopes which run from Norton quarries to Norden, on the West Alvington road. The stream which runs down on the west side of Kingsbridge divides that place from Norton. The meadows about there are called Norton Meadows, and were the property of Buckfast Abbey.

The Union House for Kingsbridge and twenty-five other parishes stands on a slope above Norden House, and opposite the West Alvington Woods. It is in Churchstow parish, and was erected in 1837, at a cost of £6,000. Kingsbridge Union consists of the following parishes, viz.:—

E	1	Aveton Gifford	E	14	Modbury
C	2	Buckland-tout-saints	S	15	Malborough
C	3	Blackawton	E	16	Ringmore
E	4	Bigbury	C	17	South Pool
C	5	Charleton	S	18	South Huish
S	6	Churchstow	C	19	Slapton
C	7	Chivelstone	S	20	South Milton
C	8	Dodbrooke	C	21	Stokenham
S	9	East Allington	C	22	Stokefleming
C	10	East Portlemouth	C	23	Sherford
E	11	Kingston	S	24	Thurlestone
S	12	Kingsbridge	S	25	West Alvington
S	13	Loddiswell	S	26	Woodleigh

Those marked E are in Ermington Hundred

„ „ C are in Coleridge Hundred

„ „ S are in Stanborough Hundred

BUCKLAND-TOUT-SAINTS
TO PRAWLE.

CHAPTER XIV.

"By breezy hills
And soft retiring dales; by smiling lawns,
Bold headlands, dark with umbrage of the grove;
By towns and villages and mansions fair,
And rocks magnificent."

BUCKLAND-TOUT-SAINTS is a small parochial chapelry, appended ecclesiastically to Loddiswell parish. The manor belonged to the Tout-Saints family in the reign of Richard I., and afterwards passed to the Hills and Southcotes, the latter of whom, after having held it for several generations, sold the manor in 1793 to the late William Clark, Esq., of Plymouth. More recently it has been the property of Mr. Brunskill.

The chapel (St. Peter) was very ancient, but was mostly rebuilt in 1779 by J. H. Southcote, Esq. It was appropriated with Loddiswell to Slapton College in the fifteenth century, and is now a curacy annexed to Loddiswell Vicarage. Having undergone alterations, such as the removal of the screen and pulpit, and the adoption of the more modern style of seats, instead of inconvenient pews, this chapel was re-opened in January, 1874.

In the parish of Buckland-tout-saints there are extensive slate quarries. Before the Dutch War in 1781, great quantities of this article were exported from these quarries to Holland, but the trade has not since been resumed.

Bearscombe, or as it was originally called, Woodmaston, once the abode of "Justice Bearc" (whose name so frequently crops up in connection with Nonconformist persecution) is in this parish.

In Worth's "History of Plymouth" is the following:—
"When Pope Pius IX. decided upon establishing the present Roman Catholic hierarchy in England, Plymouth was selected as a seat of one of the new dioceses. The first priest who is known to have ministered in Plymouth after the Reformation, was the Rev. Edward Williams, who was settled at the seat of Mr. Richard Chester, in Buckland-tout-saints, and who occasionally visited Plymouth to attend to the spiritual wants of the few and scattered Catholics then to be found there. This was a century since."

Mr. Richard Chester's residence was at Bearscombe, which is, and has been for many years past, a farm-house.*

In the adjoining parish of East Allington, is situated Fallapit, the seat of the Governor of Salcombe Castle at the time of the siege. Fallapit was a possession of the Fortescues for many generations; this branch of the family is descended from Sir Henry Fortescue, chief justice of Common Pleas in Ireland, who married the heiress of Fallapit about 1450 (Fallapit having been for several descents the property and residence of a family of that name). The heiress of this branch married Lewis Fortescue, a younger son of the Fortescues of Spriddleston, who was one of the Barons of the Exchequer in the reign of Henry VIII.

* It was at one time occupied by Walter, brother of the late C. Prideaux, Esq.

Sir Edmund, the fifth in descent from this Lewis, was a zealous royalist; he was knighted by King Charles I., and in 1664 was created a Baronet. The title became extinct on the death of his son Sir Sandys Fortescue, in 1683. Edmund Wells, Esq., whose maternal grandfather, Thomas Bury, Esq., married one of the cousins and co-heiresses of Sir Sandys Fortescue, took the name of Fortescue in 1768, and was grandfather of W. B. Fortescue, Esq., late possessor of Fallapit, who, however, sold it to William Cubitt, Esq.

The house is a large and handsome mansion, built in the Elizabethan style, more than half a century ago, very near the former one—an ivy-mantled portion of which still remains. It is pleasantly situated in the midst of extensive and tasteful pleasure grounds.

The church of East Allington is dedicated to St. Andrew. It contains three aisles, and is supported by eight gothic pillars. The pulpit and the screen have the appearance of great antiquity; the former is handsomely adorned with carved work, and bears the arms and blazonings of the Fortescues, and many families who have intermarried with them. Among the mural inscriptions in the chancel, Polwhele quotes the following as being over the grave of Elizabeth, wife of Edmund Fortescue, one of the sheriffs of the county :—

> " Here lieth a wight
>   Of worthy descent,
> Whose loss for her worth
>   The people lament;
> The Rich for her love
>   And kind affabilitie,
> The Poor for her Alms,
>   Deeds, and Hospitalitie.
>   Obit 28 Jan., 1611."

There is another inscription as follows :—

"To the memory of Elizabeth, lately the Pious
Wife of Richard Wood, Gent. She died Jan. 11, 1662.
Eliza's soule a Graffe divine
    With Clay was fastened into Wood
The Tree did suddenly decline
    The Fruit was blasted in the Bud.
The Clay which death brake off lies here, the Wife
Is now engrafted on the tree of life.
Reader, expect not long to hold thy breath,
For hearte of Oake thou see'st cut off by death.

Kenedon, in the parish of Sherford, is an ancient house
of the early Tudor period. It was formerly the seat of the
Pralls; at one time it belonged to Sir W. Elford, and afterwards it was the property of the late Luke Howard, Esq., of
Tottenham. There was once a tower attached to it, but this
was taken down by the Aldhams, who occupied the place
for some years. The following is extracted from Prince's
"Worthies":—John Halse, Lord Bishop of Coventry and
Lichfield, was born in Kenedon, in the parish of Sherford (a
chapel of case to Stokenham Church). It hath the name
Sherford from a clear stream of water running there and a
passage through it. John Halse, the Judge, was the first of
the name who possessed this seat (Kenedon) whom I take to
be a native of this county, although where born I cannot say.
In the 1st of King Henry V. he was made the King's
Sergeant-at-Law. In the first of King Henry VI. he was con-
stituted one of the justices of Common Pleas, and in the year
after, 1424, one of the justices of the King's Bench. He took
up his habitation at Kenedon, and made it the seat of his
family, which flourished there many generations in a right
worshipful degree, down to the latter end of the reign of

Charles II., when Matthew Halse, Esq., was so far imposed
upon as to make away this and his other inheritance from
his uncle (a reverend divine of his name, then living in
Cornwall) and his issue, and settle it upon his sisters,
whom he made his heirs."

In a later edition of Prince's "Worthies" we find the
following remarks :—"The sisters of Matthew Halse, whose
disregard of feudal claims in preferring them to his reverend
uncle, excites so much indignation in our author, were Amy
and Rebecca. Amy was married to Jonathan Elford, of
Bickham, Esq. * * * In the division of the property
Kenedon was the property of Amy, and descended to Sir
William Elford, of Bickham, Bart. * * Rebecca, the other
sister of Matthew Halse, was married to Henry Trelawny,
Esq. The estate of Efford was her portion."

"Let us now proceed unto the Bishop; he was second son
to the judge aforesaid; and it being his fortune (or rather
misfortune, as some may esteem it) to be a younger brother,
he endeavoured to free himself from the disadvantage thereof
by his own personal worth and accomplishments; and he did
accordingly, by the vertuous improvement of his time, and the
blessing of God upon it, grow up to be a much greater man
in the world than his elder brother was with all his estate.
He was bred a scholar; and had his education in Exeter
College, in Oxford, of which house he became fellow; and at
length grew into that reputation with the university, that he
was chosen (not by his college according to the late cycle,
but by common suffrage of the masters in congregation)
one of the proctors thereof for the year of our Lord 1432.
After this he took the degree of Batchelur of Divinity; and
on the 23rd March, 1445, he was chosen Provost of Oriel
College there. In this very reputable station doth Mr. Halse

(for I don't find he was a doctor) continue the space of fifteen years; and then his fame having reached the court, he was, by that pious prince, King Henry VI., in the 38th year of his reign, made Bishop of Coventry and Lichfield. He continued Bishop of this Diocese about one and thirty years, and died upon the Lord's-day, October 3, 1490, at what time, by computation, he must be nearly ninety years of age. He lieth buried in his church at Lichfield."

"The village of Sherford is very ancient. It once belonged to St. Nicholas's Priory, Exeter. The church (St. Martin) is a fine specimen of the decorated style, and has a lofty tower and five bells. There are stoups at the north and south doors, and in the chancel is a fine trefoiled piscina."*

Let us pass through Chillington, which is a long straggling village, with a few pleasant-looking houses in it. It is one of the many villages in the parish of Stokenham.

"This manor (Stokenham) belonged, in the reign of King John, to Matthew Fitz-Herbert; it continued several generations to his descendants, by the name of Fitz-Matthew, Fitz-Herbert, and Fitz-John. Matthew Fitz-John, the last of this family, was summoned to Parliament as a baron. Dying without issue, he gave the inheritance of all his lands to the King (Edwd. I.). The manor was then held under the Courtenays, as of the Honour of Plympton. King Edward I. gave it to Ralph de Monthermer, his son-in-law, to be held of the crown, of which the Earl of Devon complained in a petition to Parliament, and obtained redress. From Monthermer this manor descended through the families of Montacute and Poole to Hastings, Earl of Huntingdon, who sold it to the Ar. erideths. Both Sir Wm. Pole and Risdon state that this manor was dismembered; Risdon says by the Earl of

* White's "Devonshire."

Q

Huntingdon; Sir Wm. Pole says by Sir John Amerideth, son of Edward, who purchased the estate. The royalty appears, nevertheless, to have been retained, the manor of Stokenham being now vested in R. W. Newman, Esq., who purchased it of Geo. Cary, Esq., of Torr Abbey." *

The Hundred Court was anciently held here, and there are some remains of an old building called the Prison, near the church, and the site of an old manor-house.

Robert Dymond, Esq., F.S.A., has furnished some very curious particulars respecting the manor of Stokenham, "derived from the ancient deeds and documents at Torr Abbey," which he says "have never been published."

"The Carys, of Torr Abbey and Cockington, were Lords of the manor of Stokenham, from 1608 to the beginning of the present century. The earliest document relating to the manor, which I find among the Torr Abbey papers, is the verdict of the jury at a Manor Court, held 30 Sep[r]., 5th Henry VII. (1490), in reference to the title to certain lands in 'Wydecombe and Colerige,' held by John Somaster and Margery Littleton, * * * 'and, moreover, the jury say that the said John and Margery and their ancestors, from time immemorial, were seized of a fishery in the Kings' water at the Ley in the manor aforesaid twice a year—once in Lent time, and once before the end of Pentecost. And moreover the jury say that the said John and Margery and their ancestors from time immemorial had, and used to have in the Park of the King at Stokynham, afs[d.] twice a year, a deer, in the feast of the Nativity of our Lord, and one other deer in the feast of the Nativity of St. John the Baptist, yearly. * * *'

Before the sale to Amerideth it was thought probable

* Lysons.

that Sir Francis Drake would have purchased the manor (of Stokenham), as the following letter to Lord Huntingdon from his agent will shew :—

'It maie please yor honor,

We have been heere at Stokenham w^h p^{r}pose to p'cede yn sale of your lo^{ns} lands there; but being crossed by the practice of one Digbye, a busie curate newlie come to that towne, and assisted by a companie of light hedded fellowes, who sent a supplicacon to yor Lo^{dp}, which we have seen in a l're dated the Vth of this month, but the chiefe cause we take to be the very povertie of the tenants who would not deale anythinge till their messenger should return from London. So beinge stalled there and at Southpole for that tyme, we left them and rode to Yelhampton, and first we enquired for S^r ff^r Drake, who, being still at the courte, we conferred wth Mr. John Heale, to understand S^r F's mynde in the p^{r}chase of this manor, but Mr. Heale had no commishion to deale therein.'

The letter goes on to state that the writer found it difficult to deal with the tenants at 'Yelhampton,' suggesting that Lord Huntingdon should confer with Sir. F. Drake in London, 'who happilie maie be drawen to yor L^{dpns} likinge.'

The letter is dated the 14th of April, at Yelhampton, 1582.

On the 6 Sept^r, 1632, Sir Edward Cary, of Stantor (an ancient house in the parish of Marldon, between Paignton and Torquay), Knt., and his son Sir George, granted a lease for lives to Wm Gournay, of Dartmouth, merchant, of 'all that place and hole, commonly known by the name of Poke Hole, situate under the cliff at Halsand, in the parish and manor of Stockingham, neere adioyning unto the fishhouse or sellar of the s^d Wm Gournay there.' Another lease of the same year grants to the same lessee a 'fishing howse at Halesand, and the Capstander roome thereto belonging.'

The papers also comprise several Court Rolls of the Manor, recording the proceedings of the Courts Leet. The following are extracted from the presentments at the Courts :—

In 1675 Richard Hawkings, esq., was presented 'for committinge of an assaulte, and drawinge of blood fro^m Thomas Luscombe wthin the manno^r aforesaid, to ye disturbance of ye peace, and amerced in 3s. 4d.,' and again, 'Roger Parret, for his irreverent behaviour, and disturbinge ye Co^{rt}, and smoaking tobacco there after notice given him,' is amerced in the sum of 3s. 4d.' [R. D. remarks the temptation to indulge in this imported luxury was too strong for poor Roger]. In the same year, under the head of Button and Muckwell, a fine of 8d. was inflicted on 'Elizabeth ffox, widow, for brewinge ale two severall tymes without ye Lycence of the Lorde of ye Manno^r.' In 1683 we find John Ewen presented for 'sowinge of garden seeds and placinge of bees in Addle Hole.'

Michael Pope and John Lowe were fined 12d. each 'for sufferinge their hoggs to goe unringed and unyoaked, to ye annoyance of ye inhabitants of ye Leete.' 1676. Thos Paidge was presented 'for keepinge of an unruly and dangerous dogg within this Leete, wherefore it is ordered by ye Co^{rt} y^t the saide Thos Paidge doe hange or otherwise destroy the same.' 1690. 'The jury pssent Stephen Terry for commitinge of an affray, and drawinge of blood from John Earle, at Nuttiscombe, wthin this Manno^r about ye 13th day of March last, by throughinge of a stone of five pound wight, or thereabouts,' for which he was fined 3s. 4d.

About 1745 one Samuel Weekes was Reeve or Bailiff of the Manor of Stokenham. One of his letters seems worth quoting. It is dated 31 Jan., 174⁹⁄₁, and is addressed to 'George Cary, Esq., att his Tor Abby. To be left at the Post House in Totnesse with care.' It commences, 'Sir, I suppose you hear of the death of the landlady att the Church Hous in Stockingham town, Mary King;' then after enumerating the deaths of sundry persons, on whose lives tenements were held, he continues, 'its fifty to one whether the Lifes on Mr. Shath Estate in Dunson are not lost. There is no certain account of Ship nor men, since the whent out of Dartmouth —then, 'tis said, the are in Spanish prison, then in French prison: it seems there's nothing in nether of it.' Then, after a few more business particulars, he concludes, 'This from your very humble servent, SAMUEL WEEKES. I know nothing els att present. The Leay being very high, the catch many fresch water Eles at the sands side.' "

The Vicarage of Stokenham (with that of Chivelstone annexed) is in the incumbency of the Rev. J. C. Carwithen, M.A. The Church is large and antique, with a low tower and six bells. There is a National School in the village.

Sir Lydstone Newman, Bart., of Mamhead, is Lord of the Manor of Stokenham, and has a marine residence here, called Stokeley, or Stokeleigh House.

A. B. E. Holdsworth, Esq., owns Stokenham Priory estate: his residence, Widdecombe House, is picturesquely situated near the Bay.

Coleridge House, a mansion built in the Elizabethan style, the seat of John Allen, Esq., who owns the estate which gives its name to the Hundred, is also in this parish.

Stokenham includes six villages, and a few hamlets, mostly scattered along the shore of Start Bay. The villages are Chillington, Beeson, Beesands, Halsands, Kellaton, and Torcross.

Polwhele says, when alluding to a time of rebellion and revolution in 1794, "The active loyalty of every description of persons in Devonshire is beyond all former example. Signal houses were erected on the south coast of Devon in the autumn of that year, and Lieutenants of the Navy appointed to them the 18th of December following. They were situate as follows, viz., Collegrew, Start Point; Hurter's Top, near the Prawle; Westore, at the Bolt Head; Gurnose, Bigbury Bay; Berry Head, south point of Torbay; Coleton, near Dartmouth; Beer Head, near Colyton; Westdown Beacon, near Exmouth; and Dawlish Head, near Chudleigh."

Prawle Point has been thus described:—"The Prawle is principally composed of gneiss rock, which on the western side is weathered like a surface of snow which has been exposed to the sun's rays. It is everywhere broken into crags, and terminated at the point by a singular archway, through which a boat might sail in calm weather. Many years ago the *Crocodile* frigate was wrecked upon this headland, with a great loss of life."

One authority states that "here in the eleventh century the ships of pilgrims touched, on their voyage from Denmark to the Holy Land."

There is a coastguard station at this fishing village.

In the "Londoner's Walk to the Land's End," the following paragraph occurs respecting the scenery between the Start Point and the Prawle:—"Those who have been disappointed with foreign travel would do well to bend their steps to this little-known part of our own country. One may journey far before he finds so much to satisfy the eye and charm the imagination, as came before me in this day's wandering." A coastguard, whom the "Londoner" met with, remarked to him, "'Tis as rough a bit of country as any part of Devonshire, but 'tis well worth looking at. An Englishman don't know what England is till he has been along here."

The following notice appeared in the *Kingsbridge Gazette* of February 13th, 1864, headed Ornithology. "That very rare bird, the Little Bustard *(Otis Tetrax, Linn)*, was shot at Prawle on Saturday last. The bird is a mere straggler in this country; one was shot in the parish of Stokenham about twenty-five years since; and, a few years before, one at Bigbury. The Little Bustard is a bird of considerable powers of flight; the great deserts of Tartary being its principal stronghold. Large flocks of them have been seen wandering thence in the direction of the Caucasus and the Caspian Sea, also to the south of Russia, Siberia, Turkey, and Greece; and in small numbers in Italy, Spain, and France. They are polygamous; but a male specimen has seldom been met with in this country. Their food consists of vegetables, insects, worms, grain, and seeds."

Respecting *one* of the birds above mentioned, the following communication was made to Loudon's " Magazine of Natural History," and signed Charles Prideaux, Hatch Arundel, near Kingsbridge, Devon. " On Friday, the 15th November, 1839, a specimen of that very rare bird, the Little Bustard, was killed at Bigbury, in the south of Devon, which came into my possession the next day. This is, I believe, the second occurrence of this bird in that county; and it is rather singular that in the other instance the bird was bought in Plymouth market in 1804, by my brother, William Prideaux, and presented to the late Colonel Montagu, and is now in the British Museum: it was killed in the north of Devon."

START BAY.

CHAPTER XV.

" The rocky ledge runs far into the sea,
  And on its outer point some miles away,
The lighthouse lifts its massive masonry,
  A pillar of fire by night, of cloud by day.

And the great ships sail outward and return,
  Bending and bowing o'er the billowy swells,
And ever joyful, as they see it burn,
  They wave their silent welcomes and farewells."

Longfellow.

POLWHELE says, in reference to Start Point, (but we have never seen it mentioned elsewhere) "There are still the remains of columns here, it is supposed, in memory of the Phenician Astarte."

Another authority says, " The name (Start) is supposed to be the Anglo-Saxon, 'Steort,' a tail or promontory, but it is more commonly explained as the 'starting point' of ships outward bound. The point stretches boldly to sea, sloped on each side like the roof of a house, and crowned along its entire length by fanciful crags, strangely weathered and shaggy with moss. Its different sides strikingly illustrate the influence of a stormy sea on the picturesqueness of a coast. On the west, the dark cliff incessantly assaulted, presents a ruinous appearance; on the east, although moulded from the same material, it descends to the waves in a smooth precipice. Beyond this point the sea is seldom agitated by a roll from the Atlantic, the ground swell of the ocean rarely extending further eastward than the Start."

The Start Lighthouse is well known. It is situated almost, but not quite, on the extreme point of land, and at a considerable elevation above the sea; the bold, jagged rocks, however, rise high above the tower. It has now sent its warning light across the deep for more than forty years. At first it only consisted of the single round tower, at the top of which was the lantern, containing the revolving light, and also a fixed light, with the necessary apparatus for working the same. The rooms underneath were used as a residence by the light-keepers. At first *one* keeper only had to attend to this duty; but some years later, a cottage was erected adjoining the lighthouse, and a second keeper appointed to assist in looking after the light, &c.

It is the duty of the keepers to light up the lamps ten minutes before sunset, and watch them during the night, to see that the machinery which works the revolving light does not stop or get out of order. For this purpose, the night is divided into watches, which are taken alternately. It is a regulation of the Trinity Board, that during the time the lights are burning one keeper is to be constantly present in the lantern, watching them.

Up to the end of 1871, the lighthouse continued to be worked with the lamps and machinery fixed when it was first erected; but after so many years' wear the machinery had become worn and uncertain, and uneven in its action, and it was determined to fix a new lantern, machinery, and lights. For this purpose, plans and specifications of the proposed alterations were issued by the Honourable Trinity Board. The contract of Mr. Chapman, of West Alvington, was accepted for the various alterations in the masonry department, and that of Messrs. Chance for the new lantern, &c.

The alterations embraced the erection of a new cottage for the head keeper, the removal of certain of the stone floors in the tower, the perforation of the tower for new windows, and the closing of some of the old ones; the erection of a substantially-built stone store-room, for the paraffin oils used for the light, &c.

All these alterations appear to have been satisfactorily completed. The new lamp, enclosed in its dome of crystal prisms and reflectors, is considered *the best* which has yet been erected; and the contractors, the Messrs. Chance, of Birmingham, may well feel satisfied with the perfect manner in which everything has been carried out.

The arrangement for obviating the necessity of a fixed light, in addition to the revolving one, to throw its bright gleams on the sunken rocks and sand banks, which endanger vessels when they approach too near the point, is most ingeniously contrived; a portion of the light being reflected from the lamp on *the land side*, where its rays are not required, and thrown down upon powerful prismatic reflectors on the story below, and then a second time reflected, and allowed to pass through a large window in the desired direction. The light itself is obtained from an arrangement of a burner of four concentric wicks, supplied with paraffin oil.

Visitors to the Start Lighthouse will be struck with the extreme neatness, as well as substantial quality, of everything appertaining to the buildings. The apparatus and interior fittings are beautifully bright, and although some persons may imagine that the light-keepers must have much time on their hands, it does not appear to be so, the cleaning and trimming of the burners requiring the attention of both men for a large portion of every day.

A short distance from the lighthouse is the fog-bell, which was erected in October, 1862. Although this does not appear altogether to answer the object desired—that of throwing a volume of sound *far out to sea*—yet no doubt vessels enveloped in a very dense and bewildering fog, would be warned in time to keep away from the perilous reef of sunken rocks lying off towards the south-west of the light. The machinery by which this bell is rung is very beautiful. By means of a falling weight, of about thirteen hundred-weight, the huge clapper continues to strike the bell for about four-and-a-half hours without additional attention on the part of the attendants. The machinery is very similar in appearance and action to that of a large turret clock.

There is every probability, however, that ere long the fog-bell will be superseded by some adaptation of the steam whistle, as the sound thus produced is found to penetrate a foggy atmosphere further and more freely than that of a bell.

The following is extracted from a newspaper of March 17th, 1866:—

"The 'Albert Medal' is at last formally announced. It consists of a gold oval-shaped badge, enamelled in dark blue, with a monogram composed of the letters V. & A., interlaced with an anchor erect, in gold, surrounded with a garter, in bronze, inscribed in raised letters of gold, 'For gallantry in saving life at sea,' and surmounted by a representation of the crown of the Prince Consort, and suspended from a dark blue riband of five-eighths of an inch in width, with two white longitudinal stripes. It will in future be granted to such as have distinguished themselves by their bravery in shipwrecks, or on other occasions, on the recommendation of the President of the Board of Trade."

Mr. Samuel Popplestone, of Start Farm, was the *first* person to whom this medal was presented; it being given in the presence of the Queen herself, as a mark of appreciation of his gallant conduct in saving, at the imminent risk of his own life, the mate and one of the crew of the *Spirit of the Ocean*, which was wrecked at the Start Point, on the 23rd of March, 1866, when the rest of the crew perished.

On the day above mentioned, the *Spirit of the Ocean* was caught in a strong gale from the south-west, and Mr. Popplestone, seeing the danger of the vessel, dispatched messengers to Torcross, and to the Coast-guard for assistance ; and then taking a small coil of rope, proceeded along the rocks, and a dangerous sea washed him off whilst endeavouring to obtain communication with the vessel. He, however, by the aid of a returning wave, regained his footing, and from that perilous position succeeded in saving the lives of two persons. For this act, Mr. Popplestone received the decoration of the Albert medal. Shortly after this, subscriptions were collected in the neighbourhood, and a tea service, consisting of a silver teapot, sugar basin, and cream ewer, were procured. The teapot bore the following inscription : — "Presented to S. Popplestone, for heroic conduct, in saving life from the *Spirit of the Ocean*, wrecked off the Start, March 23, 1866." The presentation took place at the Grammar School, Kingsbridge.

About a couple of miles from the spot that witnessed the loss of the *Spirit of the Ocean*, but nearer Prawle Point, the *Gossamer*, a China tea clipper ship, of 735 tons register, was wrecked in December, 1868, and thirteen lives were lost.

There was a strong south-west breeze, and a heavy sea. The vessel stood too close in shore to the Start, and was driven broadside on to the breakers. Two anchors were instantly let go; but the bottom was rock and loose shingle, and they would not hold, and the *Gossamer* was soon beating on jagged rocks, sixty yards from the shore, green seas breaking over her and sweeping the decks. These occurrences had been watched by the coastguards, who, under the orders of their chief officer (Mr. Pengelly) had got out a rocket apparatus, and conveyed it to the point nearest to the wreck. The crew were so terrified that they were unable to perceive the preparations being made for their rescue, and several of them jumped overboard to swim ashore. Most of these, however, perished in the attempt; but all who maintained their position were ultimately brought ashore by the rocket apparatus. The captain and his wife were both drowned. Had there *then* been a rocket apparatus at *Prawle*, as there now is, most probably all would have been saved; but Mr. Pengelly had to send to the next station, Rickham, about two and a half miles off, which, of course, took a considerable time. The survivors were unable to save anything more than the wearing apparel they had on.

The cargo consisted chiefly of shop goods; and the stocks of very many drapers, clothiers, boot makers, and booksellers, hardware dealers, and toymen, were strewn along the coast in the greatest confusion. There were, in all, with the pilot, thirty-one on board the vessel when she struck, including eleven able seamen and five apprentices.

In June, 1870, the *Emilie*, of Altona, Captain Alhsen,

from Iquique, bound to Altona with saltpetre, went ashore about half a mile from the place where the disastrous wreck of the *Gossamer* occurred. A dense fog prevailed at the time. Immediately she struck, both anchors were let go, but the chain breaking, she drifted about twenty yards from shore. The crew, thirteen in number, then took to two boats, and pulled off clear from land, and were discovered about five the next morning, upon the fog clearing, by the coastguard. Mr. Murray, the chief officer, launched his boat, and brought the crew to Prawle. At first, the *Emilie* was standing complete, with her sails set, but on her beam ends; but she soon began to break up, and in a comparatively short time was a total wreck. Scarcely anything was saved from her, with the exception of the clothes of the crew. The coast for some distance was strewed with wreckage.

Another disaster occurred in March, 1873, when the *Lalla Rookh* fell a victim to miscalculation and fog, and was wrecked on the rocks at Prawle Point. The *Lalla Rookh* sailed from Shanghae in October, bound for London, having on board an enormously valuable cargo, consisting of 1,300 tons of tea and 60 tons of tobacco. The morning was thick, and the wind blowing with considerable force from the south-east, with rain, and it is surmised that strong currents must have set on the weather side of the vessel, causing her to drive on the point, of which her officers thought she was sailing well clear. So close on shore did she run before land was seen, that four of her crew actually slung themselves down from her bows on to the rocks, and thus escaped. The boats were immediately launched, but one of them was stove, and became useless. Ten of the crew got into the other, but it was swamped, turned bottom upwards, and the occupants were thrown into the boiling surf. They, however, succeeded in getting back on board the ship, with one exception, that of the chief mate, Mr. Groves, who was drowned. The rocket apparatus was soon got to work, and all hands (with one exception, already mentioned) were quickly saved.

The *Lalla Rookh* afterwards parted asunder, and an extraordinary sight was to be witnessed on the beach. The cargo of tea washed out, and at high-water mark lay many tons of loose tea, forming a ridge in some places ten feet high. Hundreds of entire chests were saved by the coast-guards and their numerous helpers. Bales of tobacco were floating about in all directions. The *Lalla Rookh* was 869 tons register, owned by Messrs. Adams & Co., of Liver-pool: the captain's name, George Fullerton. The crew lost everything. The mate, Thomas Groves, was a native of Kendal, in Westmoreland.

Halsands and Beesands are two very small villages, built quite on the beach, and almost entirely inhabited by fisher-men's families. Between Beesands and Torcross there is a large slate quarry, which, although not now worked, is said at one time to have produced slate of particularly good quality. There used to be, in the quarry, a steam engine, and machinery for squaring the slabs.

Years ago a noble race of Newfoundland dogs might be found in these Start Bay villages; noble, not so much on account of their appearance, for we have often seen hand-somer animals, but for their *deeds*. They seemed as essential to the fishermen here as the sheep-dog is to the farmer; but somehow they are now almost extinct.

On a dark night, when the wind is blowing hard from the east, and south-east, and there is such a surf that it would be impossible for boats to approach near enough to the shore for a rope to be thrown to any one there, the word is given to a dog, and immediately away he plunges into the waves. He may be buffeted, knocked back by the surf, perhaps lost to sight for some time; still the faithful creature will not give up, but perseveres till he gets hold of the rope, and returns to the beach, grasping it firmly between his teeth, until he delivers it up to the men (or *women*) in waiting, who then haul in the boat, which perhaps contains the weather-beaten master, who is come back from his night's toil. When once the boat is close on the shore, the dogs are on the look out for the pieces of wood, technically called *ways*, which are placed underneath the boats to draw them up on the beach. It is very rarely that a single *way* is lost, owing to the careful guardianship exercised over them by the dogs. But with all their good qualities we are bound to confess they sometimes manifest a propensity towards *cheating the revenue!* Here is an instance, related by the dog's master. "One night I was out with the dog when it was dark, and presently he began snuffing about, and then dashed off into the waves, and soon returned, lugging along something, which he dropped, and began digging a pit in order to bury it in the sand. It proved to be a *tub of brandy*, which I brought home, and was very glad of, as my missus had been ordered to take brandy." Another time, a dog, probably the same, brought in *two* tubs of this much-desired liquor, and again, "he brought in quite a lot of them"—but alas for the smuggling trade, those blue-and-white gentry, the coastguard, have pretty nearly put a stop to these proceedings, both of dog and man.

It is not only *property* which the dogs thus watch over, for many a time they have been the means of rescuing persons from drowning. Interesting facts might be recorded to illustrate this noble trait in the habits of these intelligent and sagacious animals, who well merit our respect as well as admiration. Here is a fisherman's story :—"A dog was sitting up on the cliff above the quarry, and all at once he pricks up his ears, and cuts away right into the sea, of his own accord, and brings out a little drowning child. He carefully laid her on the shore, and began licking her face, but there was no sign of life, so he thinks to his self, 'what's to be done next? I can't bring her *to*?' So away he goes to the nearest cottage, and pulls the clothes of the people to attract their attention. Guided by the dog, they soon brought in the poor child, and the means used were successful in restoring animation."

The *sands*, which extend almost uninterruptedly in crescent form for seven miles, are in reality one vast bank of regular beach pebbles, extremely heavy to walk on. The accumulation is due to the exposure of the shore to a long range of breakers, and to the circumstance of the shingle being unable to travel, so as to escape out of the bay.

A gentleman, once a resident at Slapton, says, "What Brighton is to London, Weston-super-mare to Bristol, and Scarborough to the great cities of the north-east of England, Slapton (or rather, we should say, Torcross), is to the humbler towns of Kingsbridge, Dartmouth, and Totnes. It could not be passed unnoticed in any description of the South Hams; but as Kingsbridge claims it for most civil purposes, it deserves especial mention among the environs of that town."

There are several lodging houses at Torcross; none of them grand ones, but very pleasant, nevertheless; and there is a good inn facing the sea, and quite on the beach—a great

R

recommendation to occasional visitors who flock there in
the summer time.

It is an interesting sight to watch the fishing-boats
returning home after a night of toil—first one, and then
another, and another, tiny sail appears on the horizon, until
the little fleet comes in close to the shore, where wives and
children are waiting to receive the spoils as they are handed
over to them by the weary fishermen.

You will find a Coast-guard Station at Torcross, and a very
small barn-like dissenting chapel, but there is no church
nearer than Stokenham. Torcross is situated at one end of a
long straight road, two miles in extent, which crosses the
sands midway between the lea and the sea—between the
fresh water and the salt.

Slapton Lea presents many points of interest. It is
situated in the parishes of Blackawton, Slapton, and
Stokenham. Its length from Street-gate on the north, to
Torcross on the south, is more than two miles, and it contains rather more than two hundred and seven acres. It is
fed by three small rivulets, and the water thus accumulated
forms the Lea, which has no visible outlet into the Bay, but
discharges itself by percolating through the sand. A channel
was cut in 1854, underneath the cliffs of Torcross, to allow
of the escape of the surplus water, but it requires frequent
clearing from the sand and pebbles with which it becomes
choked up by the storms of winter.

In Leland's "Itinerary" we find as follows :—"Ther is a
very large Poole at Slapton, a 2 miles in length. Ther is but
a Barre of Sand betwixt the Se and this Poole.

The fresch water drenith into the Se thorough the Sandy
Bank. The Waite of the Fresch Water and the Rage of
the Se brekith sumtime this Sandy Bank. Good Fische in
Slapton Poole."

At about a mile from Street-gate the Lea is crossed by Slapton Bridge, which divides it into two parts, called re- respectively the Upper and the Lower Lea. The Upper Lea is entirely overgrown with various kinds of reeds and other aquatic plants; but the Lower Lea is open water, with the exception of reeds growing near the shore, especially at the end near Torcross. That most voracious of all fresh water fish, the jack or pike, here sometimes attains the size of from twenty to thirty pounds, but the generality vary from three to ten pounds each. They feed mostly on their neigh- bours, the perch and roach, but they are sometimes known to pull under and devour the coots and young ducks which breed there in great abundance. The little coots may be seen swimming about amongst the reeds after their parents, almost as tame as domestic ducks. The common wild duck breeds in the meadows adjoining, and immense flocks of starlings roost in the reeds in the winter, but when summer comes you will not see one in the whole district. In the morning they separate in smaller or larger flocks, and range abroad in search of their daily food, perhaps to a distance of twenty or thirty miles; and as evening approaches they return, and may be seen dropping down in amazing numbers to their nightly repose. In the autumn, swallows, martins, and sand-martins, make this place their rendezvous, and about a fortnight previous to their departure to more genial climes they roost in the reeds in almost incredible numbers. In the winter the Lea is frequented by almost every kind of water-fowl, and some very rare specimens have been taken. The spoonbill, a pair of the glossy ibis, the little bittern, and the little bustard, have been captured in the valleys near by, and the osprey, or fishing eagle, visits this spot at rare intervals. On the sands between the Lea and the sea are frequently seen large flocks of gulls of different species; also great numbers of the various kinds of *tringa*. Now and then, in the surge of the sea, the great northern diver, which is a magnificent bird, makes its appearance; and the guillemot pops up its head from the water. On walking over the sands, you may disturb from its nest the ring-dottrel, which will tumble and roll on before you as if wounded, until you are considered to be at a safe distance from its eggs or young.

A pair of Pallas' sand-grouse were shot, in the summer of 1863, from a flock of fourteen, which had dropped on these sands, apparently in an exhausted state. Their journey must have been a long one, as their general abiding-place is on the deserts of Tartary; and not until that year had any of the species been recorded as having been taken in England. It seems sad to reflect that these distinguished strangers should have met with so inhospitable a reception on this their first appearance on our shores. Slapton Sands afford but few specimens of shells; such as there are being common to most shores. Has any one ever noticed the absence of fresh-water shells in the Lea? One would have expected to find in such a locality a great abundance and variety, instead of which there are, we believe, scarcely any. Perhaps this may be accounted for by the occasional influx of the salt water, which would be prejudicial to their existence.

The "Sands Hotel," which is greatly frequented by gentlemen-fishers, is built quite on the beach, and is occasionally, during severe south-easterly gales (like the houses at Torcross), washed by the spray, and invaded by the waves. The Lea itself is subject to incursions of the sea on such occasions, which sweeps over the narrow barrier, much to the discomfort of the fish abounding therein.

Sir William Pole speaks of "Slapton, thauncient inheritance of Guy de Bryan, from Kinge Henry II. tyme unto Kinge Henry IV. tyme:" and Leland says "Slaptoun, a praty college toward the shore, is almost in middle way betwixt Dertmouth and Saultcombe Haven. Guy Brien was founder of this college."

"What is this tower hard by, which man has dismantled, but which the compassionate ivy has mantled round? This old tower is the only part remaining of the famous chantry built by Sir Guy de Brian, one of the first Knights of the Garter. He was standard bearer to King Edward III. at the battle of Calais, in the year 1349, and was rewarded for his intrepidity by a yearly pension of two hundred marks from the Exchequer. He built this chantry, that when his worn-out frame had sunk to rest, the priests might sing masses for his soul."

The parish church at Slapton (St. James') is rather a peculiar looking one, with a low spire.

John Flavel, an eminent Nonconformist minister, retired from Dartmouth, after the passing of the Five Mile Act, to the parish of Slapton. He found an asylum at Hudscott, then a seat of the Rolles (and still the property of that family), where he preached in the great hall at midnight.

There is a farm near Slapton called Poole, belonging to Mr. Bastard. "Here," we are told, "once lived Admiral Hawkins, who sailed round the world;" and moreover, "there was a Lady Edith Hawkins, of whom village tradition still reports that she walked on a velvet carpet from Poole to the church door."

Probably this was the "Pole" which Sir William Pole describes as "a priory founded by the Lady Joane Pole, wief of Guy de Bryan in Kinge Henry III. tyme. After the dissolving it was purchased by the father of Edward Ameredith, of Pole, Esq., and sold by John Ameredith, his sonne, unto Sr Richard Hawkins, Kt., whoe dwelled their, and hath left it unto his sonne."

The village of Slapton, sheltered amid an amphitheatre of hills, is remarkable for the equable temperature of its climate. It rests on a red sandstone rock, surmounting the argilaceous slate, which principally dips in a south-easterly direction. These rocks, when decomposed, form some of the best land, and it produces exceedingly fine orchards.

Beyond Slapton Sands you pass Blackpool. Of this village the following incident is related :—" In the reign of Henry IV., the French, under the command of Monsieur de Castel, landed in considerable numbers at Plymouth, plundered the town, and burnt 600 houses, after which, according to Stowe, they landed at Blackpool, where they were immediately attacked and repulsed by the country people. On this occasion the women united with the men in the assault, behaved with great courage, and rendered important service. The Commander himself of the invading forces was slain; three barons and twenty knights were taken prisoners, and conducted to the King by the countrymen, who returned with their purses filled with gold."

At Blackpool Sands, in March, 1869, several valuable gold coins were picked up. They consist of coins of England in the time of Edward III. and Henry IV., and French coins of the reigns of one of the Charles's and Louis of France. They are in a wonderfully good state of preservation, the inscriptions being quite legible. It is supposed that these coins must have formed part of a box of specie on board a ship which had been wrecked there, and became deeply imbedded in the sand for some hundreds of years, but owing to the recent sweeping away of the sand by the sea, they have become dislodged, and are now being washed out of their deposit. These new "diggings" caused quite a little rush, and at low water every day, for a time, numbers of people visited the spot in search of the treasure. At an Archæological Society meeting at Exeter, which took place after their discovery, the coins were exhibited and commented on.

Blackpool is in the parish of Stoke Fleming, which is thus spoken of by Sir William Pole. "Stoke (called from the Flemyngs, thauncient inhabitants thereof, Stoke Flemynge) was, in Kinge Henry II. tyme, the land of Sir Richard Flemynge." In the church at Stoke Fleming is a fine brass for John Corp, 1361, and his grand-daughter Eleanor, 1391, with canopy.

You pass through both Blackpool and Stoke Fleming on your way to Dartmouth, a curious old town with narrow streets, beautiful harbour, and ancient castle; and having conducted our readers thus far, we leave them to pursue their researches, either by way of the Dart, a river which tourists are wont to call "the English Rhine," or, if they prefer it, they may walk on board the steam-ferry, and landing at Kingswear, can take the railway, and thus more speedily leave behind them

"KINGSBRIDGE AND ITS SURROUNDINGS."

APPENDIX A.

THE CHARTER, GRANTED IN THE REIGN OF HENRY VI.,
TO HOLD A MARKET AND FAIRS AT KINGSBRIDGE AND
BUCKFASTLEIGH, DEVON.

*A true copy of the original record of Chancery, preserved
in the Tower of London, attested by Jno. Bayley.*

Rex archiepis epis &c. saltm. Sciatis qd de gra nra
spali concessim' & licenciam dedim' ac per presentes conce-
dim' & licenciam dam' pro nob & heredibus nris quantu in
nob est dilcis nob in xpo abbi & conventui domus & eccliœ
be Mariœ de Bukfast in com Devon & successoribus suis
qd ipi & succesores sui exnunc imperpm heant unu mercatum
apud maneriu sive dnium suum de Kyngesbrygge in com
predco singulis septimanis per diem sabbi tenend aceciam
duas ferias utraque ear per tres dies imperpm singulis annis
duratur unam videlt apud Kyngesbrigge predict in die sce
Margarete virginis & per duos dies prox sequentes tenend
alteramque apud manerium sive dniu suu de Buckfastlegh
in com predco in die sci Barthi appli & per duos dies
prox sequen similiter tenend cum omibus libtatibus juribus
& libis consuetudinibus ad hujus modi mercatum & ferias
pertinen sive spectan nisi mercatu illud & feric ille sint ad
nocumentum vicinor mercator & vicinarum feriam. Quare
volumus & firmiter precipim' pro nob & heredibus nris

quantnm in nob est qd predci abbas & conventus & suc-
cessores sui imperpm heant unu mercatu apud predcm
manerium sive dniu suu de Kyngesbrigge in com predco
singulis septimanis per diem sabbi tenend acceiam duas
ferias utraque eam per tres dies imperpm singulis annis
duratur unam videlt apud Kyngesbrigge predict in die sce
Margarete Virginis & per duos dies immediate sequen
tenend alteramque apud Buckfastlegh predict in festo sci
Barthi appli & per duos dies immediate sequen singulis
annis similiter imperpm tenend cum omibus libtatibus juribus
& libis consuctudinibus ad hujusmodi mercatum & ferias
pertineu sive spectan nisi mercatum illud & ferie ille sint
ad nocumentum vicinor mercator & vicinaram feriam sicut
predcm est. Hiis testibus venerabilibus pribus Th. Cantuar
& W. Ebom archiepis Th. London & E. Exon cancellario
nro epis ac carissimis consauquineis nris Rico Ebor & Johe
Norff ducibus Rico Warr & Rico Sarum comitibus Henr
Bourghchier thes Angl vic necnon dilcis & fidelibus nris Johe
Nevill camerario nro & Waltero Scull thes hospicii nri
militibus & aliis. Dat' per manu nram apud Oxon xvj
die Septcmbr.

Per issm Regem & de dat predca &c.

APPENDIX B.

THE following information—much too valuable to be
omitted—was very kindly furnished by G. B. Lidstone, Esq.,
but too late for insertion in the body of the work.

"Pindar Lodge, the residence of Dr. Wolcot (the author
of 'Pindar's works'), is supposed to remain unaltered, so

far as the house is concerned, with the exception of a new
front, which was put to it by the Rev. Nathaniel Wells, who
became possessed of the property after Dr. Wolcot left it.
The lawn in front of it has, of late years, been converted into
business premises, and now comprises the coal-yards and
cellars of Mr. John Adams, and the stable-yards and small
garden used by the occupier of the Anchor Hotel. There
was also a walled garden on the other side of the road,
behind the house.

The old house, with its lawn, having two or three handsome chestnut trees growing in it, stood intact (except the
new front before mentioned) until the property was purchased by Mr. John Foale Annis, builder, about the year
1834. He divided it, and sold the house with that part of
the lawn immediately in front of it, and a part of the walled
garden, to Mr. Joseph Adams, coal merchant, who built
cellars, and made his coal-yard in the lawn. The part retained by Mr. Annis consisted of the little garden and the
remainder of the lawn : on these he built stables. This part
of the premises is now used by the occupier of the Anchor
Hotel. He also retained part of the walled garden.

After Mr. Wells' death his widow occupied the entire
premises, and she was succeeded by Capt. Crozier and Mrs.
Pell, before the property was purchased by Mr. Annis.

The barn alluded to by Dr. Wolcot in his writings as the
resort of itinerant players, has been taken down, and on its
site, on the opposite side of the street, several labourers'
cottages have been built.

The ancient entrance to Pindar Lodge must have been
through the large doorway at the end of Ebrington Street,
as the lawn ran down to the creek, which was then the
muddy beach on which sea-sand, dredged from the Bar at

the entrance of Salcombe Harbour, was deposited in large quantities, and taken away by farmers in the neighbourhood for manure.

Dodbrooke Quay then only extended so far as Quay Lane, where the muddy beach commenced.

Mr. Strong, corn merchant, owned the garden on the south side of Quay Lane, and made a great improvement by inclosing a portion of the creek, on the west side of his garden, which now forms South Place. He also built that portion of Dodbrooke Quay which lies on the west of South Place, which was afterwards extended to the point at the steps, where it now terminates. An attempt was then made by Mr. Winsor, the agent of Mr. Hodges, Lord of the Manor of Dodbrooke, to erect a sea wall, to form a road from Dodbrooke Quay to Barrack Lane and Salt Mill, then an ancient Quay; but this was resisted by Mr. John Lidstone, who claimed the right outside his field,* which then sloped down to the beach, and on which field Quay Cottage, Victoria Place, and Glena, have since been built. It was then bounded on the west by the ebbing and flowing tide. After much litigation a compromise was effected, by which a sea-wall was built by subscription, with Mr. Lidstone's consent, and continued on the beach outside of Boxhill to Barrack Lane and Salt Mill Quay.

Ebrington Street was then called Barrack Street, it being the only road from the town to the Barracks, then

---

* On the crest of the hill of this field, which was called Lower Field, it is supposed there was a row of cottages at an ancient date, as traces of their foundations were found in excavating for the new buildings. An ancient copper coin, or token, was picked up by Mr. G. B. Lidstone, among the excavations, having William Markell, 1666, on one side of it, and an ancient galley on the other. It is supposed that William Markell was a merchant who resided in the town, as there is a tombstone in Dodbrooke Church to the memory of a person of that name, of the same date.

standing on the hill above the lime kiln at Salt Mill
Quay. It was also the only road from the town to
Charleton, Frogmore, Chillington, Stokenham, and Torcross;
consequently there was a large traffic over this street, and
it was considered an excellent place of business.

The proposed deviation of the traffic from Barrack
Street, by a road over Dodbrooke Quay, to Barrack Lane,
was the occasion of much consternation among the shop-
keepers residing in Barrack Street. [This led to the
composition and circulation of some rhymes, by an anony-
mous author, but as they number seventeen stanzas, their
insertion here is scarcely desirable].

The land from the lime kiln at Salt Mill Quay to
Mr. William Date's shipbuilding yard was, about 1804,
previously to the communication being made by the road
between Dodbrooke and Salt Mill Quays, taken in from
the creek by the Lord of the Manor of Dodbrooke.

It formed a beautiful level piece of ground of several
acres in extent, and was dedicated by the Lord of the
Manor to the public as a promenade and recreation
ground.

The only erection then on it was a small house, now
part of the New Quay Inn, then used as an officer's
bathing-house.

The promenade ground continued for many years to be
used by the inhabitants of the town, without let or
hindrance.

In the year 1829, the Kingsbridge and Dartmouth
Turnpike Trust obtained an Act of Parliament to make
a turnpike road over it to Charleton, and thence to Dartmouth: and from that time the public have been confined
within the walls of the turnpike road, and numerous

erections have been made on new ground, which have completely spoiled the picturesque appearance of the place. Although the town has made great progress of late years in trade and commerce, and the improvement of its streets, it has sadly retrograded in its public walks and footpaths; so that in the winter season, the inhabitants are comparatively imprisoned in the town, for want of those conveniences for air and exercise so conducive to health."

APPENDIX C.

NATURAL HISTORY—BIRDS.

MR. HENRY NICHOLLS, who for a number of years, has paid much attention to the study of Natural History, has very kindly furnished a list of the birds which have occurred in this immediate neighbourhood—all, or nearly all, having come under his own notice.

White-tailed Eagle	*Haliaetus albicilla*
Osprey	*Pandion haliaetus*
Peregrine Falcon	*Falco peregrinus*
Buzzard	*Buteo vulgaris*
Honey Buzzard	*Pernis apivorus*
Kite	*Milvus vulgaris*
Hobby	*Falco subbuteo*
Merlin	*F. æsalon*
Kestril	*F. Tinnunculus*
Goshawk	*Astur palumbarius*
Sparrow Hawk	*Accipiter Fringillarius*
Marsh Harrier	*Circus rufus*
Hen Harrier	*C. cyaneus*

Montagu's Harrier	*C. Montagui*
Short-eared Owl	*Strix brachyotos*
Long-eared Owl	*S. otus*
Tawny Owl	*S. stridula*
White Owl	*S. flammea*
Great Shrike	*Lanius excubitor*
Red-backed Shrike	*L. collurio*
Great Tit	*Parus major*
Cole Tit	*P. ater*
Blue Tit	*P. cœruleus*
Marsh Tit	*P. palustris*
Long-tailed Tit	*P. caudatus*
Spotted Flycatcher	*Muscicapa grisola*
Kingfisher	*Alcedo ispida*
Bee-eater	*Merops apiaster*
Hoopoe	*Upupa Epops*
Chough	*Corvus graculus*
Raven	*C. corax*
Crow	*C. corone*
Hooded Crow	*C. cornix*
Rook	*C. frugilegus*
Jackdaw	*C. monedula*
Magpie	*Pica caudata*
Jay	*Garrulus glandarius*
Waxwing	*Bombyx garrula*
Nuthatch	*Sitta Europœa*
Wryneck	*Yunx torquilla*
Creeper	*Certhia familiaris*
Green Woodpecker	*Picus viridis*
Great spotted Woodpecker	*P. major*
Lesser spotted Woodpecker	*P. minor*
Cuckoo	*Cuculus canorus*

Nightjar	*Caprimulgus Europœus*
Swift	*Hirundo apus*
Swallow	*H. rustica*
Martin	*H. urbica*
Sand Martin	*H. riparia*
Pied Wagtail	*Motacilla alba*
Grey Wagtail	*M. sulphurea*
Yellow Wagtail	*M. flava*
Meadow Pipit	*Anthus pratensis*
Tree Pipit	*A. aboreus*
Rock Pipit	*A. aquaticus*
Wood Lark	*Alauda arborea*
Sky Lark	*A. vulgaris*
Snow Bunting	*Emberiza nivalis*
Bunting	*E. miliaria*
Black-headed Bunting	*E. passerina*
Yellow Hammer	*E. citrinella*
Cirl Bunting	*E. cirlus*
Chaffinch	*Fringilla cœlebs*
Mountain Finch	*F. montifringilla*
Sparrow	*Passer domesticus*
Greenfinch	*Loxia chloris*
Hawfinch	*L. coccothraustes*
Goldfinch	*Fringilla carduelis*
Linnet	*F. cannabina*
Bullfinch	*Loxia pyrrhula*
Crossbill	*L. curvirostra*
Rose-coloured Pastor	*Pastor roseus*
Starling	*Sturnus vulgaris*
Dipper	*Cinclus aquaticus*
Missel Thrush	*Turdus viscivorus*
Fieldfare	*T. pilaris*

Redwing	*T. Iliacus*
Thrush	*T. musicus*
Blackbird	*T. merula*
Ring Ousel	*T. torquatus*
Golden Oriole	*Oriolus galbula*
Dunnock	*Motacilla modularis*
Redbreast	*M. rubecula*
Redstart	*M. Phœnicurus*
Blackstart	*M. atrata*
Stonechat	*M. rubicola*
Whinchat	*M. rubetra*
Wheatear	*M. œnanthe*
Grasshopper Warbler	*Sylvia locustella*
Sedge Warbler	*S. salicaria*
Reed Warbler	*S. arundinacea*
Blackcap	*S. atricapilla*
Whitethroat	*S. cinerea*
Lesser Whitethroat	*S. sylviella*
Willow Warbler	*S. trochilus*
Chiff Chaff	*S: rufa*
Wren	*S. troglodytes*
Gold Crest	*Regulus cristatus*
Wood Pigeon	*Columba palumbus*
Rock Dove	*C. livia*
Turtle Dove	*C. Turtur*
Pheasant	*Phasianus Colchicus*
Black Grouse (male and female)	*Tetrao tetrix*
Pallas's Sand Grouse	*Syrrhaptes Paradoxus*
Partridge	*Perdix cinerea*
Red-legged Partridge	*P. rufa*
Quail	*P. coturnix*
Little Bustard	*Otis tetrax*

Great Plover	*Charadrius crepitans*
Golden Plover	*C. pluvialis*
Dotterel	*C. morinellus*
Ringed Dottrel	*C. hiaticula*
Grey Plover	*Squatarola cinerea*
Peewit	*Vanellus cristatus*
Turnstone	*Strepsilas interpres*
Sanderling	*Arenaria calidris*
Oyster Catcher	*Hæmatopus ostralegus*
Crane (seen)	*Grus cineria*
Heron	*Ardea cinerea*
Squacco Heron	*A. Senegalensis*
Night Heron, and young	*Nycticorax Europæus*
Bittern	*Ardea stellaris*
Little Bittern	*A. minuta*
Spoonbill	*Platalea leucorodia*
Ibis	*Ibis falcinellus*
Curlew	*Numenius arquata*
Whimbrel	*N. phæopus*
Spotted Redshank	*Totanus fuscus*
Redshank	*T. Gambetta*
Green Sandpiper	*Tringa ochropus*
Wood Sandpiper	*T. glareola*
Common Sandpiper	*T. hypoleucos*
Greenshank	*Scolopax glottis*
Avocet	*Recurvirostra avocetta*
Black-tailed Godwit	*Limosa melanura*
Bar-tailed Godwit	*L. rufa*
Ruff	*Tringa pugnax*
Woodcock	*Scolopax rusticola*
Great Snipe	*S. major*
Common Snipe	*S. gallinago*

Jack Snipe	*S. Gallinula*
Brown Snipe	*S. grisea*
Knot	*Tringa Canutus*
Little Stint	*T. pusilla*
Dunlin	*T. variabilis*
Purple Sandpiper	*T. maritima*
Land Rail	*Crex pratensis*
Spotted Crake	*C. porzana*
Little Crake	*C. pusilla*
Water Rail	*Rallus aquaticus*
Moor Hen	*Gallinula chloropus*
Coot	*Fulica atra*
Grey Phalarope	*Phalaropus lobatus*
Grey-lag Goose	*Anser palustris*
Bean Goose	*A. ferus*
White fronted Goose	*A. albifrons*
Bernicle Goose	*A. bernicla*
Brent Goose	*A. brenta*
Egyptian Goose	*A. Egyptiacus*
Canada Goose	*A. Canadensis*
Hooper	*Cygnus ferus*
Mute Swan	*C. mansuetus*
Shieldrake	*Tadorna Bellonii*
Shoveller	*Anas clypeata*
Pintail	*A. acuta*
Wild Duck	*A. boschas*
Garganey	*A. querquedula*
Teal	*A. crecca*
Widgeon	*A. Penelope*
Surf Scoter	*A. perspicillata*
Scoter	*A. nigra*
Pochard	*A. ferina*

Scaup	*A. marila*
Tufted Duck	*A. fuligula*
Long-tailed Duck	*A. glacialis*
Golden Eye	*A. clangula*
Smew	*Mergus albellus*
Red-breasted Merganser	*M. serrator*
Goosander	*M. merganser*
Great crested Grebe	*Colymbus cristatus*
Red necked Grebe	*C. rubricollis*
Dusky Grebe	*C. cornutus*
Eared Grebe	*C. auritus*
Dabchick	*C. Hebridicus*
Great Northern Diver	*C. glacialis*
Black-throated Diver	*C. arcticus*
Red-throated Diver	*C. septentrionalis*
Guillemot	*C. Troile*
Rotche	*Uria minor*
Puffin	*Alca arctica*
Razor-bill	*A. torda*
Comorant	*Pelecanus carbo*
Green Comorant	*P. cristatus*
Gannet	*Sula alba*
Common Tern	*Sterna hirundo*
Arctic Tern	*S. arctica*
Lesser Tern	*S. minuta*
Black Tern	*S. nigra*
Masked Gull	*Larus capistratus*
Black-headed Gull	*L. ridibundus*
Common Gull	*L. canus*
Lesser black-backed Gull	*L. argentatus*
Great black-backed Gull	*L. marinus*
Herring Gull	*L. fuscus*

Glaucous Gull   *L. glaucus*
Kittiwake   *L. Rissa*
Skua   *Lestris cataractes*
Richardson's Skua   *L. Richardsonii*
Buffon's Skua   *L. Buffonii*
Dusky Petrel   *Puffinus obscurus*
Leach's Petrel   *Procellaria Leachii*
Stormy Petrel   *P. pelagica*

APPENDIX D.

BUTTERFLIES.

MR. CHARLES ROGERS, of Plymouth (who is one of the principal collectors for the Crystal Palace Aquarium), has been kind enough to supply a list of Butterflies which he had himself captured in this district. This we should gladly have inserted if Mr. Henry Nicholls (whose facilities for collecting have been greater, owing to long residence at Kingsbridge,) had not since given a list, which includes several in addition to those mentioned by Mr. Rogers.

Brimstone   *Papilio rhamni*
Clouded Yellow   *Colias Edusa*
Pale clouded Yellow   *C. Hyale*
Large White   *Pieris brassicæ*
Small White   *P. rapæ*
Green veined   *P. napi*
Wood White   *P. sinapis*
Orange tipped   *Anthocharis Cardamines*
Marbled White   *Papilio Galathea*
Wood Argus   *P. Ægeria*

Wood Ringlet	*P. Hyperanthus*
Gatekeeper	*P. megera*
Rock-eyed Underwing	*P. Semele*
Small meadow Brown	*P. Tithonus*
Large meadow Brown	*P. Janira*
Small Heath	*P. pamphilus*
Red Admiral	*Vanessa Atalanta*
Peacock	*V. Io*
Large Tortoise-shell	*V. Polychloros*
Small Tortoise-shell	*V. urticœ*
Painted Lady	*V. cardui*
Purple Hair-streak	*Thecla quercus*
Green Hair-streak	*T. rubi*
Greasy Fritillary	*Papilio artemis*
Small pearl-bordered Frittilary	*P. Selene*
Dark green Fritillary	*P. aglaia*
Silver-washed Fritillary	*P. Paphia*
Small Copper	*P. Phlœas*
Large Blue	*Polyommatus Arion*
Holly Blue	*P. Argiolus*
Common Blue	*P. Alexis*
Grizzled Skipper	*Pamphila Malvœ*
Large Skipper	*P. Sylvanus*
Small Skipper	*P. Linea*

APPENDIX E.

PROVINCIALISMS.

WE here give a list of *some* of the provincialisms which may still be heard among the working classes in the rural districts surrounding Kingsbridge, although from the influence of modern improvement they are gradually getting out of use.

Appledrane	A wasp
Aps	An abscess
Arrishes	Stubbles
Banger	Large
Barker	A whetstone
Belving	Bellowing
Biddix	An axe
Biver	To quiver, " Bivering with the cold "
Blab	To tell
Bowerly	Comely, " A fine bowerly woman "
Braave	Good, or large, " A braave catch of fish "
Briss	Small twigs from a wood rick, used for lighting fires
Buldery	Sultry, " buldery weather "
Catteball	A ball (such as children play with)
Cauch	A mixture
Chainy	China
Chauk	A jackdaw
Chewers	Odd jobs
Cladgy	Waxy, " cladgy potatoes "
Clever	In good health
Clitty	Close, " clitty bread "
Clome	Earthenware
Clout	A blow, " a clout on the ear "
Coin	A female crab
Creemed	Shivering
Crickled	Gave way
Cris Hawk	A Kestrel

Crope	Crept
Crownin	Coroner's inquest
Cruel	Very, " cruel good," " cruel kind "
Crune	To whine
Dashed	Daunted
Dashful	Bashful
Davered	Withered
Derns	The woodwork around a door
Dicels	Thistles
Dimmet	Twilight
Dishwasher	A wagtail
Dolly moppin	An idler, a lazy fellow
Doust	Chaff
Drang	A ditch
Drasaking	Slow, lagging behind
Drashel	A flail
Dratch	Thatch
Dreskal	Threshold
Dringle	A throng, or crowd
Dumps	Melancholy
Dwam	Sleepiness, " a bit of a dwam."
Evil	A three-pronged agricultural implement
Floshed	Spilt, splashed
Frape	To bandage tightly
Furse-chat	A stone chat
Galagantin	Large and awkward
Gallied	Frightened
Gawk	A stupid person
Glamed	Hurt
Glumping	Sulky
Golden Gladdy	A yellow hammer
Grail	Offal of grain

Grainy	Proud, ill tempered
Griddle	A gridiron
Grizzle	To grin
Gruchy	To shrink under sudden pain
Grute	Earth
Grute-field	A ploughed field
Gulging	Drinking
Gulk	To swallow
Hatch	Half door of a cottage
Hedgaboor	A hedgehog
Hickymal	A titmouse
Hood	Wood
Hoodwall	A green woodpecker
Homescreech	Missel thrush
Hoop	A bullfinch
Hoost	Hoarseness
Horse-long-cripple	A dragon fly
Icybells	Icicles
Jackybread or Jacky lo'	Currant Cake
Jolter head	Blockhead
Kicketh	Stammers
Kit	All large hawks and falcons are thus designated
Lew	Sheltered
Lerrapin'	Large, straggling
Lerrip	Chastise, " I'll lerrip that boy "
Linhay	An open shed
Lodyholt	A disease in a cow's foot
Longcripple	A lizard
Long-tailed pie	Long-tailed tit
Lop	Lame

Lowster	To work hard, " he can't lowster as he used to do "
Magames	Nonsense
Make wise	Make believe
Malkin	A dirty person
Mallin'	A beating
Manch	To chew, to eat
Maurs	Roots
Mawl	To break or bruise
Mazed	Mad, deranged
Mift	Offended
Moody	Low-spirited
Mooster	To stir, " time to mooster "
Moot	To root out
Mopt	Blindfold
Mulley	A donkey
Nearts	Nights
Nimpingang	A boil on the finger
Nort	Nothing
Oft	Ought, " you did'nt oft to do so "
Old sodger	A deceitful person
Omes	Alms
Organs	Penny royal
Orts	Fragments, refuse
Panking	Panting
Pickin ears	Gleaning
Pig's loose	Pig's stye
Pilem	Dust
Pindy	Mouldy, kept too long, " the meat is pindy "
Pixies	Fairies
Plashet	A quagmire
Plimmed	Swelled

Plum	Light, soft
Pook	A rick, " a haypook "
Posses	Posts
Power	A great number, " a power of people "
Pucker	A fuss
Qualing	Fainting
Quarrels	Panes of glass
Queltering	Hot
Raked up	Awoke from sleep
Rare	Early
Rash	Rough-handed
Ream	The cream on the surface of new milk
Reamed	Stretched
Rory tory	Tawdry
Rouse	With a great noise
Ruff	Roof
Rusy-boat	A swing
Scad, or Scud	A shower, " a frisky scad "
Scovy	Uneven in colour, "this dyed shawl is scovy "
Scrimmage, or Strimmage	A commotion
Scrimping	To deal out begrudgingly
Scute	A gift
Sheerymouse	A bat
Sight	A great quantity, " such a sight of pilchards "
Skiver	A Skewer
Slammed, or Strammed	Shut with violence

Slewered away	Gave way
Slock	To entice, "my dog was slocked away"
Slottering	Dirty, wet
Smeech	Offensive smell in the fire
Smeered	Smiled
Sproil	Strength, "I've no sproil left in me"
Squat	Pressed, or squeezed
Squeaked	Spoke, "he never squeaked a word of it"
Stag	A young cock
Stewer	Dust
Stewardly	Managing, "a good stewardly wife"
Stram bang	To fling violently
Stroil	Grass weeds
Suent	Even, smooth
Swap	Exchange
Swelter	To melt
Swinging	Huge
Tantara	A disturbance
Tantarems	Vagaries
Teel	To set, "teel potatoes," "to teel a trap"
Thicka	That
Thickee	This
Tidly goldfinch	A gold-crest wren
Tidly tope	A wren
Totling	Working slowly
Traffic	Trash, "don't tell me sich traffic"
Trapes	A slatternly woman
Trounce	Punish
Unray	To undress
Vang	To take money
Vege	A journey
Vinny	Mouldy (applied to cheese)

INDEX.

INDEX.

ERRATA.

Page 56, read Progymnasmata

„ „ „ Themata Homerii

„ 96 „ 1824, *not* 1825

„ 136 „ Chapter IX., *not* XI.

G. P. FRIEND, STEAM PRINTER, UNION STREET, PLYMOUTH.